# The Next Step

*Merging the Personality, Intuition, and Soul*

Dorothy A Bodenburg M.S., MFT

To access the enhanced features discussed throughout this book,
please visit DorothyBodenburg.com, or scan the QR Code.

ISBN 978-0-9792688-2-3

9 780979 268823

90000>

ISBN: 0979268826
ISBN-13: 9780979268823
Sacred Scribes Publishing

# Dedication

To those who choose to take their next step

# Table of Contents

# Introduction

*"For the first three years, being a stay-at-home mom was fun. Now I feel depressed and guilty for wanting more in my life."*

*"Getting up and facing my day is becoming increasingly more difficult. My life is filled with too many things I have to do. I'm like a robot. I have a wife and two teenagers who want every new electronic gadget that comes out. I work hard to provide the things that are expected of me as the provider. I thought I would be happy but I'm not…something is wrong."*

*"I just graduated from a prestigious law school with honors and received many lucrative job offers in large cities. I'm getting a lot of pressure from my girlfriend and parents to take one. But what I really want to do is move to a small town, open up a one-man law office and enjoy the outdoor sports I love. I still want a family, but I don't want to sell my soul to do it. I'm so confused. What am I going to do?"*

*"When I go to church or when I am around my church friends I feel good. Then when I go to work, it seems like my spirituality needs to be tucked away. How do I live my spiritual beliefs in my everyday life?"*

*"I try to follow my heart, but every time I do, I end up defending myself, which just causes problems between me and my husband, friends and family. Then I start doubting myself."*

*"I've read so many books on spirituality and finding my purpose. All they do is make me feel like I'm a failure because I don't seem to get it. What am I doing wrong?"*

The common bond between these people and among all human beings is the challenge to find our place in this world. We ask ourselves: Why am I here? What am I supposed to do with my life? How can I make it meaningful? What is my responsibility to others? What is my responsibility to myself? If there are so many contradictory paths, how do I know which is the one right for me?

To complicate matters, we are subjected to two often opposing forces that heavily influence us and with which we may struggle: the demands of our internal and external worlds. Indeed, our lives are a reflection of the intersection between our internal desires and the demands that the external world may place upon us. The fact that we recognize and negotiate the opportunities presented by both represents our consciousness. Our identity and sense of self arise from the choices we make regarding how much sway and in what combinations our external and internal worlds create our values, beliefs, thoughts, feelings and actions.

Negotiating these choices is no simple matter. The external world is all around us. We are bombarded and conditioned by its values and expectations. Our parents, schools, religious institutions, economy, government, media and culture affect us strongly and carry with them obligations and expected patterns of behavior. The promise is: if we adhered to these spoken and unspoken rules, we will be accepted into our families, communities and nation. We will enjoy the benefits offered. We will be successful. We will be happy. So why is it that so many of us now feel so lost? That so many of us, no matter what our outward achievements, continue to ask ourselves, "Is that all there is?"

Our reactions to the external world even pull some of us in directions that may not be of our choosing. We believe we have limited recourse against the effects of poor parenting, tragic events, socio-economic status, limited education and myriad other circumstances that can arise in everyone's life. All of these infuse us with a belief that the external is a force too powerful to be reckoned with—certainly we don't have the strength to fight it. We become molded by the external world, which then limits our innate potential. We believe and act as if we are victims. We feel damaged. We resign ourselves to our "fate." Sadly, this kind of belief in the power of the external world leads to a life of mediocrity and disappointment—not joy.

Our ability to respond to the relentless demands of the external world only comes from our being able to understand, connect with, and fortify our internal world. Although we may be unaware of it, this inner world has a definite, innate infrastructure. We need to learn how it develops and also how to use this infrastructure in order to come into our own as whole, fulfilled, and spiritual human beings. **The Next Step: Merging the Consciousness of Personality, Intuition, and Soul** is a visionary and practical book for this process.

## Separation, Connection, and Unity

As a species, we evolve by understanding who we are internally as individuals and our relationship to our external environment. We observe our surroundings including our relationships to the people within it. Then we link and match the conclusions we draw from our internal world of feelings, beliefs and experiences with what is coming at us in the external world. This process is consciousness.

But consciousness is not a monolithic structure. Actually, I have found that we co-exist on three levels at all times: separation, connection, and unity. Each consciousness level can be likened to its own world. And each of us is living a different reality because we operate and create from a unique combination of these three levels. This is what makes our individual lives and worldviews different.

This book is divided into three parts which corresponds to a specific consciousness level. Each consciousness level has its own function and purpose that supports us as we explore, interpret, and evolve in the world around us. These levels also have corresponding internal infrastructures:

- The separation consciousness is expressed through our personality.
- The connection consciousness is expressed through our intuition.
- The unity consciousness is expressed through our soul.

In Part I, we explore the separation consciousness and Personality Level, which are a reflection of one another. At this level, family, friends, experiences, religion, media, and politics influence us and the conclusions we draw. This determines what we expect from others and ourselves. Also, the personality is formed which is a mask that places a boundary between our internal and external selves. Part I presents opportunities to question, review, identify, update, and change the conclusions we have made about our lives until now.

In Part II, we explore the connection consciousness and Intuitive Level, which are a reflection of one another. Becoming the authority in own lives through self-mastery and self-determined responsibilities creates new possibilities and visas we may never have imagined before. Our intuition acts as a midwife as we give birth to visions, insights and inspirations. We now develop an expanded version of who we thought we were. Hope for a more positive, fulfilling and richer life turns into action with the guidance of our Intuitive Level.

In Part III, we explore the unity consciousness and Soul Level, which are a reflection of one another. This level is potential waiting for interpretation and form. It is a world of transcendent and universal energy that exists everywhere. Everything comes from this energetic impulse that radiates within and around us. We cannot understand the vastness of this level of consciousness with our individual minds—it is far too big for us to grasp. We only access it through our souls. They are our energy adaptors and transformers. They customize and step down this incredible living pulse into a miniature that we can manage.

In each part of **The Next Step**, we explore the beliefs that represent our Personality, Intuitive and Soul Levels respectively. Then, we investigate the psychology, purpose, defining questions, motivating impulses and lessons to learn through each consciousness level.

When the Soul, Intuitive, and Personality Levels merge in our internal world, we know how to invite in the separation consciousness and use it to further our goals. But we contain it so that it doesn't crush our spirit or initiative. In this merged state, we are capable of creating rich, vital, rewarding, magical, and magnificent lives. This benefits us individually and collectively as we evolve as spiritual human beings.

## What is your choice? What is your next step?
### *How to Use This Book*

This book offers a guide for becoming who we are meant to be by living our birthright of merging our different levels of consciousness within. It is a personal journey, one that is unique to each of us. You decide how you want to approach this book. **The Next Step** provides several ways to discover, interact with, process, implement, and integrate the insights presented:

- Questions and "Check it Out!" exercises
- Points to Ponder
- Exploration and Discovery Activities

Perhaps reading a few pages a day and answering the questions as you read will provide a way to personalize and pace the experience. Or you might prefer to read a whole chapter and then go back to answer the questions that support you as you discover more about yourself, challenge your belief systems, and create new ones. You could doodle and sketch symbols, make comments, underline, and pose questions in the margins or on a piece of paper as you read. The Exploration and Discovery Activities at the end of the chapters provide experiences that support you to go into depth in your personal exploration. Journaling about the Points to Ponder at the end of chapters and any statement you want to spend more time with in a chapter, provides an opportunity to develop, expand and personalize new ideas, feelings and gain further insight.

Another possibility is to list the questions as you read. In a journal or notebook that is committed to interacting with this book, write the first response to the questions. Then later that day, the next week or following month return to the questions. You will find that each time you address these issues, you will write at a deeper level. Additional insights will appear in all areas of your life. That is the magic of entering and merging new levels of consciousness within.

For those that prefer to use a computer for answering the questions within this book or for journaling, I invite you to use the <u>www.DorothyBodenburg.com</u> website. questions and activities are available for download.

### *The Road Ahead*

Humanity is at a crossroad as we clarify and resolve problems at a scale never before seen. Swiftly changing scientific and technological advances are colliding with traditional individual and cultural values that are slow to respond to change. Transitions in demographic, economic, and environmental trends are testing our ingenuity. We are reaching a point of maximum stress on natural resources, a changing climate, inefficient responses of governments to meet the needs of its people due to decades of unchecked population, deterioration of infrastructures, and the dominance of profit-driven economics in the decision making policies of local, national and international governing bodies.

These transitions affect all of us—individuals, families, local communities, cities, and nations. However they also present us with unprecedented openings for change. The intertwining of these forces is an opportunity for us to take our next step in the evolution of man. We are capable of creating and implementing new visions and building flexible structures that satisfy the needs of the twenty-first century.

**We are the solution.**

# Part I.
# The Separation Consciousness
# And The Personality Level

## Chapter One

### What is the Separation Consciousness?

The separation consciousness is a perspective that the world and all in it is made up of distinct, stand alone units or parts. Only when and if these parts are fitted together does the whole picture appear. In the separation consciousness we use roles, job descriptions, family traditions and external influences to help us decide what is available to us. Finding and fitting together the roles that make up the various parts of our life is essential for survival and determines our existence.

### The Separation Consciousness is a World of Forms

The beliefs we use to shape our unique lives originate from the perspective of the separation consciousness. We accumulate objects that we need to provide the essentials of living: house, car, food, clothing and leisure "toys." These are all the forms that make up our everyday existence. Also, we form interactions with people such as loved ones and coworkers for the different roles and functions they may play in our lives. This process derives from what already exists and is available to us. We do not design and build our car. We select from the cars that are manufactured by different corporations and fit within our price range.

The separation consciousness is our first attempt to form a lifestyle in our family and community in order to survive and belong. While we may take for granted the forms that surround us, we need them to survive. We relate to the world of form in a physiological and psychological way. Form as a noun consists of myriad inanimate objects and living organisms. Noun forms have names and definitions such as apple, chair, Ben & Jerry's Ice Cream, and John to differentiate one from another. Verb forms pertain to the process of coming into being. This includes the traditions we use to create Christmas, celebrate the Fourth of July, enjoy summer vacations, parent, or cheer on our favorite sports team. For instance, the idea of Christmas sets into motion our gathering all the elements: the tree, decorations, Christmas music, wrapped presents. The idea is the stimulus for actions and use of certain concrete forms. Whether we are referring to the literal, concrete or processing of creating a form, our everyday lives are consumed with interacting with the world of forms

Our physiology validates the existence of the separation consciousness since we perceive forms through our senses. While taste, smell, touch, and hearing support the existence of forms, our visual perception plays a major role in reinforcing the separation consciousness. We can see the space between individuals and objects. We assume that the space is empty because we can walk between them. These solid forms provide a sense of continuity and safety, especially when we attach an emotional connotation with form. A locket given to us by our first love, a worn baseball mitt, grandmother's china all elicit powerful feelings when touched or looked at. These associations are created by past and present personal experiences, interactions with individuals and groups, and acceptance of traditions in society. They are strong influences on our lives. Since our focus is on our daily tasks in this world of forms, we do not spend time analyzing their effect on our psyche. However, our relationship to our physical world of forms does impact our perceptions and relationships. From our physiological and emotional responses to forms, we develop common and personal assumptions, beliefs, thoughts, feelings and actions. We create a perspective which I describe as the separation consciousness.

The psychology resulting from the separation consciousness creates an "us versus them" mentality. Describing and judging the differences among people, animals, things, and ideas separates one from the other. Indeed, labeling is the language of the separation consciousness. If we identify individuals according to a "foreign" nationality such as

Australian, Chinese or Tongan, we scrutinize their behavior, dress, and language. Our focus is on noting the differences. Depending on the situation, we may take another step and determine whether they are a threat to us. However, if we view the person as a fellow male or female of the human race, the differences diminish since gender is more global than nationality. An expression of the separation consciousness is the way individuals, groups, and nations define themselves. One may share common rituals and behaviors that put them at odds with others. All the past and present religious struggles demonstrate the power generated by using the differences in beliefs as the basis for determining relationships. One worldview is judged better than another. Which one will the majority accept? Who is chosen to profess these beliefs? What kind of power do authorities have to implement and enforce these beliefs? And what happens to those who eschew them?

At this stage of self-awareness we view people, places, and things through our individual perceptions of them. When we interact from the separation consciousness reality, we look at the concrete form of our friend Susan. Yet we see only those parts of her that have meaning to us. We acknowledge Susan as our friend but not necessarily a lawyer, mom, wife, or school volunteer. We also don't relate to the larger context of Susan as a fellow resident of planet Earth. Nor do we see the invisible parts that make her whole, such as her intuition and soul. The part of Susan we relate to is all that interests us. Susan is a total entity by definition of the role we assign to her. In the separation consciousness, we compartmentalize our interactions with only those parts we value. The doctor treats the liver as a separate entity from our body. We make choices for lunch without taking into account all the food we eat in the day. We relate to Mary only as our housekeeper, ignoring her family life and economic situation. We focus on a segment that is merely part of a bigger whole, yet this attitude limits our perspective of what is possible.

The associations between familiar noun and verb forms bring emotional comfort. However, this rapidly changes into habit. But such complacency in the consciousness of separation creates a cocoon-like mentality which blocks new perspectives that might improve our lives.

Indeed, we may equate change with chaos that would threaten our way of life, and thus be difficult to accept and implement.

## Beliefs of the Separation Consciousness

Living from the separation consciousness is like learning to play a new board game. We follow the rules and accept a common meaning and usage of all the pieces. In addition, the game has a beginning, middle and an end, with drama, competition, excitement, and disappointment. Each time we play, the game changes, yet the rules and goal of winning are the same. The separation consciousness also has its own rules of engagement for all who participate in it. Whether we accept, fight, or reject these beliefs does not diminish the fact that they are the determining factors we use in creating our lives. Keeping in mind the board game analogy, we can play our lives any way we want as long as our strategies fit into the content and context of the game. Let us see some of the rules, basic premises, and beliefs for the game of life in the separation consciousness.

### *Dependence on the external as a reference point*

Separation consciousness helps us find our first place in society. We figure out how we can use our abilities, talents, and preferences to make a living and find acceptance in our families and communities. We rely on external feedback to figure out how well we are doing with this important task. Since the motivation for recognition is so important in the separation consciousness, we develop only those traits that are desirable to the organizations and institutions to which we belong: the corporation we work for, the religion we follow, political parties we elect, our family traditions... We take on their attitudes and beliefs and use them as our own.

Each of the institutions we participate in presents spoken and unspoken expectations and desired behaviors that reflect its beliefs. We must behave in certain ways to sustain acceptance with these external influences. This leads to the different roles we play in different parts of our lives. We follow a script for each of them— co-worker, family member, friend, partner–that calls for us to use different parts of our self in certain combinations. The husband who is a manager may have positional power at work, but if he tries to be the ultimate authority at home, fireworks will ensue. A smart man knows that a successful father and husband are more personable, collaborative, and loving at home than at work.

We use our personality in different ways for each of the roles we play. All of us are left to navigate and negotiate with our self and others to balance the many roles that define us. Our aim in the separation consciousness is to ensure that we have a sense of satisfaction in these varied roles and a certain amount of ease in shifting from one to another. One way of dealing with this constant rearranging of our personalities is to compartmentalize. This means focusing on specific actions and behaviors that are appropriate to the role and situation at hand. This can be as easy as taking off our work clothes and putting on old grubbies when we get home. This simple act is the trigger for letting go of certain behaviors and attitudes and embracing others

How we juggle all of our roles is a reflection of our understanding of our self and our beliefs. However, while living our busy lives we still wonder how we are doing and want reassurance from those we care about that we are on the right track. We look to external feedback from friends, family, and co-workers to reassure us that our behaviors are acceptable. We also seek feedback to feel safe, since we believe that we are in control of our lives when we do what is expected of us. Since external feedback strongly influences our self-image and self-esteem in the separation consciousness, we are dependent on it.

### Check It Out!

**There is a correlation between what we are willing to do to be accepted and meet our own and others' expectations and our self-worth. Therefore it is important to assess our level of dependence on external feedback.**

- What happens to your self-image when the boss ignores your accomplishments?

- What are you willing to do to be successful?

- What happens when you are in the "out" group at work?
- What do you do so others think you are powerful?
- What are you willing to do to keep a relationship going?
- What happens at home when you feel you are taken for granted?
- What do you do to be liked and accepted by friends?

**If you change yourself to win the approval of others then dependency on the external is operating in your life. If you do not reflect on the external feedback you receive and decide which has meaning for you and then throw away the others, you will be forever dependent on situations and others for your self-esteem. You may be unable to develop your personal power, for you assigned others to define it for you.**

## *The patriarchal voice*

In the separation consciousness the patriarchal voice dictates the positional power of men and women in society. The patriarchal voice proclaims that men possess reason, intellect and courage. This gives them the power and right to make decisions, set boundaries, discipline, protect and create order for society.

Historically, the patriarchal voice has positioned women as less important than men. The assigned role for women is to care first for the male authority in the family whether he is the father or the husband, and then care for children. The needs and values of women are not a value or concern of men.

In fact, the patriarchal voice judges, limits, and trivializes women and their work as a means of keeping control. In putting down women, men attempt to elevate their own positions. They use their power to remain on top of the system. Religions, which are patriarchal in their teachings, are headed by men. The man is supposed to be the head of the household; men dominate as national leaders; the corporate world is still predominately a man's good old boys club; and men's collegiate and professional sports are more visible and financially powerful than women's teams. In our world, men are held in higher esteem than women.

This bias against women exists in everyday life in all cultures around the world: less pay for women doing the same jobs as men; the struggle to the top of hierarchical organizations; restrictions on women to be educated, drive, and hold property or public office. Even now, there is an expectation that women are responsible for the emotional environment in the workplace.

In a more personal expression, the patriarchal voice tells a woman that she needs a male to feel safe and protected, that she cannot achieve without the help of a man. The implication behind these messages is that women are incompetent, they cannot look after themselves, and their feminine qualities are less valuable than masculine traits.

If women accept help they lose their own power. They feel divided internally because to stand up for what they think is right puts them at risk. They may be alienated, which makes them feel separated from the safe road. Fear and anxiety then cause doubt about whether what is important to them is really of value. Also many women still believe that to gain power they must take on masculine traits and suppress their feminine qualities. Protection and support from the patriarchal male exacts a high price. In the separation consciousness the repercussions of "stepping up to the plate" may be too big a risk. This internal battle crushes the aspirations of too many women.

The patriarchal perspective has endured for thousands of years because it assigned roles to men and women who worked to build a civilizing social structure. Mothers and fathers taught these roles without question to generations of children. As a result, the patriarchal voice is imprinted in varying degrees in all societies, past and present.

Today, despite the fact that technology and greater access to education has changed the world, the patriarchal voice still tries to maintain its power and influence. The resistance to new ideas that develop from the growth of society is a threat to the power structure that the patriarchal voice created. It does not want change, and yet nothing can prevent it since change is an inherent part of life. These opposing forces shift the noble parts of what the patriarchal voice achieved and pull it into a destructive vortex. To survive, the stakeholders and institutions that benefit from the patriarchal voice must maintain power at all cost. Any change no matter how necessary is a threat.

Some of the most severe problems that hurt people today- financial uncertainties, competition for world resources, humanitarian and environmental disasters and many others—have been caused by those who hold power granted by the values and practices of the patriarchal voice.

In the separation consciousness the patriarchal voice dominates the way societies function. This dominance prevents the acknowledgement that there is a masculine, dynamic energy in both males and females. This masculine dynamic energy contains reason, intellect, creativity and courage, attributes that the patriarchal voice claimed for the basis of power and used and abused in its interpretation and implementation. Nor does the patriarchal voice acknowledge that there is matriarchal voice. The matriarchal voice values love, caring, connecting, nurturing and the intuitive nature. These are all qualities that enrich the human spirit. However in the separation consciousness this voice has no legitimate platform.

The patriarchal voice denies that masculine, dynamic energy and feminine, receptive energy reside within both males and females. In the separation consciousness, the patriarchal energy is only acceptable within the male, and the feminine energy is rejected. This is the source of misunderstanding, and separation between men and women. We end up just viewing each other through tired, overused stereotypes. The separation consciousness builds an opposition between males and females and the patriarchal and matriarchal voices. This creates a competition between which voice should be heard. All lose when there is an either/or perspective. Each voice has value and when both are used, one expands the other.

Only in modern society is the patriarchal voice starting to be questioned. Only recently (as compared to the history of mankind) are women and men recognizing that the strength of the patriarchal voice needs to adapt to today's values, needs and resources.

## Check It Out!

**Since the patriarchal voice is still the dominant force in our society, it is difficult to determine the extent of its influence on our personal lives. Without a new model to guide us, we are left with uncertainty as to how to delineate the strengths and abuses of this voice. Personal review is essential in order to make choices on our own behalf.**

*Review the institutions that you participate in and notice the ratio of men to women in leadership positions. Observe your tendency to choose to trust a male or female who were both considered experts. Write down the stereotypes you hold about the opposite sex and determine if one sex is more important and powerful than the other. What causes one to outrank the other? What place in society do you think men occupy? What place do women occupy?*

*If you are a woman review all your relationships with males (father, teachers, brothers, husband(s), lovers, friends, co-workers) Notice the strategy they use to get you to do what they want. What strategies do you use to get what you want from them?*

*If you are a man, review your relationships with women (mother, teachers, sisters, wife/wives, friends, co-workers) and reflect on the strategies you use to get what you want from them. Think of the strategies women have used on you to get what they want.*

**If your relationships at home or work involve power struggles between you and the opposite sex then the patriarchal voice is operating in you.**

## Absolutism

Absolutism is the desire for hundred percent certainty. Either you're right or you're wrong; either it's black or it's white—a zero sum game. Being absolutely sure about a belief, decision, or action is a desire in the separation consciousness. If you are perfectly sure about divorcing your wife, then you shield yourself from doubts or anxieties that come from this enormous decision.

You may recognize that the conflicts with your wife are based on black and white statements such as: "I cannot make a statement without her being critical and defensive." "Her friends are more important to her than me." "We are living two separate lives." "We have nothing in common anymore." "We said we wanted children before we got married, but now her career is the most important part of her life." "We don't talk, we fight." But then memories of tender times intrude and confuse you. You remember the feelings attached to certain events in the relationship... "the time she came home excited about her promotion and we celebrated, making love the first time, sharing our dreams, when she looked at me with love in her eyes, when she listened to me, when she believed in me." Now ambivalence sets in as feelings and thoughts collide.

This time of ambivalence is difficult since there is no absolute answer or guaranteed outcome for any decision. Fear of making the wrong decision that you will regret or be criticized for makes you vulnerable. In the separation consciousness, making any decision and acting on it will be judged and therefore has risk attached to it. Friends and family always offer opinions whether or not you want them. Your decision may be accepted or rejected by those who are important to you. "What will my parents say? Whose side will our friends take? Will this disturb the way my co-workers perceive me?"

Because being absolutely sure about leaving your wife prevents these feelings of vulnerability and self-doubt from arising, it is easy to see how seductive certainty becomes. In the separation consciousness, we are still dependent on the external world to validate who we think we are. Our internal world is not as solid as we need it to be. Ambivalence causes frustration, anger, depression, overwhelm, and fear. These feelings may come at unexpected times and can seem to flood us. The desire for absolutism correlates to doubt about our self and what we need and want. If only we could find the right answer then we would feel in control again.

## Check It Out!

**The way we react to circumstances and situations defines us. The decisions we make are relative to our interpretation of our relationship to our self and others. We also are unduly influenced by others.**

- Do you view situations as right or wrong?
- Do you want choices to be all or nothing?
- Do you wish life was black or white?

- How do you react to anxiety and ambivalence?

- What do you do to feel in control again?

- When you make a decision, what comments do you use to back it up? Are these familiar? "That's the way I have always done it. My religion said so. That's the way it should be. I'm doing the right thing. I'm right!"

**In the separation consciousness we are most vulnerable to exposing who we are. Absolutism is an illusion of self-confidence and conviction that is not necessarily tied to our true nature. If the desire for absolutism is something you seek it demonstrates that part of you is living from the separation consciousness.**

## Time as a reference point

In the separation consciousness, time acts as a structuring and focusing device through work schedules and designated family and free time. We go to work at 8 AM and focus on certain tasks and roles. We take a coffee break at 10 and go to lunch at noon. The school day signals that only certain behaviors and topics are acceptable until the final bell rings. During vacation, we act differently than during the workday.

Time regulates large numbers of people, which supports, reinforces and sustains the values of the status quo. Authority figures consider the regimentation of time necessary to ensure control over workers so that their responsibilities are met. At a certain time we appear at work to interact and do what is necessary to accomplish the tasks required to keep the business going. Flextime becomes an option when companies are competing for workers. Conversely, when there is more competition among workers for jobs, flextime disappears. Regimented time ensures control; flextime requires trust.

Time controls our lives almost parentally by telling us what to do and when. Think about it: How does time control you during your day? What are you supposed to be doing at 6:30 in the morning or at night? What does it mean to be out at 2:00 a.m.? What behaviors and feelings does the thought of 5:00 p.m. activate? The structuring of time gets us to conform to the producer/consumer model that dominates our regimented society. Just look at the freeways during rush hour to see how we all obey. Time is also used to make judgments about our activities. If we aren't doing what the majority of people are doing at a certain time, we become suspect. A spouse might ask his or her mate, "What were you doing up at 3:00 a.m.? Couldn't you sleep? Oh, what is wrong?" If we leave work early, it is noticed. If we arrive too late, assumptions are made about our performance.

There are so many connotations associated with time that impress upon us the right way to respond. "Time is money," is a favorite saying of the business world. Of course, what they are really saying is that if we waste time, we might not maximize profits for the company. Religious institutions give the message that idle time invites the devil. Alternatively, if we are not spending our time in a worthwhile way (as defined by what we think we should do) then we are also suspect. Again, this is evidence of the power of the external environment to regulate our thinking and influence us to conform to the accepted ways of our social institutions. These institutions let us know what is worthwhile. For instance, the concept of families is really a function of societal institutions, for they instill accepted values through parenting. Teens are forced into time frames by parents who relate the importance of using time properly. Most parents of teenagers complain that their children don't do anything worthwhile with their time. Random Internet surfing, texting, downloading songs, talking on cell phones, blogging, and watching TV are all important activities for teens but parents judge these activities as waste of time.

From this we can infer that time is also associated with achievement and how much we accomplish. The way we spend our time demonstrates to others what we value.

No matter how reassuring we are or how much quality time we spend with our children, they figure out how "important" they are to us based on how much time we spend with them. The number one complaint I get from young children is that their parents are always busy. Even if the parent is home, it still doesn't mean that he or she is giving the child attention. One ten-year-old told me that she can't remember her mother ever looking at her when she talked, because she was either opening the mail, checking her voice mails, or cooking dinner. Even if we tell our kids we are busy and don't have time, what is that saying to them?

Time also helps us make sense of our lives. Evaluating what happened in the past, is happening in the present, and will happen in the future affords the opportunity to see the scope of our lives. Reflecting on our personal story supports us in understanding our changing needs and motivations. Where did you come from? Where are you going? What was important to you in the past? What are your motivations, needs and goals now? What are you hoping for in the future?

## Check It Out!

**Looking at the time we spend doing what we think we are supposed to do versus what we want to do is very revealing. Review the past week. Make some categories such as shopping, working, chauffeuring, talking to friends, and family time.**

- How much of your time is used on activities that you think you should do versus things you want to do?

- What distracts you?

- Who is in charge of your time?

- How are you affected by deadlines?

- What is your relationship to time?

**If you feel you never have enough time and are putting off activities that matter to you then time is controlling you. It's time to control your life by making some priorities that balance your life. You can't be everything to everyone!**

Time structures our lives and makes us decide what we do or don't do. That in turns becomes the guideline to how we live our lives and who we become. By reviewing your time you can see how you respond to the real and false obligations in your life. Part of the learning in the separation consciousness is to understand the effect of our behavior on others, which the use of our time provides. Another purpose of the external structure of time is for us to start making the daily decisions about how we use our minutes and hours that, when strung together, make up our life.

### *Belief in hierarchy*

A hierarchy defines who has power and who does not. This is done through role designation and job description. A hierarchy establishes that one person is the absolute leader and thus has the most power. For instance, the family institution may posit that the man is the head of the household. Religious institutions can give one person such as the Pope the right to speak for the whole organization. Monarchies would bestow such power on their king or queen. Hierarchical power brings with it control, recognition, status and most often, wealth. All of these factors of external success are extremely desirable in the separation consciousness. Is it any wonder that so many will do anything to climb the hierarchical ladder?

The belief in a hierarchy in the separation consciousness is another way for social and commercial institutions to reward individuals who excel in supporting the goals of the organization. The boss–CEO, the man–is designated to keep the institution going. That person has the authority to control the work environment and set the standards and rewards for all employees.

The head of the hierarchy becomes the spokesperson and leader to maintain the mission of the organization. Theoretically, corporations implement their mission statement. However, the key, unspoken objective is survival. To do that, the leader must make sure the commercial enterprise makes profits so that it sustains itself. In the family organization, social expectations give the head of the family direction. And with religious institutions, the leader enforces the human-interpreted, handed-down beliefs about the relationship of God and man and how we should live. Each step we move up the hierarchy brings additional power. Authority figures are people who exercise control over and influence lives. In its purest form, authority means that a person is an expert in something the culture values and will use this expertise to help others. However, authority figures that live from the separation consciousness perspective use their position in the hierarchy to amass more personal power. The higher the rung on the ladder one achieves, the more authority; hence more power. Power and prestige from hierarchical ranking is about controlling others with continuous demonstrations of one's accumulated power.

Hierarchies have layers of policies and rules to make sure individuals conform to the institution. Judgment about whether we can stay in our job shows up in the annual evaluation. Family conflict mirrors the different perspectives among family members that seem incompatible with the direction of the head of the household. If the head of the family— is too rigid, imposing only one way of doing things, then dysfunctional behavior will erupt. Nevertheless, any threats to one's hierarchical power are unacceptable. Nonconformity is a threat to social and commercial institutions. Tension arises when individuals in the organization or family have unmet needs or when the hierarchy's policies and beliefs discount these needs. The urgency of these needs does not dissipate. Some leave the institution and others express their feelings in destructive ways. We see this in the student who acts out in class, the employee who blames others for creating obstacles instead of finding solutions, the teen who defies authority, the illegal drug user. In extreme cases, some become so alienated from the institution they seek to destroy people and property. How many examples have we seen in the news of people who have killed coworkers because they felt they had nothing to lose. That is a sad commentary on hierarchical and authoritative power in the separation consciousness.

## Check It Out!

**If you have conflicts with authority figures, then it is important to review your first relationships with authorities such as your parents, elementary teachers, coaches and religious figures. Checking out how these people made you feel is important because it taints your relationship with all authority figures.**

- What type of a relationship do you have with the authority figures in your life?

- If you are an authority figure, what is your perception of yourself from those you supervise?

- Is there a difference between your perception of authority figures and your perception of yourself as an authority figure?

- How do you feel about yourself when you exercise the power inherent in the different roles of your life?

> **Making a written list of the attitudes and behaviors you want to follow as an authority figure will help you lessen the hold of past experiences. Don't let the past dictate the present or the future!**

At this level, we use anything in our arsenal to ensure our importance. We work and rationalize that whatever we need to do to climb the hierarchical ladder is all right. This blind ambition comes from the need to prove to others and ourselves that we are special—in short, to demonstrate our personal power.

## Competition

How often have you seen a new boss begin to redecorate the corner office—even before getting to know the staff? This act demonstrates that a new person is now in charge. Competition is associated with the belief in a hierarchy. No matter the number of people in the organization, there is only one person designated as the absolute leader. There is only one superintendent in the school district of twenty schools, one President of the United States, one head coach, and one CEO. Since only one person can be at the top, we compete with others to reach that goal. We use competition to establish a ranking among ourselves and others. This ranking labels us as the "up-and-comers," the "placeholders" and the "losers." As we climb the hierarchical ladder there are fewer and fewer spots, so the competition becomes fiercer. We demonstrate to our superiors why they should promote us instead of another. We also make alliances with those who are ahead of us to assure them that we will not be a threat to their power. How we compete is a reflection of who we are. Are you admired for your determination and the way you got to the top? Was your ascent marred by selfish backstabbing, brownnosing, or sleeping with your boss? Unfortunately, in my counseling office too many people regret some of what they did to get ahead. Illicit affairs, illegal or shady financial dealings, purposely spreading malicious lies, and many other unsavory acts are performed in the frenzy to get ahead.

Competition is also associated with scarcity. Scarcity in the separation consciousness activates a fear that we will not have opportunities for the right job, to be creative, to find a space where we fit in, to have money, to find love, or to have what we value. These fears make competition a fight for survival. Then the world can seem an unsafe place because there is not enough for everyone. The competition for goods and resources, when tied to survival, causes the basest of human traits to surface. What are we as a nation willing to do for oil, food and other natural resources?

## Check It Out!

When we compete we are taking a risk. We are striving for something that is measurable and visible...the medal, the new job, a title, a privilege. When we are victorious, others can witness our triumph. However, if we lose, they also see our defeat. With competition lies the potential for success but also the risk of humiliation and frustration. As you review your attitude about competition, be sure the risks are not too high. This will help you decide how you want to respond to winning or losing.

- What have you competed for?
- What have you given up because you did not want to compete?
- What behaviors have you rationalized as you competed?
- What behaviors made you feel proud?
- What does winning mean to you?
- What does losing mean to you?
- What attitudes about competing do you retain from your early years as you competed in school?

It is important to decide what we are willing to compete for and how we chose to compete. We all have to develop and feel comfortable with our own style. If you are unsure about yours, look to others whom you respect for some guidance.

Competition is a powerful force that motivates us to stay focused to achieve a goal. The rewards for winning in the separation consciousness are recognition, status and power. When we are competing against others for jobs, titles and status, we are in a personal power contest.

It causes us to compare ourselves to them, which prevents us from finding our own song, our own uniqueness. When we are competing against ourselves without any reference to others, we are defining and learning about ourselves. Deciding how you chose to use competition in your life greatly affects your relationship with yourself and others.

## Polarized thinking

Polarity is a field created by two opposing forces. Polarized thinking results from the nature of the separation consciousness and is a major influence on the way we see the world. Examples of polarity are all around us: male-female, night-day, black-white. It influences our thinking with such concepts as good-evil, either-or, receptive-dynamic, and rich-poor. Because polarity is based on opposing attributes, it limits our thinking and inhibits creative problem-solving. Polarized thinking suggests that if it's this way, then it can't be that; or if it's that way, then it can't be this, which leads to a simplistic view of individual and world problems. The most problematic factor of polarized thinking is that there are only two options. A great example revolves around deciding on a policy for abortion. The polarized thinking of abortion proponents and opponents makes it such a difficult issue to resolve. Each side is entrenched in a polarized ideology of right or wrong. Unfortunately abortion, like so many other issues, is neither all right nor all wrong. Many factors are at work including illness, rape, personal choice, the right of one group to impose their standards on another, and so on. Is abortion a legal or religious concern? Finding a solution that integrates parts of the opposing camps is impossible unless some common ground is identified.

The separation consciousness does not lend itself to mediation or creating a position that will serve a higher purpose. Coming to a workable solution means that the two opposing positions have to give up some convictions and power. In the separation consciousness, there is only a winner and loser. The winner gains power and status and the loser is out, a situation that may also include the loss of credibility and authority. The debacle in current American politics is an example of the limitation of polarized thinking. The Republican and Democratic

Parties are each too busy trying to prove they are right and the other is wrong. This is how the political parties keep their power. The more emotionally charged the issues that they can rant and rave about, the bigger the following. The parties must emphasize differences to ensure their constituency. The party helps the candidate get elected and that, in turn, makes the party more powerful. That is a win-win situation for the candidate and the party but what about the people? Think of all the campaign speeches we hear. Their only purpose is to get the current audience emotionally charged about the issues and point out that the other party caused them. If politicians would take the energy they use for their emotionally acted out speeches and apply it to solving problems, maybe something would get done.

Politics is all about personal power. Men and women convince themselves that they want to serve, but once elected, they focus on amassing and sustaining personal power to get re-elected. And that means siding with lobbies that fund campaigns and aligning with a certain political party even if the candidate doesn't fully embrace the party line. Washington, D.C. is so intoxicated with personal power that it is isolated from the people legislators are supposed to represent.

## Check It Out!

**The inflexibility of polarized thinking prevents changes that are necessary to make a difference in our own lives. Think of attitudes that you have.**

- Where can you detect either-or thinking?

- How comfortable are you in gray areas?

- What feelings arise when there isn't a clear answer to the situation?

- What is your reaction to others who have polarized thinking?

- What decisions are difficult for you to make because you can only see one way or the other?

**If you have difficulty being decisive or are reactive to others stating their opinions then polarized thinking is a part of your life. Try substituting the world "or" with the word "and" when you are trying to figure out alternatives. Take some of one position and part of another and see if you can create a new possibility.**

## *Materialism*

In the separation consciousness, success and personal worth are associated with materialism. If we own the trophy house, the expensive cars, and the giant TV screen, then we are not only powerful, successful and wealthy, but we are also persons of worth. This belief system is evident in our producer/consumer economic model—the dominant force in Western civilization. The consequence of this materialism is the dedication to the accumulation of wealth. If we choose not to participate, others judge us as suspect and lacking. Elevating our status is the need to be special or elite by legal or illegal, moral or immoral means. What matters is that we demonstrate to others that we are powerful enough to get what we want.

Unfortunately, materialism is a widely accepted and closely watched indication of our personal power. The rise of celebrities from reality TV shows is yet another expression of personal power and materialism. It is extremely difficult to untangle ourselves once caught in the web of using materialism for status and self-worth, since we would be naked to ourselves and others. How many times have you made a decision to forgo what you really needed and opted for the producer-consumer model which supports materialism?

A client of mine, who was a talented violinist, set music aside to go into the corporate world. She plotted and executed her strategies to become a CEO at a very young age. But by the time she obtained the title, the Mercedes, and the beachfront condo she felt disconnected from herself and dead inside. She believed that going into the corporate world was the right decision, since she accepted her parents' and teachers' warnings that a musician's life is hard. What she was saying to herself was, "I can't risk being a musician, because if I'm not great and make enough money I won't have the lifestyle that I want." So she has wealth, but has lost her soul. Materialism is also thought to bring happiness in the separation consciousness. Corporations selling products and services create and reinforce this message. Think of the billions of dollars spent in advertising to persuade us of what will make us happy. According to the producer/consumer model we should buy the latest trendy car, computer, and clothes; see the latest movie, play, and concert; travel where the rich and famous go, and work to remain youthful. "If I have the 4,500 square foot house, then our family will be happy." "When we get the 54-inch high definition, surround sound TV then the kids will be happy." "If I get Botox, I will be sexy." The attitude toward materialism in the separation consciousness makes people dependent on a thing for happiness, success, and self-worth. Unfortunately, obtaining "the thing" does not guarantee anything.

## Check It Out!

**Review your spending for the last five years.**

- How many things that you bought are still in use?
- What have you determined is enough in your acquisition of material items?
- What does your house say about you?
- What does wealth mean to you?
- How do happiness and material wealth correlate for you?
- Which of your possessions enhances your self-esteem? Why?

**If you are financially strained because of your purchases or there are many items that you bought that are not now in use then materialism is part of your thinking.**

Developing criteria for what to buy and why helps us get in touch with our true needs and wants. When we buy on impulse, or on the mistaken notion that it validates the giver or the receiver in some way, it keeps us in the separation consciousness. This type of dependence on external possessions as a way to meet our internal needs undermines our connection to ourselves. It makes us doubt our right to live authentically.

## Judgment

In the separation consciousness, judgment defines and reinforces what is acceptable and unacceptable. We make a judgment to determine whether the person we are talking to is one of us or the "other."

If we agree with another on recreational activities, dressing standards for our teens, political and current events, TV shows, and how national and world problems are handled then we feel validated. The other person is then one of us. We think we have enough in common to predict the other's behaviors. This gives us an illusion of comfort.

However, if we are the group in the neighborhood that wants to save the wetlands instead of building a shopping strip that will bring in city revenue, then the opposing group is the other. It is easy to see how the beliefs that characterize the separation consciousness work together. As the two groups push for different land use, emotions build. The rhetoric becomes a powerful polarizing force...one group's opinion against the other. Then each group will justify their positions using an assortment of facts that supports their position. Undoubtedly, there is some institution with a hierarchy and stated procedure to handle the situation that each group will want on their side. Also, within each group a possible power struggle will ensue for leadership. And each group will compete for the hearts and minds of those who are uninformed of the situation and try to draw the attention of the media.

What comes from this emphasis on differences are emotionally charged statements which further alienate the groups. The situation gets bogged down with judgments which further exacerbate any resolution. Frustration, anger, and violence become possibilities along with stagnation and deadlock. Certainly, this is a reason for finding another level of consciousness to live from.

Judging everything and everyone around us seems like a national sport. Review the TV listings, look at magazine and newspaper headlines, check out the internet, read text messages and posts on Facebook, talk to any stranger. We all give opinions solicited and most often unsolicited. Our movies, books, political attitudes, clothes, entertainers, schools, and anyone in the news are all subject to judgment by others, either legitimate critics or those who feel the urge. In our personal lives we judge family members and coworkers and are judged in return. Besides emphasizing differences which cause separation, we also use judgment to justify our behavior. Those who lead violent demonstrations against abortion providers justify their illegal behaviors by judging the concept of abortion. If we live our lives from the separation consciousness, we use judgment to police others to ensure conformity. Unfavorable judgment against an individual carries a threat of rejection, or a rallying cry to get others to join in condemnation in hope of influencing an outcome.

While starting a consulting business to further the concept of sustainable resources in manufacturing, a client of mine was fired up by the possibilities of managing natural resources. During meetings with others around the world, he judged their process and insisted upon his way. He thought the funding he had behind him would serve to convince people about his approach. All he accomplished was to cause friction between two groups that had previously worked together. As a result, the whole industry suffered a setback. This chaos and uncertainty also prevented him from getting what he wanted. Judgment prevents a coming together to create something new.

### Check It Out!

**Judgment is everywhere. When our personal opinions align with others, we develop relationships. When they do not, we form judgments that keep us separated. Judgment is a driving force in personal, national and international relationships. On a personal level we can determine how judging and being judged has influenced who we are now.**

- Who judges you now and who judged you in the past?
- How do those judgments make you feel about yourself?
- What decisions have they influenced in your life?
- How does judgment control you?
- Who and what do you pass judgment on? How does it make you feel?
- How do you handle differences of opinions and judgment in your relationships?

**If you have acted on others' opinions and judgment with which you didn't agree then judgment is a negative part of your life. If you reacted to others' opinions and judgments, revisit those reactions and decide again what is right for you.**

Judgment, when used to impose our will and personal power, is an expression of the separation consciousness. But judgment, when used as discrimination and discernment to further a goal or vision that doesn't have personal power as the real objective is not an expression of the separation consciousness.

## Concrete thinking

No one understands the concept of God completely. It is one of the great mysteries of our human experience. Are we a part of an overall pattern? Do things happen for a reason? Is God an all loving or a judgmental being? How do we even know there is a God? At the separation consciousness we focus on our own self-importance and righteousness. We are working on our own personal power and are uncomfortable with the concept of God as unknowable, mysterious and illusive. The words omniscient, omnipresent and omnipotent are used in reference to God. What do those terms mean? We want our God to take on human qualities — a reflection of our humanness. We hope that this gives us some understanding of God, so at least we know the rules of engagement. Religions, just like all other social institutions, act as interpreters of what is vague and unexplained and make concrete and literal explanations so that people feel safe. We want relief from feelings of vulnerability, anxiety and powerlessness so we can think we control most aspects of our lives. All religions take on the task of making God available to us if we do what the authority figures say. We then feel comfortable; we have a right and wrong way of establishing our relationship to the concept of an all-powerful, all-knowing being or consciousness level.

Each religion has its own formula, directives and laws. The Catholics are in love with the Church and accept those who follow its absolute authority. This means living by the numerous laws and customs to maintain the Church's ideals. If we follow the Church laws and financially support it, then we are candidates for a good relationship with God. The Protestants have different churches because of their preoccupation with the true interpretation of the Bible. Each church claims that its view is the right one, and all the others are wrong. From these different readings of the Bible flow the customs and taboos of Protestantism. The Jews have 617 canon laws to follow. Also, they must make sure they do nothing to damage or dilute the cultural and racial identity of the Jewish people.

But if religion is the vehicle of the message of God, how pure can the message be if each religion preaches its own beliefs and at the same time sustains itself as a viable institution?

Let's look at another issue. Global warming certainly has the ingredients to make all of us feel anxious. Whether or not global warming is true, just facing the issues of any changing weather cycle and the ramifications of raising crops and witnessing shifting natural habitats for species we depend on is daunting. The way to relieve this anxiety is to jump on the wagon of the pundit of our choice. Conforming to some authority figure's ideas makes us think there is a solution thus alleviating fears. If ten million people agree, it must be right? How did the earth ever change from a flat surface to a sphere? Conformity gives the illusion of safety and concreteness.

In the separation consciousness we want a consensus about issues and an agreement among experts and authority figures. We want a concrete solution to problems. And we want it understandable, logical and definite!

## Check It Out!

**Concreteness is important in the implementation phase of an idea. However, it can stifle alternative thinking and limit possibilities. Review how comfortable you are with abstract ideas and a desire for literal and concrete thinking.**

- What do you want to be concrete and literal for you?

- What does God the Father mean to you?

- What role has religion played in your life?

- What is the difference between religion and spirituality to you?

- How do you handle ideas that evoke anxiety?

- How do you determine what is real in your life?

> If someone asks you if there are UFO's and you immediately reply, "Of course not. I haven't seen any!" then the desire for literal and concrete thinking is active in your life. Pause to consider other possibilities. The question "Why not?" will support you.

## Conditionality

If you do this then I will do that. This way of thinking underlies spoken and unspoken contracts in relationships. "If I have sex with my husband then I can get my way." "If you get good grades mommy will give you love and attention." "If I pretend to agree with my boss and flatter him, he gives me the choice projects." "If I do for others, then people will think I am a good person." "If I put up with your abuse, then I won't have to face my fear of leaving the relationship." "If I meet all your needs then you won't leave me." Conditionality is based on the fear that we are not good enough.

## Comparing

I am better than you or you are better than me. Comparing ourselves with others can keep us feeling inadequate. "She is thinner than I am." "He has a speed boat and a sports car and I don't." "She is smarter and gets all the attention." "He can talk to anyone and I can't." When we judge ourselves as better than we become dependent on others for validation or have to convince ourselves that we are indeed better. "Everyone said that I throw the best parties." "I think I came up with a better logo; Steve just kissed ass to get his picked." "Everyone says I can get any guy I want." Comparing thrives on our feelings of unworthiness and inadequacy. It is based on the fear that we do not have our own unique talents. If we valued ourselves and developed our abilities then it won't make any difference how others live their lives.

## Ranking

One thing or experience is better than another. If we have the better thing or the better experience then we must be better. "It sounds like you had fun but wait till I tell you about my unbelievable vacation."

"It was once in a life time experience." "My decorator said my marble tiles came from the same area that the Romans got marble to build the Forum." "I only drink red wine from France, because it is the best." Ranking is an attempt to demonstrate than we are more discriminating, richer, trendier, and intelligent. It is the desire to be superior to others—a need that covers our fear of being inferior.

*Check It Out!*

**Many other beliefs describe the separation consciousness. Use your words to add to mine. Any belief that differentiates one person from another, judges them better or lacking, and then acts on those beliefs comes from the separation consciousness. This is how prejudice in relation to gender, socio-economic position, lifestyle, race, religion, talents and abilities, and religion are created.**

## Limitations of the Separation Consciousness

If we only live within the separation consciousness, we limit our human experience. Using the external world for personal validation underlies the beliefs of the separation consciousness. This premise sets up a dependency on the power sources in society—patriarchal institutions such as religions, corporations, politics, media, government and family—to prescribe how we should act, think and feel in order to gain acceptance. All of us participate in some institution, through work, religious beliefs or lifestyle. Participation, whether wholehearted or resigned, strengthens the perceived power of the institution. After all, if so many people are participating, then how can it be wrong? That question is answered with another question: How many people in those institutions rely on authority figures to tell them what to do? In the separation consciousness, the standards set by institutions create the standards of personal worth. This limits our personal development. The premise is that if we follow the dictates of authority figures, the institution will support us. However, support is limited to implementation of the institution's purpose, not the enhancement of our own talents, goals and visions. If we don't conform, then we are rejected, that causes feelings such as unworthiness, powerlessness, and despair.

If we participate in the institution, we must fit into the structure that sustains the system. We are required to do what the institution wants, which might not be what is best for us.

The separation consciousness is not the point of reference for our whole lives. It is a passage only. Its functions include learning socialization skills, exploring our abilities and experiencing our environment. These fundamental lessons that we learn in the separation consciousness through our Personality Level comprise our self-identity. As we discern what is right for us instead of blindly accepting the dictates of the institutions we are involved with, we start on the path of personal growth. Since society is a composite, of every individual member, we do effect change through personal beliefs and choices. Understanding the purposes and lessons of our Personality Level is a necessary foundation for this growth. Then we are ready to develop and align our self and spiritual identity, which encompasses more potential for our self and others. Our Intuitive Level in the connection consciousness supports this growth.

## Chapter One Exploration and Discovery Activities

**Mentally prepare yourself to be an objective observer. Slowly walk around your house. Look in your rooms, closets, cabinets and drawers. Then go into the garage and yard.**

- What are your overall thinking and feelings of your home?
- What parts of your house activate strong feelings?
- How does your house reflect you?
- What feels uncomfortable?
- What conclusions can you make about yourself from observing your home?
- Which possessions activate strong feelings?
- How do your personal possessions affect your relationship to the physical world?

**Decide on one prized possession (example: car, racing bicycle, jewelry, antique furniture, clothing).**

- How does it define you?
- For a week put it away, don't use it, or substitute it for a lesser valued item. If this isn't logistically possible imagine yourself without it.
- What was your reaction? What conclusions can you draw?

**Observe yourself for a day as you go about your daily life from the moment you wake up to the moment you go to bed.**

- What are you happy with?
- What causes you resentment?
- What do you want that you don't have?
- What would that do for you? What would that say about you?
- When do you have the most energy?
- When are you stressed?
- When are you most yourself? Is there a difference in your mood when you are working or at home? Does your mood

change as you transition from work to home? What is the best
time of the day? What are you doing? Who are you with?
- What do you look forward to in your day?
- What would you like to change in your day?

**Think of the decisions you made today, this week, this month, this year.**
- What beliefs, thoughts, and feelings were they based on?
- What were your motivations?
- What did you want to control?
- What were the results of your decisions?
- What did you learn from them?
- What conclusions did you make about yourself based on these
  decisions?

**Review the beliefs of the separation consciousness.**
- Dependence on the external as a reference point
- Patriarchal voice
- Absolutism
- Time as a reference point
- Belief in hierarchy
- Competition
- Polarized thinking
- Materialism
- Judgment
- Concrete thinking
- Conditionality
- Comparing
- Ranking
- Additional beliefs that you have thought about that describe the
  separation consciousness

**Choose those that impact your life right now.**
- How do these characteristics influence your beliefs and
  thinking?

- How do they influence your feelings?
- How do they influence or justify your behavior and actions?
- What motivations are created using these characteristics?

### Seeing a part as a whole

**In the separation consciousness, we compartmentalize our interactions with others to only those parts of them we value. This creates a partial perspective of what is possible. List some of your friends, co-workers, family members, and also your significant other.**

- What role does each person play in your life?
- What does each one do for you?
- What do you do for them?
- How can you open your relationships to discover the "whole" of who they are?
- How can you share the whole of who you are with them?

### Understanding your relationship to authority figures

In the separation consciousness, authorities shape our lives. Our parents are the first authority figures we encounter and have the most influence on our thoughts, feelings and beliefs about ourselves and the world. From your relationship with your mother, father, or step-parents, describes how you perceived authority figures? How did they make you feel about yourself?

**Think of all of the teachers and coaches you had in school. Describe the different kinds of "authoritative" behavior you witnessed.**

- How did you interact with authority figures?
- How did you think and feel about them?
- What is the range of your experience with them?
- What did you learn about yourself from them?
- What are the conclusions you made about yourself as you review the effect of the interactions between you and authority figures?
- How has that influenced your perspective of power?

- Think of all the jobs you have had before and after you started your career. List each job.
- What was the relationship between you and your bosses?
- What did you learn from these experiences?
- How did and do you feel about yourself when you interact with bosses? What kind of an authority figure are you?

# Chapter Two

## Personality as a Reflection of the Separation Consciousness

The Separation Consciousness forms the basis of our personalities; the purpose of the Personality Level is to establish our identity. The Personality Level is the infrastructure we use to understand our function in life. We are trying to find out how we as specific human beings fit into the world into which we were born. We have come into the lives of certain parents who supply us with genetic influences and life circumstances that help in this process. Our daily positive and negative interactions with our family of origin result in thoughts, feelings, behaviors and beliefs that will affect our decisions for the rest of our lives.

Our gender, race, socioeconomic level, religion, and culture also help to socialize us. These are filtering devices that define who we are and influence what we are supposed to do with our lives.

In the Personality Level, we try to reconcile what we want with what is expected of us as delineated by the spoken and unspoken rules of society. In fact we can think of the Personality Level as a malleable, ever changing mask that represents us to ourselves and to others in our intimate and public roles. This mask exists between our internal and external worlds and is designed to mediate what our ego wants and needs with the pressure to conform to society's expectations. Sometimes our mask hides or protects our inner feelings while at other times it displays them openly. How we react to the interplay between internal and external forces and how we express this dynamic is the function of the Personality Level. This process creates our beliefs, thoughts, feelings and behaviors. Our Personality Level then becomes a framework that helps us understand, experience, and express the separation consciousness.

*What is expected of you? Will getting what you want cause you to be accepted or rejected by society? What does it mean to be white, brown, black or bi-racial? How does having a doctorate degree or a high school education affect your life? What does it mean to be a woman in society? What does it mean to be a man? How does age support or hinder what you want to do?*

We use stereotypes and labels to answer these questions in the separation consciousness. In fact, multiple labels and stereotypes can be applied to all of us. These initially direct us into roles to clarify what is expected of us and what we are willing to do. Living from the Personality Level enables us to learn about the many parts of ourselves that we express in the different roles we play. We react through role definition: as friend, mother, father, cousin, lover, and coworker. Roles are the way we identify appropriate behaviors in any situation. *How does your behavior differ with a friend, a boss, and your child?* We also develop skills and talents that are accepted and marketable to enhance our place in life. Integrating labels, stereotypes, roles and skills that we use to fit in to our community make up the Personality Level.

However, at the Personality Level, we do not operate from a whole self-picture. We only see the parts we are using at any given moment, which are dictated by the external forces of society. Living from the separation consciousness only allows us familiarity with those particular parts of ourselves. Without the ability to see ourselves whole, we are left with a limited sense of self. It is as if we are made up of many separate compartments, each of which contains only some of our feelings, thoughts and actions. *In which role are you most competent? Which role causes you to feel most vulnerable? Which do you avoid? In which role do you feel most powerful? Which is closest to your ideal self? Which causes self-judgment or diminishes your sense of self?*

The distortion drives our Personality Level to compensate for our incomplete recognition of our abilities, talents and potential. Since we are seeing only parts of ourselves, we seek recognition, approval, and a sense of belonging. Achieving these needs assures us that we are functioning members of society. This is common to all people. It helps us to recognize that we are participants in the same game of life. *What are your needs? What do you feel is lacking in yourself? What are you longing for? What are you striving for? What are you trying to prove? Which emotional need is the most powerful motivator for you?*

The Personality Level is most influenced by external forces, as I described in Chapter 1. These determine what we want, what we need to do to get what we want, and how to go about doing it. It gives us a checklist of the potential rewards, which motivates us to win the prize. The need for an external point of reference is so strong that most of us become attached to it. In fact, many of us are dependent on it for approval and validation for most our lives.

## The Psychology of Fear and the Personality Level

At the Personality Level we react and must fit into the established ways of our society. Because of this, the psychology at the Personality Level is fear. We believe that institutions which create the norms for society establish the values and rules we must follow. This external point of view is the gold standard we are trying to live up to and is supposed to be the one that will ensure success and happiness. The beliefs held in the separation consciousness as I discussed in Chapter 1 (including judgment, patriarchal attitudes, hierarchy, and time as a reference point) are pressures that push us to conform to a pre-established mold. If we are unable to perform, we become fearful that we are inadequate. These fears come from the overwhelming dogma that one set of standards must apply to all.

All beliefs in the separation consciousness are judgments about our ability to adapt to the status quo. The inherent threat to our well-being in a judgment-based belief system such as this is that others decide whether we are acceptable. They decide our worth. *Does your family accept you? Who accepts you at work? What activities do you engage in where you feel part of the group? What activities or people do you avoid so you will not feel uncomfortable or criticized?* Judgment from others gives us feedback on our attempts to act on the norms of the status quo. However, it also activates the fear that we will be rejected because of the way we live our lives. This influences our thoughts, feelings, and actions. We see criticism everywhere: Think of the slights your children experience at school because they're wearing the wrong sneakers, the family member who tells you how to potty train your child, your co-worker lecturing you to stand up to your boss, a friend expressing disbelief that you didn't end your marriage, and on it goes. The Personality Level is infested with opinions, suggestions, and advice from self-appointed pundits in every walk of life. These are forms of judgments. And all judgments feed fear, self-doubt and inadequacy. It is amazing we can function as we swim in this sea of judgments. What makes others think they know better than we do how we should live our lives?

Not only does being judged inferior cause us emotional distress, but it also puts us at risk of feeling alienated from our "tribe." The fear of separation is so strong because it activates our most basic need to belong. When we are in survival mode, we are desperate. Helplessness and hopelessness can easily overwhelm us, producing anxiety that casts doubt and undermines our confidence.

Many people are unable to overcome these feelings. Mental illness, addictions, severe depression, and even suicidal thoughts develop when we are anxious, without support and feel we have no place in this world. *When have you felt threatened by fear-based emotions? What did you do about it? What did you learn from you experience?*

Even if judgment comes in the form of approval it is still a means of establishing what is acceptable. If we are praised for meeting our sales quota, the unspoken message is that we must repeat our success to continue receiving approval. Praise, a form of judgment, reinforces the group's standards. And if we don't live up to expectations, then we fall out of favor and will be ignored, criticized or rejected. Our status will be lowered. When we struggle to find our place in the world, our uncertainty-based anxiety makes us more susceptible to others' reactions.

Janet had just moved into a new school district where she very much wanted to fit in. During her first week, her teacher called on her to answer a question about the outcome of a battle in WWII. Since she was flustered, she unintentionally made a flippant remark that caused the other students to laugh as if she'd make a great joke. Their approving reaction set Janet on a course to be the witty girl in class. She hoped this would give her a way to fit in. Unfortunately, when we only use reactions from others as a barometer of how well we are doing, we become vulnerable to feelings of insecurity, incompetence, and unworthiness. All such expressions of fear turn into obstacles in our path as we try to become authentic people who are meant to develop our innate talents. To handle the vulnerability, we try to hide our fears. One way is to use personal power in the form of control to feel more in charge of our lives and to appear competent. Sixteen-year-old Annabel was at odds with Tina, her stay-at-home mother who had a college degree but never pursued a career. Tina was against Annabel going to France for a semester exchange program. She was plagued by fears of inadequacy and therefore worked to appear as a competent in-charge mom. But Tina's desire for recognition as supermom propelled her to be intrusive. She needed to control Annabel since her daughter's success would validate her skills as great mom. However, she became so involved in Annabel's activities that the teenager felt stifled and resented her mother.

Annabel really wanted to go abroad and her father supported this adventure. But Tina could not see herself as a competent person without control of her daughter. If Annabel left, who would she be? How would she handle her anxiety and self-doubt? Tina's need to keep her daughter dependent on her conflicted with Annabel's need for independence. A family uproar ensued. Annabel's father made certain she went to France. He also left the marriage. He was fed up with twenty years of living with Tina's controlling nature. Unfortunately, Tina was unable to face her fears which caused her to be stuck in the Personality Level.

We all want to demonstrate our authority and appear strong. However, our personal power often becomes an offensive tool that we use to set boundaries in order to feel safe, visible, and respected. We hate being disregarded. At the Personality Level, what others think of us and how they act toward us becomes our means of validation.

Being perceived as too weak to get what we want is yet another fear-based force in the Personality Level. While appearing like a good person we subtly use manipulation to get what we want. Even when we are courteous, compliment others, and show kindness, our agenda is for others to treat us in ways that make us feel good about ourselves. Alternatively, we may become dictatorial and use our authority to tell others what they should do and how they should do it. We become the know-it-alls who are "experts" on every subject. *What do you do that gets a favorable reaction from others? How authentic are those behaviors? How do you act to be accepted, loved and respected? What do you have to do to be heard?*

Living from the Personality Level can be difficult because of the expectations from self and others. This measuring up activates fear and self-doubt. And, in our society, fears are deemed a sign of weakness. Is it any wonder that we go to extraordinary lengths to hide them? *How much effort do you use to hide your fears? What behaviors work for hiding and defending against fear?* Reflecting on how we react to others reaction to us and what we do about it is crucial to understand our Personality Level and helps us identify beliefs from the separation consciousness that we embrace. It allows us to stop and evaluate: *Who is really in charge of my life?*

## Check It Out!

**Think of some of the times that you have said, "No!" to your child, husband or friend.**

- List the reasons or excuses you used to back up your decision.

- At what point has fear entered into your decision?

- How it has influenced you?

**We become fearful of situations that we cannot control or when there are no guarantees. If fear is the determining factor in making decisions, then you are limiting your life. You are living from the separation consciousness.**

Some years ago, a sixteen year old girl attempted to sail around the world. So many parents responded by expressing their fear of what might have happened to her. People who were disconnected from the situation and ignorant of the circumstances condemned her parents and made statements such as, "I would never let my child do that! She's too young! Those parents are irresponsible!" All of these comments were expressions of fear. It is so ingrained in our society, but it is a narrowing and limiting force.

## Reactivity and the Personality Level

We use others' reactions to evaluate our status. A spontaneous hug from our wife, a pat on the back from the boss, a smile of delight from a friend when we walk into the room all reinforce our positive self-esteem. We feel good about ourselves when others shine their light on us.

We interpret reactions in the Personality Level through a personalized viewpoint...*"It's all about me."* This happens in the separation consciousness because we are dependent on the external to judge what type of person we are. We are in the habit of letting others' reactions dictate our moods. Their positive regard makes us preen, puts a bounce in our step, and brightens our day.

Unfortunately, the converse is also true. Unfavorable reactions to and from us in the Personality Level not only affect us but also cause reactivity. By reactivity I mean a reaction that goes beyond the intensity of the situation. We have all seen reactivity...the dad on the baseball field who explodes at the umpire when his son is called out, the over-tired working mother who finds her teens fighting about cleaning up the kitchen and screams that they are grounded for the rest of the summer, the young woman in the car ahead that flips us off because we honked since she is so busy texting that she didn't notice the light had changed and on and on. The media and Internet are filled with tidbits of dogma that are twisted, turned and spun with emotionally charged reactivity, and is used to persuade, intimidate, and bully those who don't agree. We perceive this type of expression from "authorities" as showing conviction and is accepted in our society.

However, when viewed objectively we can see that reactivity is, in truth, a response to being judged by others, feeling humiliated, and being put in a place where we believe we need to defend ourselves from a real or imagined attack. Even if the criticism has some merit–our dog really does bark long into the night–we only perceive that someone has questioned or wronged us. And since it is "all about me," we have to fight back or defend ourselves. Shock underlies this visceral upwelling of feeling. Reactivity is the shock that we are being criticized, and that we don't agree or even acknowledge the possibility of being in the wrong. We are shocked because we are unexpectedly confronted with a situation or person who challenges our very sense of self. It also makes us feel the limitations of our power to control how others perceive us or influence a desired outcome. The shock bleeds into hurt that we were attacked and that brings varying degrees of revenge, anger, humiliation, and powerlessness. We may hide these feelings (even from ourselves), but we still react to them. This is because we feel the limit of our personal power to control how people think and feel about us. We have been found out! We aren't the wonderful person we want others to see.

Whether or not we acknowledge it, hurt puts us in a vulnerable position–we are less powerful and in control than the other. We feel the criticism as a personal attack. We react to this attack, pushing us into the defensive, survival mode. We either lash out at the person whom we perceived blocked our power or feel a generalized anger at life, "them" or any real or imagined group in our society, such as authority figures, politicians, bureaucrats, men, women, cops. Another reaction to the shock is to withdraw into ourselves and restrict our lives. In this case, we minimize our desires and needs to escape from the fear of rejection, failure, and helplessness. *"My eighth grade teacher told me in front of the whole class to pretend to sing at Spring Sing, and all my classmates laughed. I never opened my mouth to sing again even though I love it." "At a regional meeting, my boss laughed when I brought up an idea about redesigning the packaging on our product. He then said, 'Where did you get that idea? From your three year old son?' I guess my ideas aren't good enough so I don't say anything at meetings anymore." Can you make a similar statement about a past experience?*

Reactivity is an ineffective way of protecting our self. The result is an either/or outcome where someone is perceived as right and the other wrong. Therefore, one person has displayed more power than the other. This demonstrates the one-upmanship belief of the separation consciousness. Reactivity diminishes when we take more responsibility for our self-image.

---

### Check It Out!

**At the Personality Level, reactivity shows us how much control and personal power we feel we possess.**

- What makes you reactive? How were you hurt?

- What were you expecting?

- If you can't identify the feeling of hurt, what emotion are you familiar with when someone wrongs you?

- Who sets you off? What does that person do to push your buttons?

- What feelings can you identify when you are reactive?

- What defenses do you use to protect yourself?

- How do you feel about yourself when the situation is over?

**If you get angry or easily hurt, are susceptible to feeling bad about yourself because someone made a comment about you, are embarrassed the way you handled a situation, then reactivity is part of your life. If you find yourself reacting, it is time to uncover the feelings and beliefs that undermine you. Remember you are the only one who can decide who you are.**

---

## Our Will and Personal Power

Learning about our personal power is best observed in conjunction with the way we direct our will. Once we determine what we want, then our power is focused through our will to do what it takes to make it happen. *What were you willing to do to get what you wanted when you were a child, a teenager? What are you willing to do to get what you want now?* The process of satisfying our wants and needs helps us understand how much personal power we have. How we approach the obstacles that inevitably appear becomes a fertile ground for us to clarify our values and recognize the intensity of those needs and wants.

Personal will, which is the application of our power, is directed by emotional needs that we may or may not know or accept. For instance, whether or not we consciously admit it to ourselves, the degree to which we need recognition is a strong motivator. It propels us to go back to school for an advanced degree, to become a workaholic, to achieve a title or a certain salary, or justify time away from family responsibilities. Even if we are unable to name the emotional need that drives us to use our will, we justify what we want. Who says that getting an advanced degree is really stimulated by an ego need or that wanting more money for the family is just about self-validation? What comes from these needs is often supported by the success labels that society has defined.

Our use of personal power to get our needs and wants met, especially the needs that demonstrate our materialistic success, is very seductive. Deciding how to use our power is our responsibility. We could spend hours debating the need and value of the goals we decide upon. For one person, promoting environmental issues is important for the preservation of civilization; for another eliminating aid to illegal immigrants is. Being proactive and reactive to the decisions, beliefs, feelings and behaviors of others and ourselves creates society.

How we use our will depends on what level of consciousness we are operating from. In the separation consciousness, which we experience at the Personality Level, we are trying to prove something to ourselves and others. The psychology of fear is our motivation. This comes from our inability to know all of who we are. At some level of our awareness, we feel inadequate. We need more at this stage, and whatever that "more" is, we are willing to use our personal power to get it. Status, titles, material possessions and family are all examples of what results from successfully using our personal power in ways others recognize. *What have you learned about yourself and power? When in a position of power, what were the consequences of your words and behavior? How did those consequences make you feel about yourself? Where has the use of personal power led you? What does it reveal to you about life?*

Human and spiritual development is about learning, expanding, experiencing, expressing and choosing, then being responsible and accountable for the consequences of our choices. The personal growth and spiritual aspect in the separation consciousness is learning the cause and effect of using the personal power of our will.

## Defining Questions

Exploring the separation consciousness as experienced by the Personality Level is a necessary first step in our understanding of what it means to be human. It is our entrée into the spiritual experience. Below are defining questions that will support you in assessing where you are in this wondrous journey.

### How much personal power do I have?

We all want power to control our lives in order to get our emotional needs met such as the need to be accepted, appreciated, and loved. In our busy daily lives, we focus on our health, parenting, work, relationships, extended family, home, and myriad other tasks we must accomplish to sustain the lifestyle we desire. In short, the question for all of us is: How do we balance our responsibilities with our emotional needs and personal choices? At the Personality Level, power and control are associated with the roles we take or are assigned. Each role, whether at work or at home, spoken or unspoken, has responsibilities. Being a project manager or planning the family meals carries an implied agreement among the people involved. The project manager has the recognized power to control workers, resources and schedules that affect the whole project. The mother, who is responsible for planning, shopping for, and cooking the family meals, has the power to control what her children eat. Responsibility, control and power are intricately interwoven.

We accept responsibility because it allows us to test our power and control over our lives. We get to see how effective we are in implementing our choices. This can result in a difficult or satisfying life. Responsibilities shape our lives by defining how much time and effort we put into each task. To one man, being a father may mean providing a big income to have the best house and private schooling, whereas to another father, responsibility to his child may mean throwing around a football or accompanying him to the library. Both responsibilities entail different behaviors. One father may work twelve hours a day while the other only eight. The relationship between each father and child is different.

Once a person accepts a responsibility, he or she focuses energy and power to achieve the stated goals. Observing how we go about achieving our goals and whether we attain them helps us to evaluate any discrepancies between our actual and perceived control and power. Another way to look at this issue of power and control is to notice our effect on others. Those people who perceive themselves to be listened to, whose advice is sought, who give their opinions confidently and notice that others follow their lead are aware of their power. Those who perceive that no one is interested in their opinions, who hesitate to act, and need someone to reassure them or tell them what to do believe that their power is limited. The perception of being powerful or powerless (or any variation in between) colors our ambitions and either supports us to take risks or suppresses our adventurousness. The latter, unfortunately, stifles our growth and causes fear-based behaviors. And both motivations create very different life scripts. *In what situations do you feel powerful? How much control do you perceive you have? What and who do you control? Who controls or has power over you? In what situations do you feel powerless and helpless? What is your perception of yourself as a powerful person?*

## What should I do? What is expected of me?

At the Personality Level, the institutions that mean the most to us influence the expectations we have for ourselves. We want validation from these institutions. They provide guidelines that say if we believe and act in certain ways, we will be an acceptable member.

If we examine our desire for reassurance, we recognize that once more, the psychology of fear is operating. Using the external as our point of reference often hinders us from following our true nature and desires. Maybe we want to make custom carving knives. However, since there is no tried and tested path to follow, there are no guarantees that this way of life will be successful. We may turn from it and go into a field that provides enough income to raise a family. This keeps us safe from criticism since we are now taking the path others recognize. Being an organic farmer and introducing new varieties of vegetables to the market was difficult twenty years ago and highly suspect. Now that organic produce is viewed favorably, becoming an organic farmer has gained prestige, thus providing acceptance for those who follow that path.

Making decisions based on "shoulds" implies an exchange. Motivation at the Personality Level is based on fear. One aspect of fear is expressed through conditionality. If we adhere to the rules of the game, then there is supposed to be some type of reward. If we follow the way of religion, it will give us certain experiences, privileges or satisfaction in return. Another way of saying this is that we do A, B, C, and then we get back E, F, and G. There is a return for risk and effort. This implied relationship is inherent in all institutions and relationships with which we are associated.

However, in real life this conditionality may not yield the rewards we expect. Many college graduates are not employed in their area of expertise or at the pay scale they expected. The corporate obsession with meeting Wall Street's ratings and predicted earnings causes loyal, hard-working employees to be laid off. Our dependence on external structures to provide what we want and need is a high risk proposition. There are no guarantees of receiving benefits and rewards for leading a life that follows "doing the right thing" as deemed by institutions or others. The need for acceptance in our jobs and relationships influences all of our decisions.

Deciding what we should do, what we are willing to do and who we want to accept us defines our life course. Where we shop, what sports events we attend, how much alcohol we consume, and where we vacation are all designed to influence how people perceive us. At the Personality Level, choices, decisions and values are in accord with the social group we want to participate in. *What expectations did your parents have for you? How much of your life is aligned with those expectations? Why or why not? What do you expect from yourself? What do you think your significant other expects from you? How do gender, socioeconomic level and religion influence your expectations for yourself? What are the differences between what you want and what you perceive is expected of you?*

### What is my motivating impulse?

The motivations inherent in the Personality Level arise from our longings for happiness, but how we define happiness is influenced by all of the institutions that operate in our society. While individuals created institutions, they are still a powerful statement of what the majority of people believe. We may align ourselves with the institutions of our choosing and can be content. However, institutions are not designed to support the needs, longings and desires of individuals. They are successful when they herd people to conform. All of us deal with the reality that some of our needs are not being met. This disconnection between what society offers us as ways to be happy and what will actually make us happy falls within the realm of the Personality Level. At this level we must ferret out who is responsible for what in our lives. *What do I expect my parents to do for me? What is my responsibility to make my wife happy? How much money is necessary for my kids to live a comfortable life? What does work mean—is it fulfilling an interest or is it just time marked to get a certain income? Is the government supposed to send me to college? What should I be responsible for?*

Since separation is the central theme of the Personality Level it comes as no surprise that our thinking and feeling are oftentimes separated from each other or linked in a way that causes conflict. Thoughts in the separation consciousness are most often expressions of dogma based on external and accepted opinions. We might have complaints about everyone and everything, but when it comes to standing up for what we believe in and actually living it, the risks are high.

Trying to convince ourselves that the prevailing dogma is right is easier than dealing with our feelings and making changes that defy set ways. We are supposed to be happy on holidays and yet we all have stories that contradict that ideal. Vacations are supposed to be relaxing, we should be loyal to the company we work for, we should try to look young forever, we should trust our government...all of these absolute sound bite rules have emotional fallout. Yet expressing and sharing authentic feelings that are outside accepted thinking but affect the quality of our lives are discounted in the separation consciousness. Deciding between the bottom line versus child care at work, adult time versus parenting, betting on fantasy football versus buying plants for the garden, eating out versus cooking in... all of these choices are motivated by our emotions. Is it any wonder our thoughts, experience and feelings collide creating conflicts and reactions?

These internal clashes prevent us from clarifying our wants and needs. If we suppress or deny them, it brings confusion and reactivity. We get angry, hurt, vindictive, controlling, and whiny when our needs are ignored. However, our unmet emotional needs and unexpressed feelings, though suppressed, will still emerge, most often in unpredictable ways. If we don't fulfill them or at least come to terms with them, then our unconscious tries to do the job in ways that cause internal conflict. This conflict is expressed with or without our knowledge. *Remember that sexy, flirty dress that looked hot in the store but is still hanging in the closet with the price tag on it? Were you still happy with the red sports car six months after you bought it? Whose idea was it to camp in the remote region near the Dart River in New Zealand anyway? How often did you use the pool and spa you had to have that takes up most of the backyard? Was the first class trip to Hawaii the best use of your money?*

At this level, our feelings and thinking are not connected in a way that propels us into action. The beliefs of the separation consciousness are too rigid. This leads us to paths that may not support us. When a couple getting a divorce, was asked why they got married, the wife said, *"Well, all of our friends were getting married, so we thought we should too."* A woman who gave into the practical advice from her parents when she was eighteen wondered, *"I always wanted to be a dancer, but my parents convinced me that I was in fantasyland. I often wonder what would have happened if I had become one. I keep thinking that at least I would be doing something that made me feel alive."* What have you done under the pressure of what you believed you "should" do? On which issues do you find your thinking and feelings on opposing sides?*

Needs and wants give rise to motivations, for they direct us to get what we think we are lacking. Listed below are the most prominent motivations at the Personality Level.

### Am I amassing power for personal gain?

We want what we want and use our power and will to make it happen. If our will is strong enough, we think we should get what we want. To demonstrate our personal power and test our will, we try to control our environment, circumstances and the people around us. As we amass personal power our status changes. Others defer to us, we get our way, and others do our bidding in a manner that satisfies us. That boosts our self-image. Even if our power comes from a job description on the organizational chart, we own it. We gain privileges, which in turn concretizes our power for all to see. What makes a person rationalize unethical or illegal behavior? What drives a person to work twelve-hour days, six or seven days a week? What motivates people to plot, scheme and politic to obtain leadership positions? Why is it so difficult for leaders to share power? What is the basis of competition? All these questions are about the need for the gain of personal power.

At the Personality Level, personal power is an intoxicant. It causes people to feel alive and to perceive themselves as more important than others. It establishes a hierarchy in which everyone knows their place. Our positions are even indicated by our attire. Techies throw on whatever they pull out of their drawers, players in corporate America don designer suits, and the Hollywood set sports the newest and latest no matter how outlandish. Power and control are addictive. *How can you feel the surge of power again? What are you willing to do to obtain personal power? What do you do now to make yourself powerful?*

There are many ways to increase personal power. Some people become experts in their field so their knowledge will bring them power. Others associate with those who already have power and try to please them, hoping that some of their power will rub off on them. Or, perhaps power will be bestowed. And then there are those who manipulate people and situations to their advantage. They steal colleagues' ideas, denigrate a rival, and exhibit dishonesty and other deceptions to gain personal power.

Control underlies greed and corruption. When power is used for ego satisfaction, it is easily distorted and rationalized. Unfortunately, when a person needs power to define who he or she is, the good of the whole is negated. The man-made horrors that we have experienced throughout history come from the misuse of power. Think of the millions of people who died in the name of God just to make one religion and its authority figures more powerful than another. Manipulation of natural resources, food, education, drugs are all examples of people in the corporate world who justify their actions in the name of capitalism but really make decisions that feed the personal power of those in charge.

People who attain a position of power have a difficult time sharing it or giving it up. Power hungry people are only validated when the external world listens to them. Once they have amassed power, much of their energy is directed toward sustaining it. The loss of power will force them to forfeit their illusionary identity. And when a person is directing a lot of time to stay in power, then he is less willing to risk change. This happens in many companies where the officers are afraid of losing their power by exercising necessary change. Although short sighted, many executives sacrifice the long-term growth of the company rather than relinquish or share their power.

Moreover, our society is intrigued with the elite, the wealthy, and those who appear to be above conventional standards. However, these same people feel powerless without the structure they inhabit. No wonder they hang on so tenaciously. Their vitality and understanding of the true source of power doesn't come from within them. People who shy away from overt power may have been overly controlled in their young lives. This could be linked to physical, verbal or sexual abuse coming from an authority figure, or the competition for control within the family which caused fighting and violence. No matter the circumstances, many people are sabotaged and made to feel inferior by those who are supposed to be the teachers, coaches and mentors in their lives. The latters' need for personal power is so strong they easily justify intimidation, fear, and violence. However, because power is inherent in the Personality Level, those who don't use overt power can still express it covertly. The teen who takes drugs no matter the consequences controls the family dynamic. Since the drug user absorbs more attention and resources from the family (that should otherwise be shared with others siblings or directed toward family goals), the family becomes confined and limited in its choices. Even if the teen drug user doesn't acknowledge his power, it is obvious. Just ask another member of the family.

Passive-aggressive and hidden behavior are other covert uses of personal power. The husband who nods in agreement about staying within the family budget yet overspends on items the kids beg for in order to be the "fun dad." The teenage girl who promises to clean her room before her friend picks her up for a football game, and then secretly asks that friend to arrive early so she can avoid the task.

Presenting oneself as a victim is yet another way to use covert power plays. Excuses as to why a person cannot take responsibility could fill ten books. All are similar in that the "victim" presents distorted facts to the person he wants to control, hoping the other will be swayed by the tragic circumstances. What the victim wants is for another person to be responsible for him.

Often people will try to obtain personal power by joining the fight for a cause. We see this throughout history. When one group—a religion, a race, nation or culture—gains control over others, those in power easily justify their behavior by declaring that their belief system is better than the other. Being part of the dominate group bestows personal power to the "in" crowd. As the membership increases, the leaders justify greater acts of control. Violence is too often used as a means of control in the name of the cause. . . Personal power and control are behind all of the wars humanity has fought in recorded history. Wars only become obsolete with the sharing of power. Does one person or group of people have the right to speak for and control the thoughts, feelings and behaviors of others? Why or why not? What does domination of one group over another lead to?

## Check It Out!

**Personal power blinds us to the consequences of our actions and allows us to justify keeping this power at the expense of others. Even if we are aware of the addictive qualities of personal power, if we only stay in the Personality Level, our power needs will become insatiable. To acquire power requires a major ego investment of time and energy. It also takes focus, political savvy, tenacity and strategy. Oftentimes those who are most controlling are unaware of this drive.**

- What is your need for personal power?

- How much do you need to be in control?

- What happens if you are not in control?

- How in touch are you with feelings of inadequacy, unworthiness and insecurity?

- In what situations do you surrender control? To whom?

In its most sinister expression, personal power leads to violence and the violation of the human spirit. In its most beneficial expression, it empowers us to act in ways that are respectful of others and our self. It is important for us at the Personality Level to learn about our strengths and weaknesses through the limits of our personal power.

## Do I desire acceptance and recognition?

We want and need acceptance from our co-workers, family members, friends and the people we care about. This affirms that we are likeable and ensures that we have a place to fit in. This helps us develop self-confidence. Also, at the Personality Level we want to be accepted by people who will enhance our status. Whether it is entrance into an elite golf club, becoming a board member for of church, or joining a prestigious professional association, the desire for acceptance is strong.

Once we acquire some sense of belonging, we seek recognition as a validation to ourselves that there is something special about us. Recognition is powerful, because it is based on something that is specific. We are good at making our sales quotas, we solve health problems, we improve an engine design, we entertain with style and flair, we run the marathon, or we create a winning advertising campaign. This gives us additional status with specific perks. In business these could include bonuses, a new title, company awards given at recognition dinners, trips, great parking spots and big corner offices. In our personal lives it could be awards from social organizations, a large group of friends, the satisfaction of achieving a long-sought goal. We engage in situations that provide us with the kind of feedback that meets our need for recognition. What makes it so important is that the people we are comparing ourselves to and competing with acknowledge us. Whether it is overt, covert, conscious, unconscious, friendly or deadly, competition and comparison are part of gaining recognition.

## Check It Out!

**The need for recognition is insatiable. When we have it, our self-image is Technicolor wonderful. But if we lose our source of recognition, our self-image fades to black and white. Somehow, our sense of self becomes dependent on the ebb and flow of recognition. If we only stay in the Personality Level, we become addicted to our fix.**

- In what ways have you been recognized?

- How did people treat you differently?

- How long did the glow from recognition last?

- What are you willing to do to be recognized?

- Can I create an acceptable lifestyle?

At the Personality Level, the lifestyle we create is most influenced by the values of the specific community in which we live. We easily see this if we travel from state to state in America or go from country to country. Each neighborhood, whether it is in Hong Kong or Orange County, has a unique style about it. Some neighborhoods look forbidding with houses surrounded with walls and gated entrances, others have extravagant landscaping, while still others have old cars parked on the lawn. Living with people of the same economic means makes it possible to be satisfied with what we have and also meet our need to belong. It makes us feel comfortable and part of the neighborhood. But what if Charlie buys a fancy new car—a foreign brand not normally seen in our neighborhood? Suddenly, there is a ripple in the status quo. If all neighbors conform, it reassures us that our material possessions are enough. Yet we also want to show off a little. Charlie gets lots attention along with some unspoken envy and resentment. There may also be some playful ribbing. But now all the other neighbors have to assess their standing in the neighborhood and their status in relation to Charlie. Think of the comments and gossip among neighbors about Charlie and his new BMW.

We are in a constant struggle between our desire to be special, to increase our status and still remain in our group. This comparing and competing mentality drives our lifestyle. Our next door neighbor installs a front yard patio. Others admire it as they see Jon and Joanie enjoying the Sunday paper under their sun umbrella. Within a short time, other patios dot the neighborhood. Whether it is patios, additions to the house, landscaping, a new boat, or sending the kids to private school, one member of the group or community affects the continuously shifting of status of the individuals within that group. This comparing and competing greatly influences the choices we make that constitute our lifestyle.

## Check It Out!

**Think of the last two places in which you've lived.**

- How did you choose what neighborhood to live in?
- What factors influence your decision to buy specific consumer products?
- How do your neighbor's choices affect your decisions?
- How do you determine how to use your discretionary income?
- What do you feel you must buy?

**If you find yourself doing similar things as your neighbors, family or members of a group you belong to, then the separation consciousness is affecting your behavior.**

### *What constitutes happiness for me?*

We all long for happiness. Even The Declaration of Independence–the foundation of the American dream–affirms that we have a right to life, liberty, and *the pursuit of happiness*. We believe that if we work hard, we can achieve anything we want and therefore we should be happy. This longing for happiness is our motivation to work hard and justifies our actions. Then we amass the accoutrements that represent this happy lifestyle. We think the new motor home will be just the thing to go traveling into happy land. We worked hard and did everything we were supposed to do and arrived at our destination; therefore, happiness should now be guaranteed.

In the Personality level, "happiness" means living in an untroubled state. In reality, however, we know nothing can guarantee happiness because we do not have control over every variable in our lives—we are not god. The motor home takes a lot of time to clean and maintain. Also, driving hundreds of miles around the country can be tedious and exhausting. We may have moments and periods in our lives when we are happy—catching that perfect sunset; strolling down the boulevards of Paris. Just eating an ice-cream cone can make us happy, but it is momentary. During the pregnancy of our first child, the closeness with our mate brings happiness that lasts several months. But remember the stress and strain on the marriage after the birth? We might be happy when we start a new job, buy a house or lose weight but to maintain happiness as an absolute and constant state is unrealistic and actually unattainable.

While in actuality happiness exists for varying periods and has many intensities, we still wish for happily ever after for ourselves and others. The preparation and wedding ceremony is a testimony to this mentality. We all know that marriage is about creating a life with another person who may have many similar as well as different beliefs. Of course there will be challenges and conflicts as we define our path. We are not happy with our mate every single day, year after year. All marriages go through trying and happy times. So how does living happily ever after come to be an expectation on our wedding day?

The longing for happiness, while real, is obviously still only a hope. However, this hope becomes an emotional expectation no matter how unrealistic. The state of happiness is intangible, illusive and ever changing. Yet we judge our lives based on whether we are happy. If the answer is no, we are disappointed, hurt and frustrated. This mentality of expecting our achievement, possessions and status to make us happy is the limitation of the Personality Level. It exposes the reality that the glorification of the individual is not enough to sustain happiness.

There can be times when we feel our lives are humming along just the way we want them to. We want to preserve this feeling no matter what. So changing anything becomes risky. And this eventually becomes a limitation. We become stuck in a certain life for fear of losing our image or false source of happiness.

## Check It Out!

**Happiness is an illusion in the separation consciousness. It is based on an incorrect assumption that once we have "arrived," we are set. That implies an absolute state. No matter how much we deny that change is ever present and ongoing, the fact is, the variables on which we determine our happiness are always in flux. What makes us happy today will not automatically make us happy five or ten years from now.**

- What did you long for when you were a child?

- If you got what you longed for, what happiness did it bring you?

- What did you long for when you started your adult life?

- What do you long for now?

- What limitations did you experience that prevented you from getting what you long for?

**If you are evaluating your life by a happiness thermometer then there is a disconnection between your internal and external values. The Personality Level is too active in you.**

Happiness means being satisfied with what we have achieved as determined by our internal values. And as we grow, our values and their priority will shift. This takes a detachment from the world of expectations, external reference points and false obligations. When we allow our self-doubt and inadequacies to drive our actions, then happiness is an illusion.

### How do my conscious and unconscious emotional needs motivate me?

Recognizing and accepting our emotional wants and needs are an essential part of the lessons to learn in the Personality Level. Emotional needs are the source of our motivations at this level. Some we are aware of. Those are the ones we make plans for and set goals to satisfy. They are our consciousness needs. However, we also have unidentified emotional needs that are out of our awareness. These are our unconsciousness needs. When people become driven by either a goal or a behavior, and they are unaware of the cause, we can always find some unconscious emotional need lurking in the background. Since they do not recognize the need, they continue striving and longing for satisfaction even if their actions are fruitless. The executive who is so focused on his job that it causes him to sacrifice family closeness cannot stop until he is aware of what he is fighting for. If his wife asks him, "Why are you working so hard and not participating in our children's lives?" he may reply, "I'm doing it for the family." However, underneath the rationalizations and words of martyrdom for his efforts, we see his own unrecognized need for a sense of worth.

## Check It Out!

Our conscious and unconscious emotional needs motivate us. How we go about satisfying them forms the basis of our uniqueness. It helps us understand ourselves and our place in this world. But awareness only comes with an honest look into our selves. As we satisfy our needs, others are able to understand our value system and clearly see our belief systems.

- What activities are a must in your life?

- What emotional needs do they satisfy?

- What patterns of behavior repeat in most of your interactions?

- What emotional need are you trying to fulfill?

- If you heard someone talking about you (without seeing you), what would be the most damaging and hurtful thing they could say?

- What would make you feel emotionally secure?

## Human and Spiritual Lessons Learned from the Personality Level

Our souls design the lessons we learn from the Personality Level. They are energy adaptors that adjust to the highest level of consciousness available to us at any given moment. We have to raise our hands and say, "Yes soul, I want to connect with you for I know on some level that you and I are one. I want to experience the highest potential that I can right now." While I will discuss the soul at length in the unity consciousness portion of this book, it is important to understand that the soul holds the potential of who we are meant to be in this physical existence. It attracts to us certain people and situations so that we learn the lessons that will help us expand and use our three levels of consciousness. Each level of consciousness holds specific lessons and opportunities. Below are the lessons to learn from the Personality Level before we are ready to open up to our more expansive Intuitive Level.

### Power Limitations

Some people believe that we are *entitled* to contributions from government, parents or employers. While others feel there are no free lunches, and only through hard work and determination will they succeed. But no matter what belief we start with, we will all encounter some limitations of our personal power, and at one point or another, we will all be unable to fulfill some part or all of our dreams. Maybe we wanted to open our own restaurant but couldn't get a business loan. Our idea of becoming a consultant was well planned, and we did have the experience, but our contacts dried up just as we quit our job and the economy tanked. We organized and paid for an African Safari—a lifelong desire—only to have to cancel in the last minute because our father had a heart attack, and we couldn't leave him alone. All of the training, hours and money devoted to opening a daycare center only produced insurmountable bills which eventually led to bankruptcy. No matter how big or small the dream, we were stymied by our limited personal power to obtain it. Whether it grew from self-deception or was realistic, the loss still causes suffering because we recognize the inadequacy of our power. Since many of us buy into the "You can do anything you want" mentality that self-help gurus and motivational speakers promote, missing out on our dream can be a devastating blow. And if we personalize our failures, our image of ourselves may be damaged or destroyed.

At the Personality Level we are the dream, we are the success. There is no differentiation between who we are and our actions. Yet, we don't have control over the economy or biology or the markets...... We are individuals, and all individuals have limitations. This realization is startling to many. We thought we were the exception, we thought we were special, we thought because we were good at one thing we would be good at everything. When we realize that we're not, we suffer.

Understanding the boundaries of our personal power is one of our most important lessons we can learn. Life is not just about us and our wants. When we meet this limit, we are confronted with the question, "What is enough?" Even the newly minted multimillionaire, the freshly-hired CEO, the sought-after artist, the best-selling author–anyone who has been successful must answer this question. For at some point, all of us at the Personality Level experience the limits of our personal power. Without the answer to "What is enough?" a desperate want for more and more to fulfill our continuous desire for power dominates life. This is especially true in our Western culture, where bigger and better are the operative words in defining success. Wanting personal power to validate us becomes a trap, especially if we try to repeat what we had once achieved to get our next fix of personal power.

The Personality Level gives us the opportunity to understand how much power we possess to obtain resources and to control our own lives and that of others. We decide how much personal power our family experiences, gender, ethnicity, socio-economic level, race and educational training gives us.

## Check It Out?

**We all know how we rate on the personal power scale. For some this is painful to acknowledge so they avoid wanting anything. This becomes fertile ground for self-destructive thinking and behaviors. Others interpret their first successful attempts at using their personal power as a signal to become grandiose and set imperious goals without thought of others or the environment. It is important to check out your own relationship with personal power.**

- What affect did your first big success have on you?

- How did it feel to have the sense of power that went along with this success?

- What have you done to reproduce it?

- How satisfied are you with the money you make?

- What limitations have you come up against? How did you deal with it?

- What is enough?

- How do you distinguish between your success or failure and who you are as a person?

**If you feel a limitation to your power is a curse then the separation consciousness is a strong influence on you. If you use limitation of power as an opportunity to learn about yourself then you are ready to expand to the Intuitive Level.**

## Learning About Self-Control

While exploring our power in the Personality Level, we are susceptible to emotional tidal waves if we personalize negative events. To personalize means to take situations or interactions to heart so that they cause us to feel bad about ourselves. This distorts our perspective and distracts us from our goals. It keeps us stuck in inaccurate conclusions about ourselves and our ability to be successful. We are left without the context of our situation which provides valid information that helps us evaluate our experience and grow. We cannot see the consequences of our out-of-control thinking and behavior. Indeed, in the Personality Level our reactions reflect our inability for self-control. Disappointment and frustration easily trigger reactivity. How we handle these emotions tells the world a great deal about who we are. For some, disappointment and frustration are immediately expressed as anger: irritation, bullying, denigration, revenge, spite, or violence. Alternatively, we may withdraw, adopting a victim mentality based on "everything and everyone is against me." Or we could make excuses. "If only the bank came through for another short loan, if we had the store on Main Street, if our supplier didn't close down, if, if....." All emotionally charged perspectives lead to feeling out of control and a diminished sense of power.

Grandiose expectations based on a false sense of duty or expertise set us up for disillusionment—another way we become emotionally out of control. As we exert the effort to actualize our goals, we are shocked and even enraged by our limited personal power. We personalize the obstacles in our way. We think that they impact only ourselves instead of seeing that others are affected as well. This leads to making excuses for our situation and shirking responsibility for our next steps. We only see what is, rather than looking behind the failure or viewing our disappointment from a symbolic perspective to understand the available lesson.

We are also blind to the context of the situation. Trends in the economy do affect businesses large and small. Factors that hurt relationships do exist independent of our wants and needs. Viewing the situation from a personalize perspective prevents us from learning from the situation. We cannot make the distinction between our emotionally clouded, personalized view and what is objectively true.

Personalizing situations makes the normal ups and downs of life more difficult to handle. It reinforces conscious and unconscious feelings of mistrust and self-doubt. Since we are externally oriented, when we fail to achieve our goals, life appears unfair or threatening. We ask *"Why is this happening to me?"*

When we are unable to identify and own the feelings (such as hurt, rejection, failure, disappointment and frustration) that leave us vulnerable and limited, we project our pain onto something or someone outside ourselves. We blame others, life, God, circumstances or luck.

When we reject or deny our feelings and are unwilling to explore why we feel the way we do, we set ourselves up for personalizing life's many jolts and limiting our ability for self-control. At the Personality Level, we have the option to make our lives worthwhile, as we go about defining who we want to be. We may not have control over all of the circumstances around us, but we do have control over taking responsibility for our feelings and thoughts.

## Check It Out!

Every situation that we personalize shows us the extent of our limited personal power and makes us feel as if we've lost control of our lives. However, no force exists outside ourselves that is intent on "getting" us. Any fear of being controlled, of the world being against us or of having insufficient power comes from our perception of ourselves in relation to others, situations and circumstances.

- In what situations have you personalized events and interactions?

- When you review them now without the intense emotions, what can you objectively see?

There is a direct correlation between encountering difficulties in getting what we want and our reactions. When we get what we want, the world is a great place. We are in control and have self-control. When we are frustrated, disappointed and hurt, the world is a difficult place and our self-control is difficult or impossible to maintain.

- How many times have you lost your self-control?

- Under what situations?

- What feelings activated your lack of self-control?

If you find yourself raging against "them," god, and specific others then the Personality Level is too active in your life.

## Awareness of the Environment

At the Personality Level, we are so involved in our own lives and getting our needs and wants met that appreciating the bigger picture and projecting future consequences of humanity's actions are not a priority. Our personal environment—our families, workplaces, religious institutions, social organizations, and cities constitute the extent of our concern. From this rather narrow perspective, we observe the lifestyles of others, their possessions and activities. This gives us clues about how we are to fit in. As we go about our daily lives, we notice the size of houses, how they are landscaped, what merchandise is available to purchase. It is as if we're browsing in a supermarket called "Life Choices" as we make our lifestyle selections. One person will take three cars, one summer home and a five-bedroom house and have no savings. Another will have no debts, live in an apartment, but take extended vacations. Especially in Western culture, the supermarket of life is packed with options. The world we occupy is the key determiner in creating our desires. What causes a person to require a three-man jet ski? Can we live without diamond earrings, the latest electronic equipment, and all those clothes jammed into our closets?

Adapting to circumstances so that we don't have to risk moving out of our comfort zone is too great a price to pay for the devastation of losing our integrity and spirit. Adapting to circumstances that retain our integrity for ourselves and others is a step forward for mankind.

## Check It Out!

**Our everyday lives are determined by the tasks we need to accomplish. Getting the kids to school, arriving to work on time, buying groceries, housekeeping, maintaining our car, having some social and family life are our main concerns.**

- How aware are you of Congressional decisions that could affect you and your family?

- What are your concerns for your country?

- How well do you understand the economic state of our nation?

- What are your feelings about environmental issues? Who should be responsible for the health of the environment?

- How do you let your voice be heard?

The Personality Level focuses on the concerns of everyday life. Our relationship to life as it exists is the determining factor. There are concrete lessons to learn from our Personality Level, and what we learn becomes the foundation for us to expand ourselves in the connection consciousness as we move toward the Intuitive Level.

## Chapter Two Exploration and Discovery Activities

Below are questions that will support you to investigate and explore beliefs, feelings, thinking, and behaviors so that you can ascertain how influential the separation consciousness is in your life.

**Look at some photographs from your childhood.**
- What do you see?
- What feelings are activated?
- What thoughts are activated?
- What memories come?
- How do these pictures compare to your internal experience of the actual event?

**Draw a design of your childhood. Use colors in abstract shapes, words written in a pattern, and images and symbols. Right after you have finished, objectively observe your work (without judgment) and then study it again the next day.**
- What is this saying to you?
- What symbols, memories, and feelings does your design connect you to?
- From this design, what can you say about your childhood?
- What is unresolved?
- Can you see a new perspective about your childhood now that was unavailable to you then?

**Write a letter to your parent, parents, foster parents, and/or step-parent from the perspective of a child.**

**Use a crayon with your non-dominant hand and print your uncensored message. Allow yourself to imagine yourself as a child. Follow your feelings. You don't have to know what you are going to say just start Dear Mommy or Dear Daddy...**

**This exercise unlocks unresolved feelings and memories that may still be influencing you as an adult. It supports you to process hurtful situations in your childhood from an adult perspective. Write as many letters as you need to release buried emotions. DO NOT SEND THEM! Reread your letters aloud.**

- How do you feel now that you have written the letter(s)?
- What feelings did you express?
- What feelings surprised you?
- What does the message reveal to you about your relationship with your parent?
- What does your letter reveal to you about yourself as a child?
- What needs did you have?
- What needs were your parent unable or unwilling to meet? Are these needs still unfulfilled? If they were fulfilled, how? If not how can you fulfill them now?

**Make a timeline of your personal history. Where you lived, what schools you went to, who were your friends, what activities you participated in, relationships, jobs. Write what your motivation(s) was for each entry on your timeline. Look for patterns on your timeline between motivations and actions.**

- What motivation propelled you into actions that add to your self-respect?
- What motivation produced self-sabotaging or hurtful behaviors?
- What is your motivation now? Does this motivation align with spiritual growth?
- If not, what motivation do you need to cultivate?
- How does one event, situation, or relationship progressively influence the next?

**Checking mood management. Make a chart to determine the range of your normal emotions and those that go beyond "normal." Start by listing all the feelings operating in your life on the continuum from violence/ severe depression to exhilaration/ elation. Then, identify a normal range of feelings between which you usually vacillate. For example, your normal range might be frustration and excitement, or anger and contentment. For a two-week period, reflect everyday on the range of your moods. Chart it.**

- How much do your moods fluctuate each day?
- What happens when your mood goes beyond what is a normal range for you?
- What triggers intense moods?
- What keeps your moods within the normal range that you established?
- How frequently do you go beyond your normal range?
- What do you do to moderate your moods?
- What words and behaviors do you use to convey your moods?
- What is the first indication to you that you are approaching the limits of your normal range?
- Once you sense or know you are vulnerable to exceeding your normal range, what do you do?
- What beliefs and/or thoughts contribute to extreme moods?
- What new beliefs and/or thoughts can you use to manage your moods more effectively?

**Understanding your personal power. Review your life in relation to the amount of personal power you think you possess.**

- What is your definition of personal power?
- What is your perception of your power?
- When have you felt powerless?
- What did you do?
- When have you felt powerful?
- What was happening?
- What are the limitations to your power?

- What beliefs would you have to change to become more powerful?
- How important is it for you to acquire power?
- How much is enough?
- What is the need and motivation for developing your personal power?
- Why do you want power?

# Chapter Three — Leaving the Separation Consciousness

## The Spark to Leave

Mastering the lessons at the Personality Level requires only limited parts of who we are. But our potential as human beings is to live beyond the limits that we and others have imposed upon us in order to express the highest levels of consciousness available to us. This truth bubbles up whenever we allow ourselves space and time to listen to our inner voice. It stirs up restlessness, discontent, shifting perspectives, and anticipation of some amorphous desire that nags at us to make itself known. We sense there is more within us ready to express itself. We want to know and live our uniqueness. We want to become the best person we can be. We begin to accept and understand that we are part of something bigger than ourselves.

These are sparks that ignite us to enter the connection consciousness and access our intuition. Choosing to align our intuition with our soul allows us to become who we are meant to be. What we create from this perspective benefits ourselves and others.

For me, the word "spiritual" describes the journey from the separation consciousness to the connection consciousness. Spiritual people use intuitive insights in alignment with their personality and soul. In fact, we live from a spiritual perspective when personality, intuition and soul become representations of one another.

The connection consciousness, as expressed by the infrastructure of the Intuitive Level, demands we stretch beyond the habitual routines of our everyday lives. But entering the connection consciousness is a gradual, courageous process. It starts when we recognize single reactions as part of a pattern of belief-driven behaviors that may not serve us anymore. We understand that living the beliefs we choose are more important than living by the many roles that have been assigned to us (or we have imposed on ourselves). We see our self from a more holistic perspective.

Recognition of the Intuitive Level can also start with instincts, gut level feelings, a knowingness that comes from unknown places within. We may start interpreting our lives from a symbolic perspective, viewing each day as a metaphor for exploring our human and spiritual nature.

## The Difficulty of Leaving

The connection consciousness is beckoning, yet more often than not, we stay rooted to the concrete, limiting world of form in the separation consciousness. Why do we restrict ourselves to just the infrastructure of our personalities? What makes us so attached to our lives, even though they are causing us emotional pain and numbing us? Many issues make leaving the Personality Level difficult. For one, our attachment to the separation consciousness reflects the way our minds function. The mind is a system, and as science tells us, most systems adhere to the concept of homeostasis in order to survive. We resist change because we fear our lives as we know them will end. Fear of the unknown threatens us. Staying with the familiar gives us a sense of security, even though it is illusory.

Thomas Kuhn, a professor of linguistics and philosophy at Massachusetts Institute Technology, observed this phenomenon in certain scientists. Only when they repeatedly failed to explain evidence that did not conform to current theoretical assumptions, did they finally admit their theories were wrong. Kuhn also theorizes that scientists respond to innovation as a community. Until the majority of its members agreed on a new theory, the community would not accept it.

We correlate familiarity with survival. If we know what to expect, we can prepare for it. So conformity to what is concrete, habitual, accepted, and dependable becomes desirable. At the Personality Level, we narrow our world to what we perceive is safe and workable. This comes from the vulnerability we experience whenever we feel separated from the familiar, or when we experience the limitations of our personal power. As a result, supporting a new idea or straying from our peer group becomes a risky proposition.

Our willingness to conform gives us the illusion of safety and control. But although conformity brings comfort, it actually limits our potential. To grow, inspiration and vision are necessary along with the emotional fortitude to defend and care for our vision. Inspiration, vision, and courage emerge from the connection and unity consciousness.

The second reason we stay in the separation consciousness is that we have not defined for ourselves what is enough. *What do you need to control in order to feel safe? How many experiences must you have to prove to yourself that you are competent?* Until we quantify what is enough in terms of behaviors and goals, we are left to repeat the same mistakes over and over. It is as if we are unable or unwilling to internalize our experiences to help us see ourselves as more than we ever thought we might be. We resist updating our self-image for fear that we might lose the need that motivated us. Without this motivation, where would we find our direction?

People who perceive the world from the Personality Level use the powerful motivation of fear to get themselves to do what they feel they must. Fear is a spur because the void is far too frightening to contemplate. We even create fear to stop the unknown from overwhelming us. Fear has kept many people alive in difficult situations. We anticipate reactions from others and interpret situations in a way that substantiates our feelings and thoughts. We do this to prepare ourselves—to maintain a sense of power we don't really have. But feeling powerful is better than feeling powerless. The latter is an attack on our sense of survival. Demonstrating to ourselves and others that we, in fact, do have some power supports our notion of dignity and our humanity.

Indeed, without a fear-based motivation, we become anxious about what to do, afraid that we will become lazy or apathetic. It is as if fear keeps us in life's race. Without it, we would not fit in. To defend against fear at the Personality Level, we develop behaviors, habits and rituals. For instance, when my husband was a high school principal, he always got nervous before speaking in front of large groups. I never knew this, since talking before a crowd seemed so natural for him. He was relaxed, funny and informative. The audience was enthralled, and I could sense his presence and power. When he first revealed his nervousness to me, I asked, "What are you afraid of?"

Reflecting on his many years of successful public speaking and through our discussion, my husband uncovered that his anxiety used to be fear of failure but now was just a habit—a part of getting ready to go on stage. If he were nervous before the event, then he knew he would be successful. Stage fright was part of his ritual to assure success. Could he trust himself to do well without it? Yes. His willingness to internalize his many past successes allowed him to generalize them to the present and future. His new self-image was one of confidence when speaking in front of groups. What he once held onto out of familiarity he was now able to shed, and this changed his behaviors—and added to his peace of mind.

The ability to determine what is enough is the first movement away from dependence on the separation consciousness and the external world. Usually, this task comes after some life experiences. We already recognize the emotional charge of achieving some of our goals. This feeling associated with our experiences helps us to identify our motivations and needs—to understand what has value in our lives. Acceptance of these needs and wants and conscious choices on how to satisfy those helps us answer the question: "What is enough?" Only then are we ready to start our journey into the connection consciousness.

The third reason we stay in the separation consciousness is fear of the unknown. Even though we want change in our lives, we are often afraid since we can't visualize what the new situation looks like or how it will work out. The only way to do this is to take a leap of faith—to walk into the unknown and make it knowable through experience. Changing our behaviors and attitudes is difficult if we can't conceive of an alternative. In the separation consciousness, we imitate others whom we believe have all the answers. Imitation is useful as a starting point for us to experience something new and it helps us overcome our initial fear of the unknown. However, if we do not individualize what we are copying, we become stagnant and self-limiting. And, of course, there is still the anxiety inherent in adopting behaviors that are inauthentic to our self.

Fear of the unknowable, the things that we can't explain threatens our sense of safety. What is God? Who is God? Where is God? What is the origin of life? Is karma real? What about reincarnation? At this stage of human development, so many unanswered questions appear outside our field of knowledge. At the Personality Level, this can be fear-inducing until someone makes a plausible explanation, whether right or wrong! Existential fear of the unknowable causes anxiety, which helps us to focus on what we can control and makes it important to feel some power in our lives.

It is important to monitor our fears because they shape how we react to new situations. If we are stuck in fear, then we are afraid to change. If we are ready to manage our fears, then we are ready to leave the separation consciousness. The degree of our attachment to fear is the barometer for our readiness to leave the separation consciousness.

## Determining When to Leave the Separation consciousness

We get a fairly accurate picture of who we are from looking at the lifestyle we've chosen. Our job, friends, possessions, religious affiliations, how we spend our time, who we love, what we watch on TV, and our aspirations are all reflections of our beliefs about how we fit into this world. Our personality reflects our perception of our lives through the lens of the consciousness of separation. For many of us this reflection is the only reality we want. However, deep within us is the wisdom of other consciousness levels.

Exploration of the connection and unity consciousness supports us to become whole and connected to something more. This challenging next step in our journey to become who we are meant to be depends on our willingness to risk the move into our Intuitive Level and live from its perspective.

We are transitioning from a world that is concrete, literal, and based on the scientific method, to one that is invisible, subjective, and intangible to most people. We are entering unfamiliar territory which can cause anxiety. It is our job to use this emotion to realign ourselves. In fact, if we feel anxiety, this is a positive sign because it lets us know that we are in the process of changing. It's like Alice walking through the looking glass. First, we need a push to get us out of our comfort zone and give us the desire to open up other parts of ourselves. This may present itself as a gradual awakening or a sudden uncontrollable jolt. Some of us embrace the new, whereas others go into the unknown kicking and screaming. How we use the opportunities presented is still our choice. Below are some clues that let us know it is time to move along on our path toward becoming a spiritual being.

### Same old, same old

By the time we've established ourselves in the work force and chosen our lifestyle, we grasped (at some level) the limitations of our personal power. We came to terms with our lives and modified the goals that did not work out for us. We rationalized why we did not get the promotion or start our own business. We justified why staying home, even after the children are in school, is still important. We accept that our lives are pretty good overall, which motivates us to stay where we are and sustain what we have achieved.

At this point we believe we know what life is all about. Achievement at the Personality Level demonstrates how well we learned the rules of the game. We used the opportunities that were available to us. From our life experiences, we came to conclusions about ourselves. Of course, we only experience what we recognize and relate to, so there are unlimited possibilities we did not explore. The soul sets up numerous possibilities to delve into the separation consciousness, but we gravitate to those that hold the highest potential to make us safe, competent, and accepted. The satisfaction of our emotional needs orchestrates our lives. We spend much of our time striving for that special thing, person, or experience we believe will make us feel good about ourselves. For instance, once we get the promotion, we put effort into making sure we keep the job as we evaluate the possibility of further advancement. However, we go on endlessly repeating the striving to progress from one level to the next. We replicate the same pattern of behavior, because the same emotional needs continue to propel us to prove our worth. We still need to be recognized as a competent leader, an idea person, or a great salesman.

We are caught in the cycle of *"same old, same old,"* duplicating identical patterns to get yet another fix for our emotional needs. Living a mechanical life that is structured by habit in this way is a result of our failure to resolve "What is enough?" If we found the way to satisfy our needs, how many times do we need to repeat the experience before we learn the lesson and move on? At what point do we say, "Yes, now I know I'm a competent person because I got the promotion. I feel confident and powerful." Finding the answer to what is enough is one ticket to the fast lane out of the separation consciousness.

## Check It Out!

**Becoming stuck in the cycle of "same old, same old" signals the necessity to stop and dramatically reassess our attitude toward life and our perceptions of ourselves.**

- What do you feel if you dare acknowledge that parts of your life are mechanical? What part of your life is mechanical?

- Where do boredom and stagnation appear?

- What don't you want in your life now? What do you want in your life?

**If you try to rationalize or convince yourself that you are satisfied with your life, the separation consciousness is imprisoning you.**

### Is that all there is? The thrill is gone.

Remember the first time you presented a great idea to your boss? Walking into your first classroom? The excitement of getting married? Publishing your first book? The purchase of your first house? Obtaining what we want is thrilling. It makes us feel alive. However, the familiarity of a situation can reduce the range of emotions you feel. The first time you publish a book, you're ecstatic. The second time, maybe not so much. The initial event builds the structure of your reaction while subsequent events refine and adjust that structure. There is still joy—but it's a different, perhaps more muted response. In truth, we can never repeat a feeling in its purest sense because no energy field replicates itself.

Moreover, eventually there is an adjustment to the discrepancy between what we thought the new situation would be like and what it actually is. This can come from the spoken and unspoken messages from our social institutions, or our own fantasies and expectations. When we first start a new venture, we still bask in the glow that comes from knowing we achieved what we wanted. The vision gives us direction and purpose, which assures us that we know what we are doing. It also becomes a rallying point for our energy and time. The mere fact that we know what we want and are going after it, encourages a sense of aliveness. We spring into action, which engages our thinking, emotions and behaviors. We are animated by anticipation.

But sustaining what we want requires a completely new skill set. Once we have achieved our goal, the everyday sameness of the situation starts extinguishing our thrill, and soon the reality of the situation becomes apparent. We feel emotionally drained from dealing with the disappointments and adjustments that keep our marriages going. We must deal with the fact that some employees see their job as just a job, and will not give us 100 percent, on top of which we now dread driving that extra twenty minutes a day to the new office. The dream house, although gorgeous, drains more money and time than we anticipated.

As we stay in the Personality Level and keep creating from the separation consciousness, we continue to get the same rewards. Recognition is still recognition, even though, at each reiteration, we may find ourselves at a different scale or level. As we repeat the satisfaction of the same emotional needs, our enjoyment diminishes. Where is the thrill? Where can we get a thrill?

Many of us who feel this numbness try to summon the energy to force a new goal. But even though we try, the excitement has evaporated. "What can be wrong?" we wonder. We furiously try to justify why the thrill is gone. Maybe we blame the job, our boss, our mate—anything so that we do not have to search too deeply within.

At the Personality Level, we want to keep the causes of our distress outside ourselves. We are looking for a fix so that we can get on with our familiar lives. In our quest, we pretend nothing is wrong. However, our feelings will eventually surface, usually emerging as an overreaction to a situation that is not the cause of our distress. Our son did not take out the trash again, so we scream for an hour about his lack of responsibility and withhold the car keys for six weeks. This is out of line. We are hurting others who did not cause our pain, and are generally irritable, spaced out, or tired. Life itself becomes a chore. In short, we are at odds with our present situation.

We start living behind the mask of who we think we are supposed to be. In this difficult time, we look for something in the external world to give us a sense of vitality. We miss the excitement that everything is going our way. Now we are most susceptible to making irrational or destructive decisions. We may find ourselves suddenly taking a romantic interest in a coworker we never even noticed before. Indeed, affairs are common at this stage, since the exhilaration of being with a magical person is so alluring. Of course, this "magical person" is only a projection of what we think we need. It will give us that temporary high, but, as we know, it also brings pain and devastation as reality sets in about the relationship and its consequences.

We might think that yet another toy will do the trick, so we buy a bigger car or a splurge on a designer purse. We decide to take an uncalculated risk in our career and start a consulting business without having saved for our everyday expenses. Our desperate need to stop this feeling of emptiness makes us deny the risks, pretend we are happy, and hide our feelings from others and ourselves. This is an expression of the dark side of the separation consciousness. We feel alienated from the familiar world that at one time made us feel good. We are lost.

When we can acknowledge the sense of emptiness that triggers our need to make our world seem okay again, we give ourselves a great opportunity to re-evaluate our lives. This is the time that we must make a choice: to re-live the old thrill from the Personality Level or begin the journey into the connection consciousness. The best choice is to move on.

> ## *Check It Out!*
>
> **Being honest with yourself may seem difficult at first. However, the relief that the truth is out is liberating. You can now create new possibilities.**
>
> - What activities used to be exciting but are no longer? How did you react to this realization?
>
> - What kind of feedback did you get when you were experiencing a thrilling time in your live?
>
> - What new conclusions did you make about yourself from your thrilling moments? What are you willing to try now?
>
> **If you did not take the time to acknowledge and accept those parts of yourself that sought and achieved the thrill then you have work to do. Revisit your accomplishments and acknowledge the talents and behaviors you used to achieve success. Until you do that, you will remain stuck trying to recreate a situation that no longer exists.**

It is no big deal. Minimizing our feelings

Even though we feel empty and are unsure what will make us feel better, we are not clueless. There are signs around us that emerge from the turmoil in our lives. Our feelings do know the truth. However, it is a life-altering decision to accept our inner feelings as a gauge of the authenticity of our lives. If we take this challenge, it puts us on the path toward a higher consciousness. If not, we are left with having to continually deal with those nasty feelings that keep pricking us. Unfortunately, when we do allow our feelings about the present truth of our lives to surface, we often dismiss them. Who wants to give up something that is basically okay if we keep *telling* ourselves it is okay? Not knowing how to transition intensifies our confusion. Then once we identify solutions, we actually have to go through the change process. No wonder we attempt to minimize our uncomfortable feelings. Although change once worked for us and got us where we are, now we will not only be dealing with our own issues, but also the resistance, from those around us. Maybe our family does not want to rethink their standard of living because we intend to go back to school or start a new career.

When we focus on the requirement for success that worked in the past, it becomes even more difficult to listen to our inner feelings. If we do anything that is out of the mainstream after we've achieved society's acceptance, others challenge us subtly or even overtly: we must be crazy to risk giving up what we have. Often we start minimizing our feelings with attitudes such as: *"It would never work," "I have to keep my family in the lifestyle they are used to," "My mate would kill me," and "It's just a fantasy."* We find real and invented reasons to deny what we now want and become too concerned about real and perceived obstacles.

One of the ways we deny our feelings is by immediately thinking about the role expectations we accepted from our social institutions. These served as our guide when we were looking for acceptance and recognition as we found our place in society during our Personality Level development. Their concreteness created a support system. But now they become a limiting burden since they demand conformity, obedience and sustainability. Individual growth and expression would threaten their existence. However, staying in a situation that is preventing us from growing has become a threat to *our* existence. So where do we look for guidance now?

As we start questioning the beliefs from the separation consciousness, we can acknowledge the conclusions we made from our own experience. This provides some space to reflect and catch up with our updated thoughts, feelings and behaviors that are supportive and release those that keep us in the separation consciousness.

## Check It Out!

**When we stop minimizing our feelings and accept them, possibilities open up. If we do follow a new vision of ourselves, it affords others with whom we are in relationship the opportunity to grow as well. When one person changes in a family or at work, the whole group is stimulated to reflect. Members can discuss any adjustments that need to be made. This meeting and the plans that might emerge from it provide an honest expression of feelings which can be resolved in ways that demonstrate respect for all involved.**

- What feelings are you trying to ignore and minimize?

- Can you articulate a new vision of yourself to others?

- What would you risk if you were to follow this new vision for yourself?

- What fears and concerns do you have?

- How would these changes affect your present relationships?

**Acknowledging your honest feelings to yourself is a private matter. Many conflicting thoughts will emerge. At this time it is helpful to decide which beliefs are important to you. The disparate beliefs of the separation and connection consciousness produce very different results. You have tried the separation consciousness beliefs, and they are no longer working for you. Perhaps it's time to try something else.**

### *Life-altering experience. It was out of my control!*

During an unexpected life-altering experience we can also recognize the limitations of the Personality Level. The death of a significant loved one, a serious illness or near-death experience, a natural or manmade cataclysm, a physically disabling accident, an unwanted divorce, being fired or going bankrupt—all of these incidents irrevocably alter our lives. Through the pain and suffering, we are thrust into a new situation we neither chose nor were prepared for. The force and abruptness by which a life-altering experience changes our lives, our sense of safety, and our feeling of control throws us into shock. We are subjected to unrestrained feelings and thoughts. Not only are we not in control of the event, we also have no control of the repercussions.

During the transitional time after the initial shock of the event, we focus on reconstructing our lives in a way that looks familiar. This helps us gain a sense of safety and control over our current circumstances and provides an illusion of order and familiarity. Our first reaction is to use all the skills that worked in the past. We might become sticklers for routine, stay busy all the time or dominate others. Trying to figure out the "why this happened" becomes an obsession. We think that if we can come to a logical explanation of the tragedy, the pain will disappear. However, with life-altering events, what worked in the past usually won't work in the present. Instead, we are catapulted into a survival state.

This may all sound terribly negative but there is a silver lining. The process of reconstruction forces us to find and use parts of ourselves that were unavailable to us in the past. Our experience has shaken our worldview, but now we start thinking about what really matters. We may decide that all of the time and effort necessary to live a certain lifestyle is less important than spending time with our mate before he or she dies. Suddenly, it does not matter how big our house is or how many "toys" we have, or what our title is. Who cares what car we drive? Does it really make a difference where we went on vacation? In times of difficulty and uncertainty, we start examining our choices—the decisions we'd taken for granted. Instead, we begin asking more important questions: What is really important to me? If I only have a short time on this earth, what do I really want to do? If I will only see my loved one for six more months, what do I really want to say or experience?

Tragedy forces us to *stop* in our tracks and start seeing our lives in a non-habitual way. This is a valuable opportunity to grow and learn more about ourselves and other ways of being in the world. Some of us will take great advantage of this break in the routine, whereas others may only be open to acquiring the necessary coping skills to get them through so they can return to their previous lives. Although life will not automatically be the same, it will be motivated by the same old needs that prevent true personal growth.

When life presents tragedy, we hope we will extract meaning from the suffering and recognize that our experiences brought to the surface strengths we did not know existed. We are resilient, complex individuals who possess a soul that guides us to connect to parts of ourselves that are waiting for development. Life-altering experiences set the stage for us to move into the connection consciousness. Trying to understand them from the separation consciousness confines us to inadequate, limited answers.

Our social institutions are not designed to be compassionate to an individual during a time of personal upheaval. The consciousness of separation is tolerant only of those who continue to participate in the impersonal world of consumer and producer. As a society, we are uncomfortable with others' pain and unsure how to comfort or even know what is acceptable. After the initial week or two following the life-altering event, after we've performed our token acknowledgement by sending flowers and a card, making a short call or e-mail saying the standard, "I'm sorry this happened to you. Let me know if there is anything I can do for you," we distance ourselves from those who are suffering. In the separation consciousness, there is no place for the emotionally and physically wounded. This is the unspoken message from those who are supposed to comfort us. It tells us to get over it, get back to a normal routine and acceptable behavior, because too much emotion for too long shows weakness and makes us squirm. Since compassion and acceptance are not a part of the Personality Level, during painful times we are more receptive to the consciousness of connection, where life-altering events become major opportunities for personal growth and transformation. Our pain and suffering is dignified and acknowledged as part of the transition process.

During a life altering event we are more open to accept that our soul is our champion guiding us to new vistas. Entrance to the connection consciousness is a step into hope for a new life and anxiety of the unknown. Whether your entrance is by choice or by surrender, it is a precious gift from the soul. The journey into the connection consciousness brings many treasures.

## Check It Out!

**We try to hide from ourselves the limitations of our personal power and control over our lives. This is why we are so unprepared for the bumps on our life path. If we view these as only tragedies questioning why they happened to us, we are holding the beliefs of the separation consciousness.**

- What were you reactions to a life altering experience?
- Trace the progression of your feelings and determine where you are now?
- What came of this difficult time? What still needs to be changed? What needs to be strengthened?
- What did you learn about yourself?

## Chapter Three Exploration and Discovery Activities

### Points to Ponder
**What do you think and feel about the following statements?**
- We must walk into the unknown and make it knowable through experience.
- The way we design our lives is based on the satisfaction of our emotional needs.
- When we become familiar with something, it is hard for it to maintain the charge we first got from it.
- The problems of today give us a great opportunity to re-evaluate our lives. They provide the motivation and focus to examine the present in order to change the future.
- The willingness to accept our inner feelings as a barometer of the authenticity of our lives is a life-altering decision.
- Entrance to the connection consciousness is a step into hope and anxiety. Hope for a new way and anxiety of the unknown.

### Think about the present and the future.
- Where in your life are you operating from the separation consciousness?
- Where in your life do you still feel alive and vibrant?
- What still brings you a sense of purpose?
- What would you like to stop doing if you could? What prevents you?
- In which areas of your life are you still growing and developing?
- What are your challenges right now?
- What does your future look like?
- What do you need to do now to prepare for the future you want?

# Part II.
# The Connection Consciousness and The Intuitive Level

## Chapter Four

### What is the Connection Consciousness?

The connection consciousness is the integrator of all the separate events and experiences in our lives. This supports us in making sense of our everyday life. It is in this consciousness that we embrace a more expansive perspective of our self. A bigger picture appears that opens new opportunities and possibilities.

Living from the connection consciousness is the next step in personal and world evolution. It moves us beyond the either/or mentality of the separation consciousness into the mentality of inclusion. It discards judgment and encourages acceptance. Expressing our authentic thoughts, feelings and behaviors and making conscious choices from the Intuitive Level takes us beyond the conditioning of our social institutions to the clarity of who we are becoming as individuals and collectively as the human race. We learn to be our own authorities for what is best for us, which in turn changes the collective consciousness. We develop self-acceptance, self-love, and self-respect and treat others with respect. Our internal and external realities become a reflection of each other. Our life is one of participation, meaning and hope.

### The Connection Consciousness is a World of Symbols

The use of symbols in the separation consciousness has different intentions and purposes than in the connection consciousness. In the separation consciousness, symbols identify by using names, brands, and labels. They can consist of a graphic design, a combination of letters or a material object. Institutions use symbols for anything that has accepted conventional meaning: company logos, foundations, religions, and cultural traditions. The use of symbols in the separation consciousness stimulates the messages associated with them. These messages come from marketing slogans, traditions and history. They in turn evoke feelings, thoughts, and actions. Symbols are an effective way of influencing opinions and gaining market share based on the scope and frequency in which they are displayed. They also compete for the hearts and mind of believers.

In the connection consciousness, on the other hand, symbols are the bridge from one level of consciousness to another. In particular, symbolic stories such as myths and legends have been used to explore universal human traits since the beginning of time. Interpreting symbols is akin to switching from life on a regular movie screen to viewing it in 3D and surround sound. It provides richness and a scope and depth of experience that ignites possibilities.

Symbols can come from our dreams, visions, imagination, and environment. They are representations of vague perceptions of a consciousness level we are connecting with. Symbols can represent the expanded version of whom we see ourselves becoming, the solution to a problem we have wrestled with, a way of organizing a body of information to create a system or discover a pattern where none existed before, and an opportunity to observe from an eagle's perspective a personal problem. Our interpretation of symbols becomes an expansion of our consciousness. It frees our minds and hearts to see beyond the immediate. We see what we have not seen before.

The symbols we generate for ourselves are meaningful when we interpret them subjectively. They become a litmus test for our thoughts, feelings and actions. From the knowledge and wisdom we gain from interpreting the symbols that call to us, we decide when and how to participate in the world. We make choices that are right for us.

Every one of our experiences has meaning and value. Even everyday events are open to symbolic insight. If the car battery dies, symbolically we might ask, "What is cutting off our energy?" We come home from the movies and find the toilet tank has cracked and water is an inch deep in the bathroom and hallway. What emotions were held in that now need to flow? Or, what emotions are causing us to be self-destructive? Alternative medicine advocates widely accept the association between specific illnesses and thoughts and feelings. Heart attacks can symbolize pent-up emotional pain, hip problems are associated with fear of moving forward, and back pain connotes a lack of support.

Visions, inspirations, images, realizations, insights, gut-level feelings, a sense of knowing, instincts, synchronicities, possibilities, "ahas" and coincidences are the language of symbols in the connection consciousness. Indeed, our soul speaks to us through this language. We use it to understand the relationship between our internal and external realities. As we develop and trust our intuitive ability, our consciousness expands. When we honor and act on these insights, we build a bridge between our personality, intuition and soul, and they become a reflection of one another. We dance among the co-existing consciousness levels within.

The symbols in our meditations, dreams and visions that we receive from our soul and interpret by our Intuitive Level guide us and give us direction. I once had a dream in which a Native American woman smiled and waved to me to follow her. I observed her as she went about her life as a medicine woman. I saw her healing the sick and troubled, interacting with tribal leaders, telling stories to the young, enjoying a passionate relationship with her mate, and laughing, teasing and playing with her women friends. I received this vision when the opportunity presented itself for me to expand my spiritual workshop schedule. At the time, I was traveling to Europe and Asia as the demand for my workshops was growing. I was tired and getting sore throats on a regular basis. Through interpretation, the message of the dream reminded me to balance my life and incorporate all the elements that the medicine woman had shown me. With further interpretation, I realized that I did not have a personal community. I felt rootless and out of balance. I could see that expanding my workshop schedule was not my soul direction. In fact, it was time to end this activity. My soul had defined another direction for me.

In the connection consciousness, the value of symbolic insight is so important that our self-image and even our lives shift permanently once we rely on it. *What are your dreams telling you? What symbols have meaning for you? What is your relationship with symbols? How do they function in your life?*

Objects imbued with meaning can also become important symbols. When we wear the earrings that our boyfriend gave us, we might choose to associate them with love. Often I suggest to clients that they assign a certain meaning to a piece of jewelry or something in their workspace. For one woman, a round pendent reminds her that she is whole. A man keeps on his desk a picture of himself standing on a mountaintop. This reminds him that he has the courage to take more risks in his life. Whatever issues we are working on — trust, compassion, self-acceptance — an object assigned a certain meaning becomes a symbol that activates what we choose to remember and feel. Using symbols in this way supports us in making changes we value. In fact, symbols are powerful change agents. They are flexible enough to allow space for possibilities while at the same time providing guidance. They are witness to the treasure of aligning and merging the consciousness of the personality, intuition and soul.

Choosing to try on and incorporate the beliefs of the connection consciousness is a life altering event–one with unlimited possibilities to create an existence that has heart and meaning.

### *Beliefs of the Connection Consciousness*

Think of people whom we called geniuses like Da Vinci, Einstein, Galileo, and Hawkins. All acknowledged that their ideas came from their intuition. Once they received the initial spark, they worked hard to bring it into form. They lived from the connection consciousness, receiving these ideas, and only then used the separation consciousness to bring them into a form that others could understand.

The connection consciousness magnetizes the people, opportunities and resources we need to manifest our hopes and dreams. It is as if a hidden hand guides and supports us. This is the acceptance of the invisible world and our innate ability to connect to many different levels of consciousness. If we choose to participate in and explore the connection consciousness, we will experience the following beliefs in our own way with our own timing.

### Internal Perspective

In the separation consciousness our lives were conditioned on our willingness to subjugate our uniqueness in order to fit into the parameters set by social institutions and their authority figures. Understanding ourselves through this lens kept us focused on and attached to the external world which became our barometer for appropriate behavior.

But participation in the connection consciousness begins when we no longer rely on the external world to determine what is right for us. After learning the lessons of the separation consciousness, the importance of following the dictates of the external world diminishes. Suddenly, we are at odds with many of the beliefs that the social institutions espouse. We can no longer limit our lives to others' expectations. Our desire to explore the connection consciousness is the next step in our growth. Here we learn to accept our internal reality. Its cornerstone is of our own interpretation of what matters and has meaning for us. It was created through the wisdom that comes from our Intuitive Level as we clarify and align our beliefs, thoughts, and behavior.

Our internal reality provides the fortitude for us to see a more comprehensive perspective of who we are. The degree to which we follow our intuitive insights, determines the strength of our internal reality. The stronger our internal reality, the more authentic our external lives.

Shifting from an externally based reality to an internal one is like stepping onto another planet. We feel exhilarated, depressed, confused, afraid, joyous, restless, and hopeful all at the same time! Suddenly, we see life in a new light. What we once thought was so important doesn't hold us anymore. What we believed we needed to control and accomplish leaves us shaking our heads. We become objective, observing how we are living our lives. We question. Why are we doing what we're doing? Who set the expectations we are living? Everyday situations provide the opportunities to decide what our values are and how we choose to live our lives.

As we gain clarity, our internal and external perspectives align, our daily activities, jobs, and relationships represent the values we hold. Authenticity might mean changing professions, going back to school, leaving a relationship, altering our lifestyle. Nobody says this will be easy. It may be painful to give up our hard-earned vacation because we decided that we need the money for tuition or to live on while we search for the job that allows us to live by our values. Resistance to these changes reflects our fear. What will we lose if it does not work out? If we associate change with loss this fear leads to an inauthentic life, which is actually a death sentence — our own. We become part of the denizens of living dead on this planet.

In the connection consciousness, change is associated with hope and wonderment. "I wonder what my new job will teach me. I hope that my new beliefs will lead me to a rich life. I'm curious where my new business will take me. I wonder what it will be like to truly be myself in my marriage. I hope my relationship with my mother improves now that I am clear about my values."

This important shift — understanding that the external is a projection of our internal world — is revolutionary when we truly embrace it. It makes us realize how much power we possess for creating our lives. The ability to live from this freeing idea is monumental–akin to finding our own soul blueprint and living from its knowledge and wisdom. The challenges we all encounter along the way are worthy of great poetry and drama, for it takes faith, stamina, courage, commitment, humility and more to travel this path and experience the depth of the connection consciousness. Where is this internal reality? Where is it residing in you even though you may not recognize its profundity? How can you connect to it? What is it?

### The Unconscious

Our internal reality emanates from our unconscious, which by definition is unknown to us. While we draw conclusions about our experiences which become part of our internal reality, what is unconscious is most powerful–a function of our souls. The soul brings us situations and circumstances to render what is unconscious consciousness so that we can grow. Using symbols from intuitive insights, our soul helps us connect to those parts of our unconsciousness that we are ready to know, develop and use.

The unconscious, as revealed to me and validated by my work with many clients, is the reservoir of all past, present, and future lives that were lived, are living, and will be lived by humanity in the time/space called earth. Carl Jung has taught us that the "collective unconscious" is a pool of experiences, wisdom and knowledge of all human experiences. And it's available to all of us. We enter this pool through our intuition in the connection consciousness. In so doing, we have a wondrous opportunity to expand our self-image as we tap into the unconscious part of the self. We glimpse the enormity of who we are once we develop and align the infrastructure of our three levels of consciousness — personality, intuition, and soul.

The difference between Jesus Christ, Buddha, Mohammad and the rest of us is that these prophets accepted their expansive consciousness. They realized that they coexisted on many different levels at the same moment. Merging the Soul, Intuitive and Personality Levels so each becomes a representation of the other allows for the full integration of the separation, connection and unity consciousness. This is what the great masters did; they expressed the highest level of consciousness available. We have those same opportunities. We can lift the veil of the separation consciousness, which exists in linear time, to reveal the timelessness of the convergence of past, present, and future that is available in the connection and unity consciousness.

Delving into our internal reality, we find an unlimited world of experiences that are available for us to learn and grow from as well as issues that are ready for resolution. My clients' souls reveal to me all the lives that have or will be lived, in relation to a particular theme. Perhaps a client's soul-theme is courage in this lifetime. If this is so, his soul creates the circumstances and connections to people who will help him investigate the concept of courage. When my client becomes conscious that courage is his theme, his soul activates the unconscious to start feeding into his conscious mind memories, feelings and attitudes that reflect the experiences of past, present and future lives or the experiences that are in the collective consciousness. Then, with guidance from his Intuitive Level, he comes to some new understanding of the power of courage.

Once we come to a new perspective, we can choose behaviors, attitudes, and feelings that demonstrate our new understanding. We think, feel, and act differently. This brings others into our lives who are now in alignment with our beliefs. Internal work that magnetizes external change is a gift from the soul.

Moving from the internal world to the external is a delicate balancing act. It is the process of updating who we were, who we are right now, and who we are becoming. This is the time for honest self-reflection as to what is working in our lives and what is not. It takes courage to act on our internal perspective once we connect with it. While this realization and the ability to create our reality is the spiritual task of the Intuitive Level, it is also the foundation for the Soul Level. We accept the fact that we are creators of the world—an astounding concept. It is joyous to find that we possess within ourselves the guidance system to assure our passage from the external into the internal world and to also connect, integrate, and make them congruent. When we start noticing the changes that seem to appear magically in our external lives, we realize that we possess the power to create our own reality. This is truly evidence of the fact that energy has consciousness and that consciousness produces form. WOW!

## Check It Out!

**Developing a strong internal perspective that will support you starts with exploring your thoughts and feelings to uncover what is true for you. This look into self is done without judgment (which would ensnare you in the separation consciousness). Instead an accepting attitude allows you to recognize the correlations between your internal and external realities.**

- What relationships in your life now have heart and meaning?

- Which ones are based on false obligations or denial of your truth?

- What do you have to face in your significant relationships?

- What must you acknowledge and admit about yourself to yourself?

- Are you in the right job for yourself?

- What issues have you taken a stand on that you are proud of in your job and personal relationships?

- What are the consequences of living your values at work and at home? What are the consequences to you personally when you do not live your values?

## Self-Mastery

The first step to self-mastery is self-exploration. The Personality Level is developed through reacting to what already exists and has form. Whether it is the family, school or corporate structure, the political system or religion the form is sustainable; it exists and therefore has history. How we react to the rules of social structures provides us with a great deal of information about how we interact in the world. We start discerning what works for us and what doesn't. We may feel safe working in a corporate setting where we know what is expected as delineated by a clear job description. Or we might feel frustrated and angry that we are limited to the tasks assigned to us and that we do not have input into the decisions that affect our work group.

In the family, we might react with rage or submission to the pain of emotional and physical abuse, which leaves us diminished as a person and angry at the world. Alternatively, we might feel hopeful about life and ourselves if our parents recognized us as a soul in a child's body and supported us to grow and learn how to connect to our own uniqueness. Some religions include concepts that make us feel as if we are sinners by our mere existence and others empower us through understanding our innate connection to the Divine. Each and every experience in the Personality Level is based on our reaction to what already is.

Self-mastery is the realization that instead of reacting to our external environment, we choose our responses. If our mate comes home angry, we can react to his anger by getting angry ourselves, in which case a fight would ensue. We can ignore or avoid him and allow tension to build—leading to an even angrier outburst later. We can walk on eggshells and try to appease the other. However, all of these reactions are about personalizing and adopting the other's mood as reality instead of seeing ourselves as independent beings with our own thoughts and feelings. When we respond to a mate's anger, we choose our emotional state as well as how to communicate with him. If we choose compassion, we neither add to nor manipulate his mood. "It looks like you are angry about something." This is a response to our partner's emotional state. It acknowledges him and yet lets him know that we are not going to take on his feelings.

To respond instead of reacting means we are in charge of our own moods. We take the time to figure out what thoughts, feelings, and situations activate us to lose control of our own emotions and become reactive.

Self-mastery also means becoming free of our dependence on institutions and authority figures to tell us who we are or should be. This is the time to take charge of our own destiny. We do this by starting the difficult but necessary process of weeding out thoughts, feelings, and behaviors that no longer serve who we are becoming. Gone are the easy outs of someone telling us we are important, needed and loved when our inner self doesn't believe all the accolades. No more excuses or thinking like a victim that comes from dependence on the external world. This only leads to disappointment when we don't have the lives we feel entitled to. It is our responsibility to develop self-respect, self-acceptance and self-love. We must look into the mirror of our internal reality and choose what matters so we can become who we want to be.

The journey to self-mastery is directed by our soul through the messages we interpret intuitively. It is an ongoing process of reflecting upon and clarifying our thoughts, feelings, and actions. Developing mastery over self is the willingness to say yes to life, and to rely on our dreams and intuition to see where they lead us.

Any expansion of self requires that we discover what abilities we possess, accept where we are, and then do what we must in order to follow our dreams. We may take that computer design class, sign up for a novel writing class to develop the book that is at the edges of our awareness, or open an art gallery. Our soul created these dreams and the desire to follow them in order to set up our next arena for growth. Our desire to pursue an avenue that has heart and meaning presents the perfect opportunity to learn the lesson of self-mastery.

The movement to the Intuitive Level is the movement toward choice. What do I choose? What do I want to create in my life? What do I need to do to live my values? Who do I want to be? These choices are aligned with our intuition of what is right for us. When using our intuition, we make meaning from the circumstances and coincidences that our soul designs for us. Self-mastery is essential for us to use our ability to receive, accept, and act on our intuition by creating authentic responses to our environment.

*Check It Out!*

**Through the impulse to achieve self-mastery, we realize that we can change. We can let go of limiting thoughts, choose to respond to others instead of reacting, and connect to our soul for motivation and inspiration. We become empowered by our gift of choice.**

- What have you chosen to say yes to in your life?
- What happens when you say, "No" to new opportunities?
- What are the parameters of your comfort zone?
- What does your comfort zone do for you? Does it limit you?

## Authenticity

Authenticity means being honest with ourselves about our motivations (the "why" of what we are doing) and intentions (precisely "what" we plan to do). Reflecting on situations helps us gain clarity so we can distinguish between momentary emotionally charged thinking (reactiveness) and what is right and true for us. When we incorporate self-reflection in our daily lives, we observe which situations and people we still react to and which we respond to in accordance with our emerging internal reality. At the end of the day, mentally rehearsing or writing out alternative responses to reactivity create a support system that builds authenticity.

List the facts. *What happened? What did I say? What did I really want to say? How could I have responded instead of reacting? What emotions did I need to activate to control my reactions and act authentically?*

Another way to build authenticity is consistently choosing what is right for us. Each authentic behavior and action builds our base in the connection consciousness. When we consistently interpret and express our symbolic insights, we are on the route to authenticity.

We each have four "bodies" that receive intuitive insights:
- the **mental body** experiences a sense of knowingness
- the **emotional body** experiences a gut level feeling
- the **physical body** experiences instinct
- the **spiritual body** experiences visions and inspiration

All four are ways of interpreting our connection to the abstract world of the connection consciousness. We develop abstract concepts by integrating interpretations from our mental, emotional, physical and spiritual bodies. Sorting through the perspective of each brings a clarity and authenticity that we feel viscerally and cerebrally. It is an act of courage to willingly express what we perceive as authentic. *What do you do to make sure you are clear? What is still making your reactive? What is your process to gain clarity? When are you clear about your intentions in work, home and play?*

Other times, our intuition helps others who are having difficulty connecting with their own intuition. The link between us and another may be so strong that we pick up messages from their soul to deliver to them. Remember a time when you were talking to friend when words came out of your mouth that surprised you and were meet with an "aha" from the other? My husband has that ability.

Intuitively I received the message that I was to attend the Jungian Institute in Switzerland for a study seminar and personal retreat. This came out of nowhere, since I had no knowledge of the Jungian Institute, although I always felt a strong connection to Jung's soul. I tried to suppress the message because it would have meant leaving my family, private practice, writing and consulting. Two minutes into my discussion with my husband, who did not want me to go, he looked directly into my eyes and said, "You need to go." I felt the hair on my arms standing up as what he said resonated with my internal truth. Although there were logistics to resolve, I trusted the concept of authenticity. It turned out to be a wonderful growth-producing experience, one for which I am so grateful. We are all capable of living and perceiving from our Intuitive Level.

### Taking a Quantum Leap

In the separation consciousness logical thinking and proven evidence is the standard bearer for the acceptance of new ideas. In the connection consciousness, ideas are received from other than proven evidence. They are interpreted and then their value is determined. The belief that unlimited possibilities are available to connect with at all times and from anywhere is the cornerstone of taking a quantum leap. This is embedded in all the beliefs in the connection consciousness.

A quantum leap connects us to a specific level of consciousness that resolves issues we're struggling with. It is like logging onto a computer that contains all the known and yet–to-be-known information available to man. We can pick the file that has the instructions and encouragement to proceed. Once we open it, we also open the windows of our minds to see a new picture. This mixes and moves our energy field around. The movement of energy that comes from connecting to a consciousness level other than the one we're presently in provides us a creative opportunity. We see other perspectives and participate in the exciting and at times anxiety-provoking process of airing out our beliefs. Then we connect our adjusted beliefs to the expanded energy field provided by our leap.

For instance, Alice was working on changing her repeating pattern of attracting men with close relationships with their mothers. She held the belief that if a man had such a relationship with his mother then he would be equally attentive to her. However, that was not the case. Actually she found herself playing "mother" to a series of emotionally dependent men. That meant her needs were not being met. She finally realized that their "close relationship" with their mothers was actually a dependent relationship. The only way for her to keep a relationship going was to act as a super mom.

As we worked together, Alice became receptive to the concept of the infrastructures within: the personality, intuition and soul. She started drawing symbols of her relationships with men. Her interpretations of these symbols brought a connection to a new level of consciousness. It became clear that she wanted a relationship to discover her role as a woman. How was she to balance being supportive of another with being her own person who gets her needs met? Alice was confused because she didn't know herself. This one quantum leap, or "aha" moment, started her journey.

First, Alice recognized that healing this issue was her responsibility and that projecting it onto another person prevented change. She began to acknowledge her feminine or receptive attributes. It then led her to clarify her relationship to her own male or dynamic attributes. As a result, she dismissed stereotypes about men and women and what relationships can and cannot do. She became a self-confident person who made authentic choices.

The triggering from an "aha" is like weaving the frayed loose pieces of our energy field into a whole, complete pattern. It creates new connections that keep changing and rearranging as long as we focus on transforming a confining belief into one that reorients us toward a more comprehensive perspective.

Depending on our unique style of being in the world and our connection with our Soul Level, we can expect that quantum leaps will be natural part of our lives. Many people seeking enlightenment use various methods to achieve this leap in consciousness, devoting themselves to spiritual teachings, prayer, meditation, yoga, or other practices that sustain internal focus.

Another way a quantum leap in consciousness can occur is through an event that causes confusion and breaks us from our familiar reality. In times of crisis, our normal defenses are down and our energy field is more malleable. Some of what we call calamities in our lives—losing our job, death in the family, illness, financial ruin—are opportunities for us to make quantum leaps. Our attention is focused on the traumatic event, which diverts our energy from our habitual reality. Feeling emotional suffering and the desire for it to stop also shifts our energy field. As a result, the soul releases energy from old patterns and supports new connections. Our pain is dignified and has meaning since it opens us to embrace a higher consciousness level. The next step is to integrate, express and act on the conclusions from our "aha's."

Taking a quantum leap is also about connecting to new parts of ourselves that we denied, repressed, or did not even know existed. Our willingness to take the new job, get married, risk opening our own business, or start sculpting is the beginning of exploring a higher consciousness level. As we deepen and expand our participation in life, ignition occurs and energy flows. This creates new connections. Exploration and integration of our insights brings additional parts of our selves together to support yet more insights as the process of growth continues. It is an upward spiral of evolution. This changing, rearranging, reconfiguring, and expanding is unpredictable, exhilarating, scary, wondrous, mysterious, and joyous all at the same time. Who would ever miss the best ride of our lives?

## Check It Out!

**Albert Einstein said that we never solve a problem in the same consciousness level in which it was created.**

- When have you experienced an "aha" moment? Did you willingly allow it or was it "forced" on you? How did it affect your life?

- What have you done to take a quantum leap, to solve a problem in your life?

- When were you forced out of your comfort zone due to an unexpected event? What was your reaction at the beginning, middle, and end of the situation? What did you try to hang on to? What did you learn about yourself? What were some new beliefs and thoughts that you still use?

Experiencing "aha's" helps you see if you are using your Intuitive Level to its fullest. If you are not experiencing "aha" moments, then start listening to your intuition and risk taking an action based on it. You can start with baby steps like voicing who you know is calling on your cell phone before you even look at it or commenting when you and another were thinking the same thing. Think of these leaps as a treasure chest of beautiful jewels each available to activate new insights and visions that will enhance your life. We connect with one and then another one and another and.........we are ever expanding

## Uniqueness

Just as no two people living on this earth are the same no two internal realities are identical. By our willingness to say "yes" to life, we form connections that rearrange our internal perspective. We intuit possibilities by using our symbolic sight, noticing nuances and seeing behind the accepted meaning of labels to unveil ever expanding patterns and connections. Uniqueness comes when we express our internal reality through the creation of visions, thoughts, feelings, and actions. Interpreting what we perceive in our own way allows optimal functioning—the alignment and merging of the Intuition and Soul Levels.

Developing our unique perspective comes from being open to opportunities and using symbolic sight that recognizes things are not always what they seem. It's not settling for the status quo. It is looking at life from fresh eyes with no preconceived expectations.

Let's examine the concept of war. We can view it as barbaric—the random taking of human lives because of differing values and beliefs. Or we can see it as a noble endeavor of emancipation. Whether war is right or wrong is only a matter of opinion, and right depends on what side we are on.

However, if we use our Intuitive Level and view war from a symbolic perspective, then we see more than a win/loss scenario. We recognize that both sides endure similar experiences. The authority figures that mandated war are questioned, criticized and/or praised. People shift focus from everyday living to the conflict. Insecurity and fear of the unknown surface and are expressed in a variety of ways. Everyone feels suffering and pain from loss of love ones, homes and possessions, and a way of life. What was once habitual and familiar no longer is. All of these responses to the effects of war shift our energy field. Armed conflict changes the status quo and causes the decrystalization of rigid energy structures. The energy released from this shift is now available to be reconfigured and integrated in new ways.

We recognize that destruction and creation are taking place simultaneously in a unique way. When we enter war, we focus on the opposition in order to learn about and defeat them. While we may be judgmental and only focus on the differences we are trying to eradicate, we are also seeing another culture. We learn about how they deal with adversity. We note differences in customs, traditions, religions, food, music, dance, art and dress.

New patterns emerge from the fertile, freed-up energy that at first seems chaotic. From experience and reflection, new thoughts, feelings and perspectives arise. War is symbolically the end of one consciousness and the beginning of another. Do we need war? Not from the connection consciousness. Only when we live from the limitations of the separation consciousness that breeds either/or thinking will war be a means for change.

One of the prerequisites to uniqueness is the willingness to move out of either/or thinking. Without a new stimulus, we repeat the same old patterns and allow the pendulum to swing back and forth. One way we can bring a unique perspective into form is to identify with an idea, feeling, and/or experience and observe and interpret our response to it. How did the experience make us feel? What thoughts were triggered? What conclusions did we make? What did it say about us to us? For example, suppose we read a book. The Personality Level reacts to the story, the plot, the characters, but the experience stays outside us and has no lasting effect. In the Intuitive Level, we connect to the author's energy field as well as the energy of everyone else who has read the book. This connection between the book—which is a part of the author's energy—and all the people who now share it creates a new energy field that did not exist before the book was written. The way we integrate our response to the book (which is really the energy field) is ours uniquely. At the Intuitive Level, this deeper understanding of the comprehensive ways that we connect provides fertile ground for us to see things in unique ways. Living from the connection consciousness affords richness in our lives.

---

### Check It Out!

**As each of us opens up to our Intuitive Level and embraces the unique ways we interpret and express our experiences, our lives become brilliant paintings with rich colors and dramatic shapes. Our creations, whether they are inventions or ideas, created individually or in groups, affect the consciousness of the whole human race. This process of integrating and including the new and unique is a job for all of us.**

- What is your hope for a better future?
- How do you allow yourself to see new ways of changing, rearranging and bringing in new perspectives in your job, relationships, thoughts, feelings and behaviors?
- What is unique about you?
- How do you ensure you look for the uniqueness in others?

---

If you cannot see your uniqueness, then it is time to slow down and take the time to think and feel before acting. It is time to question what can be. It is time to imagine and reinvent your life in those areas that are stagnant.

## Intentions

An intention is a determination to act in a specific way to achieve a desired outcome. All the energy that contains our thoughts, feelings and actions must be focused on our intention. This takes dedication, trust in our self, and learning from each step of the process. Our commitment to our intention at the intuitive level supports us to minimize any distraction that comes our way. It's akin to the sports metaphor of "keeping our eye on the ball." Our intention becomes the forefront of our lives while we also handle our everyday obligations with integrity and authenticity.

What is known to science is just a fraction of what is. When we are on the edge of the known and the unknowable, we walk in the field of possibilities. This is where the wonder and excitement of the world resides. The Intuitive Level supplies a plethora of possibilities available to us within the confines of time, space, and our place in this universe. Our intuition, relying on symbols and insights, interprets what is possible from among the infinite variables. Then the Personality Level individualizes our ideas and feelings and makes them so specific we can identify, describe and name them. The last step brings into some concrete form what has been up until now only imagined. Setting our intention is the process of aligning the three consciousness levels within so that each does its part in the movement from energy to form. As we learn to align our whole energy field, our unity, connection and separation consciousness, we manifest our intentions.

The freedom to set our intentions brings a responsibility for how we focus our energy. If we intend to create a loving environment in our marriage, we first generate loving thoughts and feelings to activate the vibration of love. We need to be in the state of love. Then we decide how to demonstrate love such as showing appreciation, acknowledgement, caring and respect for our mate. At this point we generate specific thoughts such as, *"I love my husband," "I open us to love energy," "I feel the flow of love within pouring out of my heart," "I connect my love with the love within my husband."* These words represent our state of love within. *What words and thoughts put you in a loving space?*

Now we summon feelings that support the state of love, such as appreciation, happiness, peacefulness, gratitude and openness. We try to generate these feelings to put our emotional body in the right place to flow the energy of love. *What feelings are necessary for you to feel to move you into the state of love?*

We design our actions to support and represent our thoughts and feelings. The choices of actions are unique to our relationship. For one couple, a homemade dinner is an act of love. For another, it is setting aside time to talk over the day or showing affection through frequent touching. We see how creative we all are when it comes to expressing our thoughts and feelings through actions. They represent our internal reality, and the way we express them is an act of creativity. Couples build a common language through actions. That is why each relationship is unique. It is the meaning a couple attaches to the words and actions they use between them that make a relationship.

However, if we do not consciously form intentions, our energy is left to just react to situations and scatter. Reactivity can lead to blame, rationalizations, hurt, anger, passive aggressiveness and all the other defense mechanisms that inhibit the creation of anything other than separation. We are prone to reacting when we are out of touch with our feelings and thoughts–when we use only our Personality Level. But, by reacting and not consciously choosing what we want to create, our lives seem controlled by forces outside ourselves. This produces a sense of being separated from our self.

We need connection and alignment with our soul, intuition, and thinking and feelings from all levels of consciousness in order to focus and sustain our energy to create. Think of how you generate ideas. *How do you treat your ideas? How do you decide which ones to implement? What is your process from idea to implementation? Which emotions sabotage you? Which emotions keep you inspired? Who has inspired you? What events in your life made a difference?*

When we achieved our intention, we then reflect and concretize our learning. Next is the release of our creation, since we learned the lesson through the creative process we just completed. The act of going back into the void to receive our next marching orders, inspiration and/or preference to do something is difficult after feeling the focused energy of doingness.

Many of us confuse letting go of what we've achieved with giving up the power we summoned to create our objective. Therefore, instead of reflecting and allowing what has filled to empty (so that we can access the next step from our Intuitive Level), we start making decisions only from the Personality Level. This draws us to the faulty logic that the next step is to make something bigger and better. Also, letting go may feel like being out of control. We could become fearful that we might never again possess this level of power. However, holding onto what we created through our intention may or may not be what we need for our growth. When an intention is realized, it is imperative to reflect and check our alignment with our soul. This alignment and connection is the source for unfolding the next intention for us to create.

---

### Check It Out!

**Envisioning and manifesting intentions that come from the Intuitive Level is the function of the connection consciousness that is a world of symbol. It supports us to see ourselves freed from the "shoulds" of life to find our own path. We find it through the intuitive process, which starts with symbols or pieces of an abstract idea, feeling, or instinct. This symbolic process becomes more whole and concrete as we allow our hearts and minds to participate in the reality of the connection consciousness.**

- How do you define intention?
- What is your distinction between an intention and a goal?
- How do you use intentions in your life?

---

Intention comes when the heart, mind and soul are focused in the same direction. If you find yourself goal-oriented (or feel guilty if you don't realize your goals) then it is time to use the concept of intention. To start ask yourself: *What do I think about it? How do I feel about it? What insights are coming from my intuition? What are my instincts telling me? What feelings are coming from my body when I think about it?* You need to allow all parts of you to have a voice and then resolve the differences among the voices. Then, your intention will become clear to you.

## Focus on the Present

Being in the present means that we are so absorbed in the here and now that the concepts of past and future do not exert an influence on us. That means, we are not thinking about what we are going to make for dinner when we are talking to a less-than-interesting coworker. Nor are we daydreaming about what we are going to do on the weekend, or conjuring a romantic interlude for the evening. This drifting off happens when we are disengaged from the present.

Being focused and participating in the present involves using the appropriate combination of all levels of consciousness. This is how we experience our power. Think of a time when you were focused. *What did that feel like? How would you describe your productivity, outcome, sense of aliveness and confidence? What happens when there are nine million things going on in your head?* The effect on ourselves, others, and situations during the times we focus on the present is powerful. It is like the juggler who for one second has all three balls in the air so well synchronized that it appears as if they are magically moving on their own.

As we become more comfortable with our emergence into the connection consciousness, we start feeling a new satisfaction with our lives. We interact from a deeper awareness. We no longer move so quickly to the next task. Instead we savor the nuances and shades of complexity within any given moment. Each holds a richness waiting to be discovered and experienced. With this attitude, we acknowledge the value of being alive and the unlimited opportunities that are always available to us to express, experience and expand. We take what we see before our eyes, as well as the unspoken information we interpret through the Intuitive Level of our four bodies.

Our teenage son barges through the front door, runs up the stairs to his room and slams the door. We follow Jason and inquire, "What's up?" While listening to him try to convince us that nothing is wrong, we sense his anxiety and insecurity. We intuitively know that he is hiding something because he fears he will disappoint us when we find out. Also we intuit his feeling of being overwhelmed about his dilemma. If we were in the separation consciousness Jason's actions and defensiveness would most likely lead to a fight. However, intuitively we know he needs support. As soon as possible, we might arrange for some simple family activity. It might be asking for his help with our computer, going on a bike ride, shooting some hoops—any activity that Jason feels comfortable with and connected to us. This provides a chance for him to start talking when he is ready.

At work we might be explaining a new project to our subordinates. If we are focused totally in the present, our intuition helps us understand how each member of our team is truly reacting to this new idea and not just giving lip service. We see that one team member is contributing ideas that massage the boss's ego. Another team member is alert and looking as if our idea is the best thing since sliced bread, when really she is hiding her lack of experience. From our full use of our Intuitive Level in the present, we understand the motivations behind the words and actions of others. We then can respond effectively.

Living from the connection consciousness in the present, we also are aware of our connection to others' energy fields. We interpret the energy configurations that flow among us. Unconscious gestures, word choices, inflections, and posture are symbols from our inner reality. They provide a wealth of information. *What does it feel like when you are focused in the present and using your Intuitive Level? When have you felt totally involved in something and lost all sense of time? What did that feel like?*

Observation of the present provides insight as to what parts of us are living from the connection consciousness and which are seduced by the separation consciousness. To accomplish this takes answering some hard questions such as: *What beliefs do you hold within that are causing you to repeat the same destructive patterns in intimate relationships? What feelings are hidden within you that contribute to being passed over for a promotion? What tone of voice and behaviors may cause others to think you are arrogant, or controlling, or manipulative, or sneaky? When do you feel authentic? When have you spoken assertively and respectfully? What happens when you have a clear intention?*

How much we remain in the present depends on the alignment of our four bodies (spiritual, mental, emotional and physical). Each participates from the Intuitive Level to bring what we intuitively know is possible into form. If our four bodies are in conflict because they are residing in different levels of consciousness that have divergent perspectives and realities this splits our energy field and throws obstacles in our path. We become disappointed, confused and can't understand why we didn't succeed since the new idea came from our intuition. The incongruence emerges in such behaviors as making excuses for not following through, procrastinating, minimizing what we want or sabotaging a project.

For instance, if we are trying to get our idea across for the new advertising campaign while carrying the tension of an unresolved martial conflict, both efforts are doomed to mediocrity (at best) and probable failure. Even though we think we are giving our all during the presentation, parts of us are really engaged with the emotionality of the conflict at home. Actually, at some level we are processing what the fight was about, dealing with our pain, and trying to figure out what we are going to do. Part of us is in the past reviewing what was said and another part is in the future imagining the consequences. We are only partially in the present and therefore only using limited parts of ourselves.

Strain on the physical body is another consequence of splitting our energy field because we are not focused in the present. Our physical body (which expresses itself through behavior and actions) responds to our thoughts (our mental body), the interpretation of our energy (our spiritual body) and our feelings, which is (our emotional body). A disconnection among our four bodies creates conflicting agendas. The physical body, asks, "What agenda should I focus on and flow my energy? What should I do? Where are we heading?" The physical body is then left to decide without the input of the other bodies. And without a clear direction, the unconscious mind takes over. Again we are left to wonder why things don't work out as we intended.

If we aren't consciously creating, then the unconscious mind takes over. Conscious creation means focusing our whole energy field in the direction set by our intention in the present.

## Check It Out!

**Allowing ourselves to truly process the present is about using our four bodies to give us feedback. All too often we are in situations where we just react emotionally, mentally or physically and miss what our other bodies experience and perceive. Our willingness to integrate all the information available from our four bodies is the intuitive process. This receptivity and connection to our full Intuitive Level allows us to view our world from a wholeness perspective. Wholeness is the total participation of all parts of us and all levels of consciousness in every interaction, which requires us to be in the present. This**

**brings empowerment. Review conversations with friends, family and co-workers.**

- What percentage of your present beliefs is created from the past, present and future?

- What is it like to be totally in the present?

- When you project into the future, how does it feel? What do you see?

- When you reminisce about the past, what do you think about and feel?

- Where do you spend most of your time thinking and talking about (past, present and future? )What causes you to be pulled in that time perspective?

## Flexible Structures

Imagine having a great idea such as taking up scuba diving. We may think how much fun it would be and envision ourselves swimming near colorful coral reefs in some exotic locale. However, if we don't build a structure that includes where to get lessons, how to pay for them and the trip, and a timeframe for when to actually go, and the energy we summoned simply dissipates. Then we are left with no action, and the idea is gone and forgotten. Or we might get excited about leaving our job and striking out on our own. Again, without an intention and plan—which are the first steps to building a structure for us to flow our energy—it won't happen. We then end up feeling disappointed in ourselves and convinced that our lives can never change.

A structure is the product of focused energy that once implemented converts into form. If we didn't have containing structures, our energy would simply stay in energy configurations or dissipate rather than manifesting. Structures reflect and carry the level of consciousness from which they were created. Individuals who join together to create a structure, (whether it be a business, family, or relationship) reside predominately in one of the three levels of consciousness). As the people interact one level of consciousness predominates. This consciousness level sets the foundation of the structure, which then contains all the beliefs and attributes of that consciousness level. Those that are adopted create a unique culture and environment.

In the separation consciousness, structures are rigid. This occurs because only limited possibilities are available. A corporation starts with a mission statement. Then those in power set up an organizational chart and define policies to carry out the mission. And that is how it stays. No matter what is learned from experience, the set way prevails even though other ways of running the corporation may make it more efficient and hence more profitable. Structures in the separation consciousness resist change because power is defined and delegated by certain people who want to retain theirs. Any feedback that suggests changing the status quo threatens their power.

Structures created from the connection consciousness are flexible; they have mechanisms in place to anticipate and support change. Updating is essential to keeping a structure flexible. Periodically, we review the alignment and authenticity among our visions, intentions and actions. We confirm that our actions represent our intentions as we implement our vision. Then we check our vision to ensure it includes what we learned through experience. We then make adjustments to align the current structure with our insights. Maybe we don't need as much money in the advertising budget and instead can use it for research. Now we can extend our child more freedom since she demonstrated her understanding of our parenting practice of responsibilities equal privileges. We recognize now that team meetings are not as efficient as meeting with only the people involved in solving specific problems. Some of our CEO's responsibilities can shift to middle management because of feedback we've received. We had our artwork in galleries and now know that Facebook and links with various art-related websites are better settings to display our paintings. Flexible structures are living entities that process information and continuously redesign systems for the delivery of the visions they were created for.

We see the difficulty of rigid structures in our society trying to meet the problems of our world today. Our financial and political institutions were created from the separation consciousness some hundred years ago and more. At that time, the separation consciousness was more appropriate to building a modern nation and world. The transition from rigid, old structures that have a long history to flexible, new structures requires fluidity. And it can be a daunting task.

Flexible structures will replace or rearrange responsibilities for those in power whenever a shift in vision occurs. We see this in our educational system which is a rigid structure that has not fundamentally changed what is taught or how in the last two hundred years. Our children are deficient in the skills that they need to move into the future. But as more of us create from the connection consciousness, we will be able to build flexible educational structures that reflect who we are becoming. The next step for human evolution is for all of us to tailor the beliefs that reflect the connection consciousness.

## Check It Out!

**Flexible structures are living spirals of evolution. They respond easily to change allowing the manifestation of our ever-changing internal reality. We process our experiences and integrate the insights received through our Intuitive and Soul Levels. And, the spiral continues to expand in the never ending process of: inspiration, vision, implementation, alignment, reflection, updating.**

- How do you respond to structures?

- What does a structure need in order to be responsive and organized?

- What do you define as a flexible structure?

- What is your experience with flexible structures?

- Are you able to create your own structure, or are you more comfortable going into an established structure?

- How have you been received when you present a system change at work or even at home?

If you feel safe and comfortable being in a traditional structure that doesn't make noticeable changes then a part of you needs support from the separation consciousness. If you are yearning to try new ways of doing things and want to participate in the frontline of discovery and innovation then parts of you are comfortable in the connection consciousness.

## Shared Power

We reside in two worlds when we first start learning about shared power. The separation consciousness requires that we follow the goals set by the institution we are working in. The connection consciousness requires that we make choices that ensure our authenticity. How does the project manager resolve the conflicting agendas between the oil company he works for, to take the smallest financial hit on land that is court-ordered for remediation and yet act with compassion toward those who are being adversely affected by the toxic land? How does the marketing manager steer her team away from using sex to sell products to teenagers? How can a screenwriter demonstrate the value of an inspiring movie that may not fit the tried and profitable formula of violence and sex? It takes self-respect, courage and self-mastery of personal needs to align and merge with the power of our Intuitive Level in order to share power.

Here is why. In the separation consciousness, personal power is understood to be the ability to control ourselves and others to get what we want. Abuses of personal power are all around us. Just read the newspapers to find stories of people and governments that are trying to control their environment and others to meet their own elitist and self-serving attitudes. Unless shared power becomes an important value in all societies, we will continue to march toward oligarchy. Who exerted what power to get us into the wars of the last one hundred years? Who was manipulated to set the compensation packages of executives at four hundred times that of workers? How much control do lobbyists and special interest groups exert over politicians at the expense of the rest of the nation?

On the other hand, sharing power takes a person who is living from the connection consciousness where everyone has the power to live their uniqueness, which benefits all. Power in the hands of a few prevents decisions that are for a common good. Only when we share power with others are we able to create the best possibilities for mankind. Through our Intuitive Level, we contribute based on our talents and abilities. We accept that living an authentic life brings satisfactions that have true meaning for us—the ones that really matter. We respect others' abilities instead of being threatened by them or competing to show that our skills are more valuable. Respect for self and others and a solid self-esteem are necessary for power-sharing.

One of my clients was just named CFO of a large company. Helene was competent, experienced. However, when it came to her relationship with the older male owner of the company, she acted like a little girl desperate for her father's approval. Helene's unconscious emotional need drove her into a subordinate relationship with her boss, where sharing power was impossible. Thinking she was being prudent, she checked in with him too often before making decisions. In reality, however, she did this to alleviate her insecurity.

Who was in charge? Who had the power? Her employees figured out that Helene didn't. Some of them formed informal subgroups to make decisions while others forged relationships with the owner, bypassing her altogether. These subversive reactions to Helene's behavior led to chaos and conflict in the company.

Helene was stuck in old fears and the same old reactions. Relying on others to validate her power prevented her from using her Intuitive Level. Unfortunately, this minimized her effectiveness. She did not stop to reflect on which parts of her were living from the separation consciousness and which were living from the connection consciousness.

In therapy, as Helene contemplated her experiences, learned from her successes and failures took responsibility for her development and recognized that the source of her power was her connection to her soul, she constructed a new internal structure that mirrored who she had become. She took responsibility for her own sense of power. Her boss's buy-in was no longer a measure of her self-esteem. Helene now felt empowered to present her ideas and make decisions. This, of course, instilled confidence in the owner of the company who was then willing to share power with her. She also created a reciprocal power-sharing relationship with her staff.

We use the laser beam of personal power from the Personality Level for the satisfaction of our own needs. But power from the Intuitive Level is like a cloud of energy dancing around us. It is defused and loosely structured, allowing flexibility for making the necessary connections. There is room for reflection and learning, adjusting our vision and updating our goals. This allows us to maintain authenticity and confidence, thus inspiring others to share power with us. At the Intuitive Level, our power focus is for intentions and goals that result in personal satisfaction as a by-product and not the main event. This is possible only when we assume responsibility for our own worth.

Inherent in shared power is the value of process. Moving from vision to implementation provides an opportunity for us to learn where and when our actions derail. Another benefit of shared power is it brings together people who use their abilities and talents. This enhances creativity because others join us in doing what has meaning and joy for them.

With a common vision and agreement upon distribution of responsibilities, all we do is our part. The need for us to martyr ourselves to prove our competencies–whether in a marriage, relationship or organization–disappears. We trust the process. If each person does his or her part, we achieve the goal. And if that does not happen, we cherish the opportunity to learn from the experience.

When we are acting from our alignment with our soul energy through our intuition, we connect with an energy field that is so powerful it draws in others. When we express our soul energy, our influence inspires others to see alternatives to the same old tired ideas. We are vibrating at a higher level of consciousness, and those who can connect to it will. That is part of the magic and mystery of the connection consciousness. It seeks to link those of like vibration to manifest a common intention. This comes in the form of coincidences, chance meetings, perfect timing, and other synchronicities. Think of a successful venture. *How did things fall into place? What went smoothly? What parts were difficult? When were you in the connection consciousness? When were you in the separation consciousness?*

Sometimes we find that our level of consciousness is out of sync with others in our group. They might require additional opportunities to learn from the separation consciousness. While we can stay in the situation and try to help change the energy field, it is up to our soul whether we still can learn from this situation or if it is time to leave. That is one of the wonders of the connection consciousness: it helps us see what situation is best for our development as we evolve in the highest expression of our soul and spiritual identities. And any growth in our development changes us and our world view, which opens new possibilities.

## Check It Out!

**Shared power is a win/win situation. It allows us to be authentic and respect the uniqueness within all. It also is a fertile ground for new ideas that can resolve important issues for man.**

- What does it feel like when you are sharing power? How do you feel about yourself?

- In what situations are you able to share power?

- What methods of communication would benefit a connection to share power with another?

- Have you been proactive and expressive of your thoughts and feelings?

- Have your intentions, thoughts, feelings and actions been aligned with the common vision? Why or why not?

- Are you able to trust yourself? Are you able to trust others?

- What prevents you from sharing power?

- What are your fears about sharing power?

If you find sharing power becomes a competition to win control, then part of you is holding onto some beliefs from the separation consciousness that is getting in the way of your growth. Start by listing your strengths so that you remember your uniqueness. Then check your emotions to review when in your life you felt dismissed, rejected or powerless. It may be time to update your reality about power. When you have a clear intention, any decisions are then made from inner power.

## Unlimited Possibilities for Inclusion

Each time we interpret the messages from our soul through our intuition, another fiber is woven to strengthen the connection between the infrastructure of our consciousness levels of personality, intuition and soul. As we trust in this connection, our perspective expands, and we see a multitude of diverse options that were unimaginable when we resided in the separation consciousness. When confronted by these illuminated moments, we scratch our heads, wondering why we didn't see what was always right before our eyes. This clarity of perspective invokes awe.

In the separation consciousness, our perspective is constricted due to the power of institutions to limit thinking to narrow alternatives which fit their culture. The right answer is the one that is acceptable to the establishment and the wrong one challenges it. While this mentality might sustain the status quo, it blocks opportunities for new solutions to problems. And history repeats itself. How much longer will we support the idea of military force being used to determine foreign policy? How much longer will our natural resources be depleted? When will governments create systems that empower people? What is the price we pay when polarized and rigid ideology is used as the basis for political parties? What vision is needed to align special interest groups into a bigger picture?

The answer to these questions comes when a critical mass embraces the connection consciousness. As the energy builds, it magnetizes people, circumstances, timing and resources to set up conditions for implementation to take place. Sharing power and perspectives while respecting all those involved integrates the best solution, bringing in a higher consciousness—a more expansive perspective which then facilitates change.

Only from the perspective of a higher consciousness do we see the world from a different point of view. We need the courage to implement new possibilities that feel unsafe, are as yet unproven, and may cause us to risk the familiar. We must remember, though, that personal growth and spiritual evolution are inherent within the human psyche. It is a force that cannot be denied. It is part of our heritage to move from human beings to spiritual beings—beings that see what can be possible.

When we imagine new possibilities we learn to live with anxiety and ambiguity, which is really just energy waiting for direction and focus. When a new idea comes, the energy to implement it is also available. As we go through the steps to implementation (which takes clarification and purposeful behavior), we are using the energy we accessed when we envisioned the idea. However, all the new available energy is not immediately put into action. This surplus feels uncomfortable because we do not yet know where to focus it. So we identify it as anxiety.

If I put a chewed up ball of bubble gum on the table, it can represent the ignition of an idea with the amount of energy that is needed to manifest it. If I get an idea and do nothing about it, the bubble gum ball just sits there. But if I press and spread the mass, it will cover more space. Similarly, if we focus our thoughts, feelings and actions on an idea, it spreads, attracting others to the cause. The movement of action from bubble gum ball to some larger mass can produce anxiety since there is no guarantee if the energy will stay intact. Or it may be spread so thin that it cannot sustain its form. This movement into the unknown is another aspect of anxiety.

Remember a time when you thought of an idea or had a gut-level feeling. *What were your emotions? What was the range of thoughts? How did you handle the excitement and doubts at the same time?* We can experience this anxiety as fear or excitement. As we develop our plan and start the necessary actions, our emotions can evolve. We feel excitement because we know our next steps. At the same time, we experience fear because we are unsure of our next step and cannot guarantee success. The mind triggers the idea through our relationship to our intuition, and then the emotional body is put on alert that energy is necessary to manifest it. Our emotions direct energy for us to use. Think of the energy burst or drain when we are exhilarated, angry, joyful, depressed or anxious. Our emotional bodies are our energy suppliers.

Ideas for manifestation come from all points on the continuum between the separation consciousness's black-or-white mentality and the possibilities and potential that comes from the connection and soul level consciousness. The wisdom of our souls recognizes that any new possibility that is so different from what we are familiar with automatically is met with resistance since the separation consciousness is the predominant level in this world. The unity consciousness operates from the unlimited energy of the cosmos. The soul easily interprets the readiness of humankind and all life forms to accept a certain new possibility. The hope and trust that there is always another way is the foundation of the "and/both" mentality of the connection consciousness. As we choose to participate in the connection consciousness, we envision a widened perspective of life.

Our intuition sparks the expanded version of anything that is already in form. This is a never-ending process of unlimited possibilities and the basis of our evolving human and spiritual identity. We are continuously growing, changing and recreating who we are. This exciting (though at times difficult) process is the reason and function behind the connection consciousness. We visualize our spiritual development as an expanding spiral. Every time we initiate an idea, learn from the experience and add it to our ever-expanding view of the world and ourselves, we see the next level and another part of the bigger picture. This expanding viewpoint is actually the result of our deeper connection to the unity consciousness. The more comprehensive our view, the more we are aligned and merged with our soul. An expanding spiral is a good symbol for us to visualize and meditate on to invoke spiritual development.

Our intuition has the ability to inspire us to expand and enhance what is already in form. In the connection consciousness, everything that is created and brought into form has an inclusive "and/both" mentality. Anything we intuit, think and feel has the energy available to create a form that represents it. It also has the space on earth for it to exist. The world is constantly expanding and including all that is realized and recognized by all living things. And since the universe is connected to a higher consciousness, it is always expanding as well. Evolution is the natural expansion of connecting to and processing unlimited consciousness levels. Our willingness to develop our Intuitive Level supports us in this fantastic journey to more.

## Check It Out!

**The belief in unlimited possibilities becomes more real to us as we constantly open to our intuition—the vehicle for our visions, imagination and desire. Whether in our personal and/or professional life, the attitude of "and/both" keeps us in contact with our intuition. We are asking our intuition for new and different perspectives to apply to the situation at hand.**

- What do you feel about the situation you are in?

- What do you feel and think about the people involved?

- What is your body telling you?

- What images, symbols or metaphors are available?

- What are your motivations? What is your intention? What are the motivations of others?

- Who benefits if this works or doesn't work?

- What more can you see and understand once you made the initial decision?

**These are important questions to answer. We reflect, process our experiences, and then apply our learning to create solutions that represent a higher consciousness. If you find yourself trying to use tried and true behavior and answers then it is time to ask yourself:**

- What's another way to look at this?

- How can I change this repeating pattern?

- What is really going on?,

- What do I think I need to defend?

**Now is time to update your opinion of yourself.**

- What's another way to look at this?

- How can I change this repeating pattern?

- What is really going on?

- What do I think I need to defend?

**It is time to update your opinion of yourself.**

## The Co-Existence of Light and Shadow

We live in a world where polarities exist. They show us what potential exists within the parameters of our existence. As we progress on our spiritual path, we choose what we connect to. On this journey, the light is our guide. It is the symbol for enlightenment and living a life from the highest consciousness level that we perceive. However, no matter how much enlightenment in our lives there is also shadow. This is the part of our self that has been damaged. Whatever we have done to defend or strike back from that hurt constitutes the shadow.

At the Personality Level, light and shadow is an either/or concept. "Shadow" connotes judgment–evil, the dark forces, and even the devil. It is something to avoid, repress, hide, and deny. Indeed, given this meaning, who would want to acknowledge their shadow parts? But this thinking undermines us. How can we be authentic when we hold such a large secret inside? The condemnation associated with our mistakes (emanating from our shadow), manifests in guilt and shame which causes us to feel defective. We may even express these feelings as self-hatred.

In fact, avoiding our weak parts causes us to overcompensate. We try to appear authoritarian to retain some sense of power and to offset our deficits. The businessman who is frustrated at work becomes a tyrant on the soccer field when coaching his son's team. The woman who finds it difficult to parent her disobedient teenage daughter is a no-excuse manager. An uninspired teacher becomes a martyr in her community's Citizen Emergency Response Team. All too often, those who compensate for self-loathing end up taking rigid positions.

Because connecting to our shadow threatens our self-esteem, we create defenses against it. This is the basis for bullying. Not only are bullies insecure, but they also fear their feelings of unworthiness and inadequacy. Their defense mechanism is to adopt behaviors that intimidate others. For just a second while in the bully persona, they feel stronger than the other. This gives them a false sense of power and superiority. In that moment, they are disconnected from their fears. Also, bullying behaviors keep people away so the ugly secrets and self-loathing can stay forever locked away.

Think of a block of granite sitting in a stream. The water must go around it, which affects the flow and direction of the stream. So it is with unprocessed events and situations in our lives. They distort the flow of energy from our soul, to our intuition, and personality. *What part of you do you think is defective? What shame are you holding inside? What are you feeling guilty about? What are you trying to hide? What do you do with your weaknesses, shame, or guilt to separate it from your awareness? What prevents you from connecting with it?*

On the other hand, at the Intuitive Level, we choose to connect with our shadow to further our growth. At this level, our shadow becomes those parts of us that are out of our awareness, isolated, and cut off. For whatever reason (inadequate self-esteem, ignoring our power source, wrong thinking, negative feelings), we were unable to face what we did or what happened at the time, so we pushed it aside. Either we deliberately repress them or they are in the unconscious awaiting discovery. It then becomes our conscious choice to connect to the parts of ourselves that we perceive as "weakness" and "error" in order to glean the lessons that were unavailable at the time of the situation might have occurred.

*What is your relationship to your faults, and weaknesses? What events have you not come to terms with? What do you do to repress your shadow? What defenses do use? How can you develop a relationship with your shadow that reflects the connection consciousness?*

The connection consciousness generates a psychology of hope. We see connection to our shadow as a learning opportunity. This allows for more energy to be integrated into our whole energy field. From this perspective, we eagerly examine our shadow. Maybe we finally acknowledge that we are controlling after years of denying what is so obvious to everyone else except ourselves. While accepting this part of us shocks us at first, asking our soul to support us during this investigation brings comfort. Asking our soul to help us feel self-compassion prevents us from directing barrage of criticism against ourselves. After all, beating ourselves up just causes us to suppress what we just unearthed. Compassion comes in the form of accepting that at the time of the situation we were in a different space. We made decisions then that reflected where we were in our development. By connecting with our shadow, we get a chance to redo our perceptions. We see that our controlling behaviors originated from our feelings of unworthiness and inadequacy. We ask ourselves: *Where did these feelings come from? What or who made me feel so bad about myself in the past? What was happening around me when I felt defective? What did I do to deflect the pain? What do I do now to prevent these painful feelings from arising in me again?*

Once we investigated the what, where, how, and why of the shadow situation, we work in tandem with our Intuitive and Soul Level to recognize that our conclusions about defectiveness are untrue. No longer do we react and personalize the hurt, disappointments, and frustrations that remind us of our relationships to our parents or lovers or any traumatic event that influenced how we see ourselves today. We release the old emotions and forgive ourselves for the fact that we did not know another way. We neither had the skills nor the strength to respond differently at that time.

We change our perspective when we forgive ourselves or others and when we start forgetting about the painful situation. Each time we remember it, we give it energy. Our thoughts create energy structures and the only way an energy structure will release its charge is when all the energy in it has seeped out of it. If we are holding a belief about our unworthiness, for instance, we must look at it from all angles over a period of time so that all of the nuances and intensity of the feeling are eradicated or reformed. By denying the belief energy, we learn the lessons we need to. This creates a new point of view about the underlying feelings that caused the regrettable situation in the first place. Even if we know this was an intentional destructive act, we were still living from a perspective that did not include self-responsibility. At the time, the external may have seemed overwhelming and often condemning. After self-exploration, it is now time to choose to create appropriate thoughts, feelings, and behaviors that align with the soul.

We are responsible for connecting any energy we released as a result of forgiving and forgetting to our Intuitive and Soul Levels. This causes the energy to become flexible and vital since we are linking it to a higher consciousness level than the one in which it was created.

This causes an expansion of our whole energy field. At this point, we gain clarity about our past motivations and actions and take responsibility for their consequences. *What do you need to do to take responsibility for your past actions? What were your motivations for the shadow part of you to take charge? What were your fears at the time the shadow was forceful? Will you forgive yourself?*

Shadow parts also refer to those parts of ourselves that are dancing in our unconscious and out of our awareness. Our soul is in charge of when and how to bring these to our attention for additional growth opportunities. This can be in the form of symbols, dreams, visions, or circumstances and opportunities. I believe that the soul also brings to our awareness conclusions made from past lives or a specific connection to the collective unconscious. These extraordinary associations are tailor made because we are ready to use this symbolic information to resolve an issue that is primed for resolution. They come when we have learned the lessons of the Personality Level and are experimenting with the beliefs of the connection consciousness so that we can process our shadow parts.

The soul determines when a shadow part is ready for activation, connection, and integration. I have seen clients find unknown talents hidden within them. One left a corporate job to become a professional artist, another stopped managing a chiropractic office to develop and successfully market natural skincare products, another quit the police department to open a gym and became a personal trainer, another resigned her teaching position to create educational aides and yet another put away her law shingle and wrote contemporary women's fiction and on it goes. Our shadow is fertile with potential and possibilities. *What is hovering around your peripheral awareness? What are your dreams saying? What synchronicities are happening in your life? What do you long to do? Do you say "yes" to new opportunities?*

When we accept the co-existence of shadow and light we affirm our humanity. Yes, in this world there are those who consciously choose to align with the shadow—those who need personal power to cover their fear of powerlessness. These individuals and groups profess absolute dogma. They become evangelistic, working to influence (or force) others to adopt their thinking. Immediately, an oppositional position forms. We are either for or against them. Fundamental Muslins and Christians both claim to possess the only right way to God. We see the ramifications of this type of thinking in the world today.

Individuals create their own shadow when they stay separated from the consciousness of their intuition and soul and only live from the Personality Level. Think of how many suffer from broken relationships, difficulties at work, and tragic consequences from holding onto old, rigid, absolute beliefs. The physically abused woman who stays with her husband, the unhappy couple who stays married and lives quiet lives of desperation, the person stuck in a job he or she hates. All these people are living in their shadow of separation.

But we also know people who are upbeat, desiring to grow and embrace life. Their light is bright, and they hold a beacon of hope for all of us. They trust and take the calculated risk to live their soul focus. The man who made millions in the start-up craze and is now using his money and time working on devices that aide the handicap, the doctor who is a member of Doctors Without Borders, and all the unsung heroes in everyday life who are dedicated to helping others.

Recognizing and accepting shadow and light reaffirms that every situation is available in the wholeness of the human experience for everyone's specific learning. It is essential to recognize the shadow and light of people we interact with. It helps us understand which consciousness levels are available in the interaction. We are then able to choose how to connect and respond. It's not to say that we spend our time looking for another's shadow; it's just when it does appear, we are not surprised, disappointed, or judgmental. The shadow just is and therefore acceptance is required. This awareness gives us clarity about the others intention and motivations. We then must choose what, how, where, when and why we decided to connect with the other. We must choose where to align our energy. *From what perspective do you choose to see the world and yourself? How well do you match your intentions and motivation with others? What blinds you to the reality of where another co-exists in their consciousness? What level of consciousness do you connect with others?*

If you are judgmental of others then there is a strong possibility you are afraid of facing your own shadow. First draw or assign a symbol to your shadow even if you cannot yet admit that you have one. Put it in your heart as a symbolic gesture that you love it because it is also a part of you. Remember that the energy that is your shadow is just that. It can be washed and surrounded by love so that it becomes more flexible. Look at it and give it a voice. Seek its origins and if amends need to be made, do so from the connection consciousness beliefs. Allow your intuition to guide you. We are all imperfect human beings learning from our misperceptions.

As we understand and incorporate the characteristics of the connection consciousness in our perspective, we are ready to explore and create our Intuitive Level.

## Chapter Four Exploration and Discovery Activities

### Points to Ponder

- In the connection consciousness, the value of symbols is so important that once we see ourselves through symbolic sight our self-image and even our lives shift permanently.
- Through the growth we experience to achieve self-mastery, we become empowered by our gift of choice. We realize that we can change, let go of limiting thoughts, choose to respond to others instead of reacting, and connect to our souls for motivation and inspiration.
- Clarity means that we understand and know our motivations and intentions.
- Authenticity means expressing how we truly feel, the reasons why we feel a certain way, and the actions that support and are congruent with our thinking and feelings.
- Authenticity is a simple equation: vision + thoughts + feelings = behaviors/actions.
- Our soul activates only those new parts of ourselves that we are ready to connect with and integrate.
- As we start living a new perspective, our souls have already designed the passage and structure for us to flow our energy.
- Our normal defenses are down in times of crisis. This allows our soul to decrystalize old patterns to support new connections. Our energy field is more malleable and receptive to higher levels of consciousness.
- Uniqueness comes from a state of openness to symbolic sight that knows things are not always what they seem.
- When trying on a new perspective, we need to think about it, feel it, and experiment with it without preconceived notions.

- Setting our intention is the process of aligning the three levels of consciousness within, so that each does its part in the movement of energy to form.
- Intentions focus the flow of our energy.
- Relationships are the meanings a couple attaches to the words and actions they use between each other.
- Using our Intuitive Level fully in the present, we understand the motivations behind the words and actions of the other.
- By observing what situations and people are drawn to us in the present, we see a mirror of our internal reality.
- Conscious creation is flowing and focusing our whole energy field in the direction set by our intention in the present.
- A structure is the product of focused energy that transforms into form when implemented. It is like a container that holds the energy field in time and space for manifestation to take place.
- Structures reflect and carry the level of consciousness from which they are created. The level of consciousness that is predominant is the foundation of the structure.
- A flexible structure has a mechanism that anticipates and allows change.
- Respect for self, others, and a solid self-esteem is necessary to share power.
- Inherent in shared power is recognition that process is valued as an opportunity to learn and grow.
- The expanded version of anything that is already in form is sparked by our intuition.
- An expanding spiral provides a growth symbol for us to visualize and meditate on to invoke our spiritual development.
- There is always a space for us to bring into form our soul intentions. Anything we intuit, think or feel has the energy available to create a form that represents it.
- We live in a world where polarities exist as a way of seeing the potential within the parameters of our human existence.

- Unprocessed events and situations in our life distort the flow of energy from our soul to our intuition and personality.
- Forgiving is letting go of the energy that keeps something alive so that we can focus the energy to learn the present lesson.

**Read a biography or autobiography of someone you respect and admire.**
- What situations did you identify with?
- How did the person handle adversity?
- What were the attitudes, feelings, and actions that supported the person to fulfill his/her authentic visions?
- How did the person develop the courage to live authentically? What motivation supported the person to be authentic?
- What did you learn and how can you apply what you learned to your own life?
- What new motivation can you use to live authentically?

**Observe people around you in all the arenas of your life.**
- Who do you perceive is authentic?
- What characteristics do they display that you identify with?
- How do they handle conflict?
- How do they manage their emotions?
- How do they share power?
- What is their communication style like?
- What skills can you apply in your life?

# Chapter Five

## The Intuitive Level as a Reflection of the Connection Consciousness

In the Personality Level, we are like worker ants doing the tasks that are expected of us with a single-minded focus. But in the connection consciousness we understand that we are a part of something greater than ourselves. We can use many terms for this powerful realization: "a grand design," "higher intelligence," "higher consciousness," "all that is," or religious terms that denote an expansive pattern. Scientists have recently announced that the universe is four times larger than we previously believed. As the cosmos expands, we also expand by connecting to and integrating different levels of consciousness. The connection consciousness posits that all that exists in the natural world—from the immensity of the cosmos to individuals to microbes—is connected by an invisible force. Our entry to this expanded field of connection consciousness is our Intuitive Level.

The Intuitive Level expands beyond the routines of life. We learn that our personal power in the separation consciousness is insignificant compared to our potency in the connection consciousness. As we participate in life in the Intuitive Level, our vision expands. We find value in a simple act. We recognize the kaleidoscope of life and its many facets that bring beauty and richness to our lives. Life becomes meaningful and every single day matters. We use symbolic insight to interpret our experience. Indeed, the guidance we receive in the Intuitive Level fills our world with wonderment. Possibilities multiply exponentially; shifts in perspectives cause previously unknown patterns to emerge and self-mastery spurs us to fertile visas. Hope and courage are our companions. To deny the full use of our Intuitive Level is to cage our heart, mind and soul.

Being in the Intuitive Level is akin to seeing our lives from an eagle-eye view while at the same time fully participating in every moment of day to day existence. No longer do we focus on only specifics or perceive events as separate units. We now enter into the abstract, conceptual, perspectives where we value personal interpretation and used it to gain clarity. We notice patterns in what we believed were unrelated events, feelings, thoughts, and instinct. We see partial images, visions, and symbols that inspire and evoke our creativity. Now we connect all of our separate pieces, all of ourselves, into a bigger context. This leads to fresh conclusions and possibilities.

My vision was corrected through laser surgery by shaping the cornea of the right eye for distance and the left one for close up. This, I realized, was a great metaphor for shifting from the separation to the connection consciousness. Viewing our world from the separation consciousness, we see through the capacity of our physical eyes. If we wear glasses, we depend on the power of the lenses. If we take off our reading glasses and see the distance, or even if we have progressive lenses, each eye has the same task. However, with mono vision, one eye sees far while simultaneously the other eye sees near. Think of the range of vision the mind is integrating. The separation consciousness lets us see within a limited range while the connection consciousness enhances and expands our vision. Here is another perspective.

The brain is capable of receiving input in many ways at once and can synthesize the information instantaneously. As we are talking to others, we listen from our Personality Level, which gives us the literal, concrete, "seeing is believing" data. But at the same time, our Intuitive Level picks up unseen and unexpressed feelings, thoughts, motivations, images, and symbols. The brain integrates all of this information immediately and makes it available to us so we can apply this new expanded perspective as we continue the conversation. Intuitive insights are available to us at all times when we live from the connection consciousness.

We use more of ourselves when we live in the connection consciousness because we are continually finding and linking to unknown and undiscovered parts of ourselves. We realize that now, instead of being limited to just five senses, we possess a sixth sense.

## The Psychology of Hope and the Intuitive Level

As we become familiar with the concept of connecting to different levels of consciousness beyond the seen world, the psychology of hope ignites within us. We are no longer stuck in a life that cannot be changed. Our ability to connect with multiple levels of consciousness, to see another perspective and find alternatives is the psychology of hope. Infinite possibilities await us.

No longer are we blinded by our own knee-jerk reactions that are caused by personalizing situations. Reactivity is akin to swathing our bodies in plastic wrap and trying to breathe. We suffocate with destructive thoughts and feelings.

As we gain self-mastery, we are open to the possibilities that emerge from our intuition. We then can choose how to respond. Shifting our perspective to the Intuitive Level is like a warm tropical breeze caressing us. There is room to relax, reflect, decide and plan. We have space to discern between our internal and external reality which reminds us who we want to be and the values we choose to live by. It is now possible to become a spiritual human being.

I counseled a couple that was discouraged with their relationship. While they loved each other, the interactions between them conveyed hurt, anger and scorn. Their frequent fights over emotionally laden and misunderstood comments caused a rift. Each felt alone. Both hoped that there was a way to regain the connection and trust they had once enjoyed.

A communication pattern that encourages authentic expression of feelings—the basis for an atmosphere of intimacy—was lacking. Jon was overwhelmed and unsure of what, when, how, and if to respond to Lisa's emotions. Not knowing what to do lead to frustration and often anger. Lisa took Jon's inability to understand her emotions followed by his anger as rejection and a judgment against her. In their frustration and hurt, both ended up reacting to each other's words. This led to a repeating cycle of emotional pain and withdrawal.

Expressing their feelings and the thoughts and beliefs that caused them was the most difficult part of their communication. Using the psychology of hope *-that there is always another way-* both committed to expressing themselves and understanding each other in different ways. Lisa started using a journal to process and clarify her feelings. Once she had some insight, she could easily decide what she chose to do with them. Jon also started a journal to explore and expand the range of emotions he could identify with. As both owned their feelings, they were able to determine the underlying issues that caused them to become reactive. This was their opportunity to unveil hidden expectations and assumptions they held about themselves, each other and marriage. As Jon and Lisa created successful strategies to take more responsibility for communicating within themselves and with each other, hope turned into trust.

The psychology of hope gives us room to maneuver around, explore, and experiment without self-defeating judgments. This frees us to respond authentically to all circumstances and situations whether they are painful or filled with joy. And when we respond authentically we define what matters to us. The psychology of hope also supports us to open our minds and hearts and experiment with the beliefs of the three levels of consciousness so that we can choose what is right for us. The psychology of hope encourages us to seek the answer to the question "I wonder...?" At the Intuitive and Soul Levels, we know that the energy fields our soul sets up and connects us to are filled with possibilities. We interpret these connections and then create what inspires us.

## Purposes of the Intuitive Level

The Intuitive Level is the messenger and interpreter of the Soul Level. It is where we find our own truths so that we can become authorities within our own lives. Only we can know what is right for us no matter how much we are barraged by unsolicited opinions from others and our external world. Our Intuitive Level has the important task to change our Personality Level so that it aligns with our Soul

Level. It can guide and influence our thoughts, feelings and actions in the Personality Level. It is the great integrator between the world of energy in the unity consciousness and the world of form in the separation consciousness. Through the world of symbols, our Intuitive Level allows us to interpret the abstract realm between energy and form. It is the link between spirit and matter. Our willingness to receive the insights, visions, epiphanies, and "aha's" from our soul coupled with our ability to interpret these through our intuition supports us in our evolution and growth. It helps us become spiritual beings. Once we start adopting the beliefs of the connection consciousness and developing our Intuitive Level, our soul participates more wholly in our lives. Below are the purposes of our Intuitive Level.

### Establish self-mastery and self-authority

Self-mastery is the first step toward becoming our own self-authority. Life skills (decision-making, mood management, communication, building and sustaining relationships, and assertiveness) are the basic tools that build the foundation from which we relate to ourselves and others. Developing and refining these-skills is essential for self-mastery. While we each have our own style, competency allows us to align the Personality Level with the Intuitive Level.

All of the problems that we experience in the Personality Level stem from a lack of self- mastery and self-authority. Competency in life skills is the antidote to lurking fears of not being good enough. We hide from our feelings of insecurity by becoming controlling and defensive. Instead of facing the reality that we must do the trench work of personality development, we want the external world to be responsible for giving us the benefits without the work. When that doesn't happen, we are prime candidates for destructive behaviors to ourselves and others. Think of all of our complaints: Our friend seems distracted at dinner instead of attending to what we are saying. Our husband wasn't as passionate as we'd wanted on our anniversary. Our boss didn't acknowledge our Herculean efforts. We weren't invited to lunch when our sister took mom out for her birthday. Our wife didn't check in with us often enough at the neighborhood barbeque. No one at work noticed our new hairstyle. Our kids forgot to thank us for taking them to the beach, and on it goes. If we have not mastered life skills, we personalize and overreact to these everyday situations. We have emotional outbursts that express disappointment and hurt in the form of anger. We injure others with our words. We are disrespectful to subordinates or superiors. We abuse authority by controlling others. All this does is let everyone know that we are stuck in the Personality Level.

Of course our view of our self is distorted at this point in our development. Instead of accepting that we need to change the behavior that is causing disappoint and emotional suffering, we want others to validate us. If we don't take responsibility for learning life skills, why do we expect others to validate what we don't possess? If we cannot control our anger why would we assume others should treat us with respect? This discrepancy from "what I do and how I should be treated" is self-defeating. It sets us up to rage at others and to complain that life is against us.

Groups that are organized for a specific cause use lack of life skills as a justification for entitlement. Entitlement is the expression of their not taking responsibility for themselves and expecting others to make up for their failings. They blame others for the deficient life skills that cause them to feel separated from society. They think that they are treated differently, don't have the rights and opportunities others in society enjoy or they go unrewarded for their contributions. Because of their perceived deprivation, they want society-at-large to give them what they feel they are due. Instead of taking personal responsibility to create their own sense of worth as they become competent at life skills, they feel entitled to be treated special. They feel disadvantaged and believe that their situation will never change.

There is no moral distinction associated with entitlement. Ask any special interest group–whether illegal immigrants, CEO's, banks, lawyers, the Catholic Church, the rich, the poor, the middle class–they will list why they are entitled to exceptional treatment no matter the cost or the effects on others.. Entitlement is personalizing judgment from society and reacting to how we feel others should treat us.

Without self-mastery we are limited to our Personality Level. Personalization and entitlement are both expressions of people who can only view differences and compete for status, power and worth. Unfortunately, this feeling of separation originates within the self, since we are separated from our three levels of consciousness.

Life skills teach us to objectively handle any situation we encounter. Our ability to stay calm when others are angry, clearly articulate ideas that are true to our values, state well-defined intentions, take actions that represent our thoughts and feelings, and follow through with our goals demonstrates our ability at self-mastery.

We become responsible and accountable for the way we act when we live in the connection consciousness. When we ask ourselves, "What do I want to create in this situation?" fear stops and hope can bloom. We are now in the psychology of hope where guidance is available from our intuition. By asking for guidance as we seek how to respond creatively, we open ourselves to the connection consciousness. We affirm that there is always another way.

Becoming an authority for ourselves starts by paying attention to how much the external world influences our opinions and decisions. Then, we start trying on and eventually adopting values that reflect the beliefs of the connection consciousness. By asking ourselves to discern what we think and feel before acting, we can ascertain whether our actions represent our values. Reflecting on the consequences of our actions on ourselves and others ensures we are creating what we intend. How we walk in the world and engage with life are choices. Acting on what we learn from experience, we accept responsibility for ourselves. Regardless of what influences us, we are responsible for our actions. By accumulating experiences and learning from them, we become our own authority.

Depending on the external for guidance is addictive, seductive, and easy, so vigilance is necessary for self-authority. Social networks, TV, the internet, conversing with friends and simply going into any store to buy necessities inundate us with persuasive messages. Wherever we turn others are always waiting to influence and give opinions. If we do not clarify our own thinking, we become susceptible to these external influences. And we become separated from our self and lose our uniqueness. This is akin to selling parts of our soul. If we are not our own authority we have no internal compass; there is no clarity to act.

Expressing our authentic thoughts, feelings, and behaviors and making choices from the Intuitive Level takes us beyond the conditioning of social institutions to the clarity of who we are becoming. External reality loses its power to define us, and our internal reality becomes the reference point for living.

## Check It Out!

We become authorities for ourselves when our external values reflect our internal ones. The process creating this congruency is our spiritual journey. Observing our own participation in our daily lives helps us evaluate the pull of external influences.

As we progressively detach from external forces and become more objective relying on our internal reality, we can catch ourselves personalizing, feeling entitled, or wanting others to validate us. The next step is to determine which life skills require a refresher course.

- What triggering events activate personalization and over-reactivity?

- What happens when you personalize?

This is the time to ask the hard questions to figure out what is really going on.

- What am I feeling? Whose emotions are on display? What did I expect? What is causing the pain? What am I responsible for? What thought is causing this reaction? What do I choose to do about the situation?

- What do you feel entitled to?

- What life skills do you need to refine?

As we learn self-mastery and express the guidance we receive from our Intuitive and Soul Levels, we become an authority for our self.

- When did you feel confident about a decision that you made for yourself?

- Evaluate the alignment of your Personality and Intuitive Levels. Was your thinking and feeling congruent? Were the Personality and Intuitive Levels congruent?

It is essential to master life skills so we can implement insights we value from the Intuitive Level. Listening to our spiritual, mental, emotional and physical bodies as we interpret our experiences gives us the necessary insights to become self-authorities. When there is a congruency among them we feel a vibrational sense of rightness. We then use our self-authority for discerning the specific way to live what is right for us.

### To live by our intuitive insights

As we choose to live from the connection consciousness, we desire to live more of what is possible for us. We want to explore who we are meant to be and what matters and has value in our lives. This flight toward an expanded view of who we are right now and trust in who we are meant to be is the spiritual journey. It is about new realizations, trying out the reality that we create from our expanded understanding of self, and then detaching from what we've created so that we can move on to learn the next lesson from our Intuitive Level. In this ever- widening spiral of expansion and growth, we choose to be the best we can be. Expansion comes from interpreting symbols, images, dreams and messages that come from our souls. It is the Intuitive Level that facilitates this process of interpretation which clarifies our direction and decisions. We have all experienced intuitive insights that we did not take seriously. In the Intuitive Level, we listen and say "yes" to these precious gifts.

Allowing our Intuitive Level to guide us puts us in a space that is devoid of stress and false obligations. This provides room to imagine new possibilities. We accept that problems and obstacles exist to help us learn and master certain skills. We appreciate each choice we make that is authentic and aligns with our values and intuitive sense of what is right for us. We move to a life filled with creativity, meaning and purpose. We become conscious of our own worth as a part of the grand scheme in life. We are at peace with ourselves and the way we are living our lives—all the result of living from the connection consciousness and expressing ourselves through the Intuitive Level. Indeed, we feel alive.

Relationships among people who relate through the beliefs of the connection consciousness are based on respect for self and others. With self-mastery we no longer need to render interactions a platform for self-validation. We are connected to others by choice through a common goal, idea, or project. Each person has the desire to contribute while also acknowledging the uniqueness and talents of the others. Diversity is acknowledged. Individuals appreciate the part the others play in the dynamic of creating together. Discussions may be lively—even passionate—but they are without personal attacks or underhanded manipulations. When we work in a group, as individuals, our goal is aligned with the stated purpose that is clear and accepted by all. The simply guideline is, "How does this help achieve the goal in the best possible way?"

Intuition is a receptive and dynamic process. Breathing is a great metaphor for understanding this process in all of us. Just as every breath we receive is a life-sustaining force that integrates in our bodies with purpose and function so do we receive inputs from multiple levels of consciousness at all times. The dynamic way we process this input (and what we exhale to the atmosphere as a result) is influenced by the filters we create to help us discern what has value, what form to use, and what needs to be released. The Intuitive Level provides a filter to create this kind of rich life.

## Check It Out!

Intuition is part of our infrastructure to give us a range of information from survival to creating. Animals and plants also have their consciousness—their own ways of sensing and relating to the environment for survival. This unseen yet undeniable force is inherent in all. We have the choice to develop it. Even if you do not feel confident to follow your intuition, just write down any insights that might arise. Then check in hindsight to see if they could have helped. By listening to and gradually learning to trust our intuition, we open to a new way of life.

- What is your attitude about intuition?

- What do you think is the source of your intuition?

- Where in your life does your intuition operate?

- What prevents you from expanding the use of your intuition?
- What messages from your intuition did you follow?
- Who supports your intuition?

## Defining Questions

The Intuitive Level like all of our levels is a fertile ground for learning. Below are the defining questions that support us in the exploration of our Intuitive Level in the connection consciousness.

### What am I connected to?

Acceptance that we exist in other levels of consciousness renders the interrelatedness of all things real and reassures us that we are part of a grander design. This awareness challenges us to evolve in our understanding of who we are and who we are meant to be. Our intuition provides us a vehicle to explore our connections to other consciousness levels, which reveals our potential.

Recognizing the extent of our connection is a humbling and empowering experience. When we realize that man is the link between different levels of consciousness and has the ability to bring insight and action into physical existence for the higher good of all, we see our true potential. And, we are humbled when we honor and marvel at the consciousness of all living things and recognize that they also have a purpose within the whole design. From microbes to human beings, we are all interdependent in the grand experiment of manifesting the potentials of existence.

Whether we are linking with another (through a new relationship) or to our own intuition to become inspired, connection is the way to obtain what we need. This sense that we are connected at all times becomes more real as we observe how efficiently our Intuition Level works. Indeed, relying on our Intuitive Level, we choose where we focus our energy and attention. We accept the need for a life that is our own and move from conformity to originality. Now we no longer depend on defined gender roles to automatically create the structure of our marriage. We can live in a remote area of the country and open an Internet business. Turning a talent into a small business becomes worth the reduced income. Living in a foreign country turns into reality instead of laying fallow as a far off dream. Participating in city politics because we feel so strongly about zoning ordinances takes on great importance. This then is the beginning of new possibilities; new ways of seeing the world, new actions that reflect our appreciation that we are part of the continually expanding cosmos in which we live.

Compartmentalization which is active in the separation consciousness works against us in the connection consciousness. We only playact at different roles when we compartmentalize. This keeps us separated from all parts of ourselves and inhibits expansion. We can be a nurturing person when we visit our sick grandmother for twenty minutes, be a tyrant at work, be a church elder, spoil one of our sons, demean our mate, and give to charities. So who are we and what do we stand for? Since we are only reacting to different roles, we cannot integrate all parts of ourselves. Authenticity has no compartmentalization; we are who we are in all situations. Our values are constantly expressed by our behaviors. When we create from our Intuitive Level we become aware of the power of aligning intention, feelings and action. In all behaviors we recognize what we are connected to and why. We know what has meaning.

## Check It Out!

**Our willingness to explore new insights and visions determines the expansiveness of our connections to other consciousness levels. For some, the acceptance of being connected to a higher power provides comfort and inspiration. For others, the quest to seek the new leads them to uncharted realities. Whatever our choice in experiencing with connection is, it guides us on our spiritual path.**

- What do you want to be connected to?

- What level—from potential, to possibilities to probabilities—are you most comfortable with?

- Are you a visionary or an implementer?

- How can you use your Intuitive Level in all steps of vision to implementation?

- What do I choose? Who do I want to be?

Our choices from the Intuitive Level do not simply emerge from our will to make what we want come to pass. Nor do they arise from our personal desire for power or our need to prove we are adequate. (In fact, we identified and worked out most of those issues as we mastered the lessons of the separation consciousness.) Rather, they come from a sense of rightness, a gut-level feeling, a knowing that we are doing what is good for us because our desires are generated from the heart.

The Intuitive Level ignites our desire to live our uniqueness and express the purest and highest consciousness level that is available to us. We hope that we connect with what we need in order to achieve our goals: guidance, inspiration, people, opportunities, circumstances, and resources. When we open the surfing school for young girls, the family activity camp, the retreat center, the shop for custom handmade shoes, or the workshops for young teens who are interested in designing clothes these choices come from the joy of doing something we love. Hoping, believing, and taking action can bring us lives that radiate excitement, meaning and abundance. Acting on hope through our Intuitive Level is the first step toward becoming spiritual beings. *Think of situations in your life when you wanted and needed a question answered—how was it answered?*

There are so many possibilities. We just happened to be drawn to a book at the bookstore; or we ran into someone who provides a link to the person who has just the experience, information, and associations that propel our project forward; or we simply got a flash of insight upon awakening. Our intuition is in operation when we acknowledge and observe our sense of knowingness, and it is evidence of our connection to other levels of consciousness.

Accepting our Intuitive Level as an unlimited resource amplifies our hope about the choices we make. It supports us to go beyond self-imposed barriers and limitations—the "I can't. . . " and "I'm afraid I don't know how to. . .". It also affords us to act with courage, and trust which bring new thoughts. "It may be difficult and I know I can still do it." "Even though this feels scary, I know this is right for me." "If I stumble I know I will find the help I need." "It feels so good to be doing something I love, I don't care how hard it's going to be." The

Intuitive Level can ignite in us a desire to dedicate ourselves to those issues in this world that could use a new perspective and aligns with our soul desire. Pick a cause that opens your heart and allows your soul to sing. *First how would you come to a compassionate perspective within yourself before acting? What would you like to see changed in this world? What can you do about it from a personal level? What can you create to bring others together for a common cause?* Being plugged into our Intuitive Level is like switching from using kerosene to a nuclear reactor.

### Check It Out!

**Connecting with higher realms happens when our wants and desires are aligned with our quest to become who we are meant to be. Creating what we want is now more real and possible, since we have the backing of our Intuitive and Soul Levels.**

- What do you want to create in your life?

- What happened to the dreams you had when you were a child? A teenager? A young adult starting out in life?

- Can you find a way to reconnect to them now?

Acting on a dream, vision, or desire is an indication that the Intuitive Level operates in your life. Wherever you are in implementing your dream, honor it as you make a plan to take the next steps. It is not the speed of the journey that is important. Rather it is the journey itself and the learning that comes from it which matter most.

## What is my source of power?

In the separation consciousness, the source of our power was expressed through personal power and will. Amassing personal power brought us recognition and status. But at the Intuitive Level, our desires do not exist solely for our personal benefit. We receive intuitive impulses to create that encourage and inspire us. These inner messages are our souls showing us other possibilities. No longer are we dependent on others' reactions to validate us. We have defined for ourselves "What is enough?" Our self-image and self-esteem are intact. We are responsible since we are becoming self-authorities. We understand that energy becomes power when we direct it.

The acceptance of where we are in our evolution is freeing since it allows us to stop striving for some amorphous goal or status. We feel comfortable in our own skin. We learn from our emotions and create alternatives that we never thought possible. Finally, being defensive when someone gives us unsolicited advice is no longer an option. We choose not to personalize the comments (or see them as criticisms) and instead listen and evaluate what resonates with our intuition. Then we let everything else float away.

Since we no longer need personal power to prove ourselves, we enjoy sharing it. We collaborate with others through a common vision and appreciate their talents, skills and abilities. In shared power there is an acceptance of our own talents and those of others. Therefore there is no competition for status or control. We don't have to dominate conversations, push our personal agenda or hold onto our own fixed ideas. The mutual respect among ourselves and others reflects the self-respect we have developed.

Power originates through our contact with different levels of consciousness. The spiral of power starts at the most limited level in the separation consciousness. It expands in potency as it expresses itself in the Intuitive and Soul Levels. This potency amplifies the magnetic field that attracts energy vibrations conducive to our soul agenda. It also repels those vibrations that are not. At each level, we interact with the wisdom and perception that is available to us. With increased clarity, we create connections with multitudes of consciousness levels. If we learned the lessons of the Personality Level, the insights we receive from our Intuitive Level are clear. We use them to create something of value that contributes to our area of influence. No matter how difficult a situation, our Intuitive Level allows us to look beneath the surface to understand the more telling reasons for people's actions. We recognize that our awareness is expanded and that we are in an energy field where it is commonplace to receive insights. When we speak with others, we are guided to share perceptions and see our circumstances from a deeper perspective. Not only do we understand the content and context in interactions, we now also understand motivations. Also without the binding obstacles of false obligations, we now view possibilities from our connection to the power of the Intuitive Level.

When we recognize that our source of power is our connection to a higher consciousness level, we understand that it is unlimited. We choose to connect to higher consciousness levels. Embracing the Intuitive Level beliefs and living from their perspective facilitates our connection to unlimited power.

---

### Check It Out!

Accepting that we are part of a greater design than just ourselves is the basis for the Intuitive Level. While we may know that intellectually, living from this space may be quite different. In everyday terms it means checking our motivations and making sure we are not personalizing or becoming defensive. When we operate from the Intuitive Level, we suspend judgment and reactivity so we have the space to listen to and interpret the messages that come from our intuition.

- Think of a time in your life when you were reactive and let your emotions control you?

- What were you trying to defend about yourself? What did you feel inadequate about?

- Think of a time when you stayed in control of your emotions as you listened to the other person? How did you respond?

- In which situations do you feel confident to listen to content and context, observe body language, and sense motivations without getting ready to react?

---

You are in the connection consciousness when you understand the whole picture and recognize how all the pieces fit together. Your personal need for power is suspended while you interpret all avenues and then choose how to respond.

## Motivating Impulses

Living from the connection consciousness shapes our motivations. Below are some of the Intuitive Level motivations.

### A reason to hope

The hope that we can create the kind of life that supports us to be who we are meant to be is the motivating force in the Intuitive Level. The power to choose how we respond to the circumstances of our lives creates a structure in which our uniqueness grows and thrives. Hope fortifies us emotionally so we can create our vision. What kind of job do we need to get or create so that we are using our talents? What kind of a lifestyle do we need to nurture ourselves? What makes empowering relationships that support personal growth for all? How do we want to use our creativity? What are the values that we want to live from? Who do we want to be? Just the fact that we ask these questions is an expression of our hope that through our choices we create meaningful lives.

### To be free

In the Personality Level, we answered the question, "What is enough?" Once that question is answered, we get off the wheel of striving. Now our unique life begins. We are free from the dictates of our upbringing and the false obligations of external forces. As we benefit from the growth we have achieved, we also accept that our personal changes add to the collective consciousness. Everything we do affects the whole. We also come to realize that the institutional system in the separation consciousness is necessary for those who need its structure to help them with the lessons available in the Personality Level.

The beauty of our human experience is that when we use up what is available for our growth in one situation, there is always more for us to experience in the next. Entering into the connection consciousness opens us to freedom from perceived restrictions to our desires. It moves us toward freedom to create. This desire for freedom from roles and stereotypes toward freedom to experiment with new approaches and lifestyles stimulates all the beliefs we held about our world and ourselves. It tests and refines us. We shed the old beliefs as we create new ones from our intuition. We all have the desire to remove the shackles of conformity and become our authentic selves. Developing our skills for self-mastery and self-authority allows us to unfurl our wings and fly. Unfortunately, some of us get stuck in life experiences to the point that we feel we live in a tar pit. The effect of the past clings to the present and future. We can get stuck in a reality shaped from past pain, sadness, and disappointment. Learning the lessons from this suffering is the way to release the old and be free to live the present. Freedom to become our authentic selves arises when we are authorities for ourselves and have the ability to follow through.

*Check It Out!*

**We want the ability to be free from our personal baggage, to be free from the stereotypes assigned by the Personality Level. We want the labels to stop affecting our lives. We want the freedom of not having others' projections define who we are.**

- What do you want to be free from?
- What do you want to move toward?
- What do you want to be free to do?
- How can you make this happen?
- What old beliefs from the separation consciousness are posing a threat to you?

### Desire to create

The desire to create is innate. Through clarity from our intuition and careful self-reflection, we progressively become clearer about the values we want to live. Our creativity becomes joyful as we understand that this is our natural state. The creative process whether it is to develop smooth interactions with your mother-in-law or to paint a masterpiece is a reflection of the consciousness level we reside in. If fear, doubts and negative beliefs are getting in the way of the process, we must confront those feelings and thoughts. The first step is to recognize those interrupters come from the past.

In the separation consciousness, we flexed our creative muscles within the confines of particular social institutions, using limited portions of our creativity when asked to come up with a more efficient accounting program, ways to cut the budget, or design new software for a game. Those in authority dictated the parameters for our task to ensure that the goals of the company were met.

As we progress in our lives, we move from predominantly self-serving or rigid values, (which come from the Personality Level) to self-actualizing values that come from our heart and soul. We are taking the next level in responsibility for creating an authentic, rich life. We must come up with a process to transition from vision to implementation that is true to our values.

When I counsel couples experiencing marital problems, we first review what they think marriage is all about. Each partner expresses assumptions that most often reflect the separation consciousness. However, when we view marriage from the beliefs of the connection consciousness, the partners realize that they are the creators of their own union. This perspective brings them clarity about their common values and the kinds of flexible structures they want to design for the benefit of the relationship and each other. The question, "What do we want to create?" becomes the central focus. *What are your relationships like? What in them comes from the "should" perspective? What in them comes from a choice of what you want to create? How do you create a relationship that enables both of you to grow? What is your reaction to the statement that you are a creator? What thoughts and feelings are activated? How does your body react to this concept?*

Being a creator and claiming this energy within us makes us accountable to ourselves. Blame no longer finds a place in our lives.

## Check It Out!

Since our lives do make a difference in the grander scheme of life, it truly matters what choices we make. We alone need to decide from what level of consciousness we want to create.

- Who do we want to be?

**Think of a time when you respected yourself.**

- What value were you expressing?

- How did you feel about yourself?

- How do you want to create your life so that everything you do is authentic and in alignment with your soul?

- In what ways can your express your beliefs?

- What form can your talents take to create an expression of your beliefs?

**What do you need to fortify yourself emotionally during the creative process? Write out the scenario of how you feel and what thoughts will support you as you go about your creative expression. You need to release the old and create a new perspective. It is like writing a script that you can refer back to when the going gets tough.**

## Creating an authentic self and lifestyle

The more courageous we are to risk living from our intuitive insights, the stronger is our bond to the connection consciousness. Being authentic infuses us with Soul Level feelings such as courage, commitment, trust, gratitude, peace, and compassion. Experiencing these emotions puts us at ease with our world and our self. At the Intuitive Level we are discovering what it's like to live in the flow when we are following a soul focus and not a specific goal.

But beware. When we start our new creative pursuit of being a photographer or owning a coffee shop, suddenly our Personality Level can rear up and take over and doubt makes an appearance. However, the consequence of slipping back into the separation perspective is like slamming into a wall. Being shocked, stressed and confused, we try to use our old defense mechanisms. When we are on the path of personal exploration, the consequence of jumping off puts us back into the past. While we resurrect our past behaviors, we also resurrect the attitudes that cause our pain. Since, we are different now, reverting to old behaviors just triggers suffering, like shoving our feet into shoes that are too small. Once our energy field expands by living our intuitive insights, it experiences great difficulty fitting back into an old, smaller structure.

Striving to fulfill our dreams is a great laboratory to develop our intuition and learn about the connection consciousness. Taking off from work for a year or two to go sailing to the South Seas, for example, becomes a valuable opportunity to hope, trust, learn, and grow. Deciding what job will best help us to expand our skill set so that we can do something we truly enjoy is more important than money. Rejecting the promotion that pulls us away from our family is done from a sense of satisfaction that we know what is best for ourselves. Acknowledging our talent as a writer, artist, photojournalist, and acting on our dreams and longings is what our Intuitive Level is all about. Our hope and trust in ourselves aligns with our soul calling.

At this level, we are involved with the joy of the process. Full participation in creating our lives brings us confidence, satisfaction, and enthusiasm. Every bump in the road to fulfilling our goals is met with wonderment. Since we are connected to higher levels of consciousness, we know we are guided. *What can I learn from this situation? I wonder what other possibilities are available? What is another way?*

Even in our everyday interactions, we have the opportunity for authenticity. Being true to ourselves and courageously living our own truth develops self-respect. As we make choices from the Intuitive Level, our external reflects our internal world. We are moving toward a state of being. We create the emotional field and select the words and thoughts that fortify our intentions. This causes synchronicities in our lives since we are operating from the energy vibrations of the connection consciousness.

Living from our soul truth inoculates us from the producer-consumer model that dominates Western civilization (and is also now encroaching upon Third World countries). We no longer are attached to the "must see, must have, must do" mentality. Choosing to live below our means in order to spend time on what we value empowers us. We are our own self-authority to create a supportive lifestyle. Trusting and hoping that personal integrity and authenticity leads us through difficult times is a choice we must make. We are no longer victims of circumstances and events. Being honest and authentic with ourselves supports us to live a life that satisfies and sustains us.

*Check It Out!*

**Practice phrases and words that empower you and then insert them into your conversations. Also, when you can get more clarity by rethinking the situation, if appropriate go back to the person and clarify what you meant. A simple, "I was thinking about our conversation and I want to clarify what my position is now........." Even if you are unable to redo the conversation, the fact that you reflected on it and came to a more authentic understanding within yourself, loosens the hold of limitations and fears.**

- What must you change in your life to become more authentic?

- Reviewing your lifestyle, what is in integrity and what is not?

- How can you make yourself more authentic?

- Where in your life are you the most authentic? What is it about the situation that supports your authenticity? What causes you to be authentic?

## *Learning from responding and being proactive*

In the separation consciousness, our need for validation makes us dependent on others' reactions to define who we are. When our "shoulds" don't materialize, we become reactive and our emotions hijack our brains. We say and do things that hurt others because our fear of losing control makes us vulnerable to appearing weak or wrong. *What emotionally charged situations have you regretted? What are you like when you are emotionally charged?*

In the connection consciousness, we learn how to create through clear soul intentions. As our internal life becomes a reflection of our movement toward becoming a spiritual being, we are not attached to outcome. The process is the act and art of creativity. The day an artist sells her work is the day her creative and learning process from that painting is over. This experience then integrates in our energy field, which expands it. Reflecting and being objective in whatever ways that we are proactive allows us to perceive subtle nuances processed through our Intuitive Level. The insights we receive become the basis for choosing how to respond to a situation. We are not in control of others' reactions, but we are in control of how we choose to respond.

Many situations are out of our control: an unexpected divorce, being fired, caring for our elderly, sick mother who is without resources, a flood or a fire. Accepting the facts of the situation is the first step in responding. In the Personality Level, blame, denial, personalization and reactivity cause paralysis and pain. Roles and false obligations keep us limited and don't allow for creative alternatives. But responding involves all of who we are in the present. We access and honestly acknowledge what we can and cannot do, what the situation means to us, and move in the direction our soul is guiding us. Checking the congruency among our spiritual, mental, emotional and physical bodies reassures us of our soul direction.

We are then ready to respond and be proactive in an authentic way. Telling our elderly mother, "I've worked out a schedule to visit once a week and call on Saturdays and Wednesdays," is an honest statement. She is then clear about how much time we can spend with her. With this in mind, she then has the opportunity to decide what (or who) else she wants in her life. When we express our participation level in any situation, we also empower others to become proactive. There are no mix-ups, or hurt feelings based on the unspoken assumptions of how an adult child should treat a parent.

Responding and being proactive prevents a victim mentality. Our response implies that the others are capable of making decisions for them self. They feel empowered. By being true to ourselves and acting on our truth, we share power with others by acknowledging their value. Anytime we are acting in a way that stresses us, such as playing the martyr, we are in the Personality Level wanting some type of validation from the person we are trying to help. Responding from clear intentions keeps us in our Intuitive Level—the very place that gives us the most options and strength.

## Check It Out!

Being authentic preserves our physical energy. So if you are drained, check all of your activities and see where you are leaking energy. If parenting is energy consuming then it's time to delegate more tasks to other family members. This can start a new creative effort to be a team and not a group of individuals living together. All privileges for kids and teenagers are based on responsibility and accountability. So if you are too tired as a parent then check to see what fears are lurking in your head that prevent you from being a parent who is CLEAR and strong enough to lead, coach and mentor. We close the wounds that leak energy when we are doing what is right and authentic for us.

- What do you put energy into?

- Do all of these activities align with your soul values?

- Where are you exerting energy that is not authentic for you?

- What activities have you been proactive about? From what level of consciousness was your desire to do them?

- How do you know when you are being inauthentic?

## Chapter Five Exploration and Discovery Activities

### Points to Ponder

- The psychology of hope-that there is always another way- gives us room to maneuver explore, and experiment without judgment threatening to defeat us.

- Hope is knowing that when we create our own internal reality that it magnetizes and synchronizes our external world.

- The psychology of hope underscores the belief that every individual's unique capacity to reason and to impose self-control from within is a major force in creating true democracy.

- Self-mastery is the first step toward becoming our own self-authority. Developing and refining life-skills such as decision-making, mood management, communication, building and sustaining relationships, assertiveness, is essential for self-mastery.

- Self-mastery is conscious awareness of how we choose to respond in any given situation and interaction.

- Our Intuitive Level encourages us and facilitates the interpretation of symbols, images, dreams, and messages that come from our soul.

- From microbes to human beings, we are all interdependent in the grand experiment of manifesting the potentials of existence.
- Intuition is the evidence of our connection to other levels of consciousness.
- Power originates through our contact with different levels of consciousness.
- In the Personality Level, we answered the question, "What is enough?" Once that question is answered, we get off the wheel of striving. Now our unique life begins.
- Everything we do affects the whole. It is like a wave that goes through the cosmos.
- Checking the congruency between our mental, emotional, physical and spiritual bodies in the Intuitive Level assures us of our soul direction.
- Being authentic preserves our physical energy.

**Think about your personal experience and relationship to intuition. Intuition is how we receive messages from our soul and gives us the ability to understand subtleties of whatever we choose to connect with. The depth and scope of our connection to our intuition determines our alignment with our soul intentions.**

- What is your personal definition of intuition?
- What is your personal experience with intuition?
- How do you connect with it?
- How do you know your ideas and/or information is coming from your intuition?
- When do you use it?
- How do you use it?
- How did you use your intuition as a child and teenager?
- What area of your life do you see your intuition most active? (personal, professional, family matters, planning, creating etc.)
- What messages from family, friends, teachers, and others did you get about intuition?
- What messages about your intuition were influenced by movies and books you read when you were a child? Teenager? Adult?

- What is your hope for your intuition?
- Which of your four bodies is more intuitively orientated?
- Which body needs support to develop your intuition fully?
- How do you use your intuition in the creative process?

**Activity 1. How can your intuition support you in developing self-mastery and self-authority?**

# Chapter Six

## Merging the Connection Consciousness by Developing Our Intuition

It is a major internal shift for us to move from the separation consciousness toward embracing the connection consciousness. Everything about us changes. What was once familiar is no longer, and what is unfamiliar is now our hope. This process is a heroic journey that has no timetable or concrete guideposts.

However, we do know that a shift is taking place because our lives change. We let go of some friends but draw closer to others as we reconfigure whom and what we trust; our interests, motivations, and needs evolve; we think and feel in new ways; our relationship to our self deepens. It's common in this process to pause to examine our lives. *What am I doing? What am I responsible for and to whom? Why am I willing to stay in toxic situations? What is possible? What is important to me? Am I expressing my authentic thoughts and feelings? What makes me happy? What are my hopes? What motivates me? What gives me emotional fortitude and courage? What has heart and meaning for me? What does love really mean?*

As human beings, we use thinking, emotions and actions to interpret the world we live in and then react to those conclusions. Our four bodies (spiritual, mental, emotional, and physical) give us distinct and useful perceptions. Seeing through these different perspectives helps us discern what is relevant in a world that overwhelms us with input.

In the separation consciousness, we experience our four bodies separately. We think, we feel, we have set religious beliefs and we view the body as our servant to act in the way we demand. This compartmentalization places thoughts and feelings at odds with each other and endangers the body with stress and strain. In the connection consciousness, we seek to understand the perspectives of each of our four bodies and integrate them according to our intuitive guidance. This affords interdependence among them. At this level, if we slip back to feeling self-doubt, our spiritual and mental bodies remind us of our purpose by flashing our vision or sending inspirational thoughts that give us strength.

As we learn about the connection consciousness, we accept that maybe all four of our bodies will not be at the Intuitive Level all the time. When we are in a difficult spot, reflecting on the perspectives of our four bodies helps us assess the consciousness levels of our thinking, feeling and actions. The best way to do this is to slow down and listen to what is going on with our four bodies. *What are the conflicting perspectives of your four bodies? Which one is trying to bring some limited aspects of the separation consciousness into the connection consciousness? Which is acting from fear? Which is acting from hope and trust? What thoughts do you hear from your self-talk? What emotions do you feel and then express with your behaviors? What feelings are at war with each other? When your thinking is clear, what are you feeling? What feels right to you? What is your inner voice or soul saying to you?*

Each of the four bodies needs to develop a relationship to the connection consciousness. Moreover, because of its unique perspective, each body makes this connection differently and in its own time. Some of us might think our intuition is just a gut-level feeling while others think that knowingness is what intuition is all about. Most of us do not recognize that the Intuitive Level exists in each of our four bodies. Our soul helps with connecting and transferring information and learning among them. The heart and soul integrate all of our realizations, experiences, and "aha" moments as we fully participate in the spiritual process. Integration creates a synergy of energy that coalesces into our own understanding of the connection consciousness.

## Merging Our Four Bodies Into the Connection Consciousness

The on-going process of integrating the learning of each body and its subsequent realizations reminds me of a kaleidoscope. As we turn it, it makes new connections rearranging the bits of colored glass into beautiful patterns and designs. Similarly, through the new connections we make to our expanding perceptions and ourselves, our energy configures and reconfigures all the time. It does not matter if the connection is a new "aha" moment or if it comes from the intuitive part of our emotional, physical, mental or physical body. New connections stimulate our energy field, which in turn affects all parts of us in an unending cycle—spiritual evolution taking place through new connections.

The sections below give us some ideas about how to get all four bodies to participate in the emergence into the connection consciousness.

### *Spiritual body*

The acceptance of a universal energy that exists in and beyond our physical existence and connects all that is seen and unseen, known and unknown is the spiritual attitude that supports the connection consciousness. This concept of universal energy means that there is a grand design in which we participate, even though we cannot perceive its totality or understand it fully.

The concept of an infinite consciousness is quite daunting. How can we have a real spiritual connection with something so immense? We do this by progressively connecting with myriad levels of consciousness within the infinite, interpreting its wisdom, and living from its perspective. The Personality, Intuitive, and Soul Levels are all examples of different levels of consciousness, each with its own reality, awareness and potential. The segmentation of the infinite and our willingness to connect to the parts we are ready to accept supports a working relationship with the grand design.

We use representations for infinity and all the different vibrations within. In metaphysics, the beings, guides, and non-physical teachers who exist in different dimensions symbolize the understanding of existence of dimensions other than our own. Although the description of God in religion refers to an omniscient, omnipotent, omnipresent energy consciousness of the infinite, we also add human characteristics to the concept. It helps many people feel more connected to a symbol that is familiar to them rather than pure consciousness.

Other representations of the infinite consciousness depend on religious and cultural interpretations of this energy, hence the multitudes of names such as God, God the Father, the Chi power, Tao, the Great Mystery, the Oneness, the Force, The Holy Spirit, the Universal Energy and many others. Personifying this infinite energy represents our innate desire to bring into form something that we instinctively relate to, accept, and know. Most of us feel that if something is in form, it is more real. All of us, however, are describing the unity consciousness that holds what we call the Infinite.

Knowing the Infinite is like an elusive dream—something that cannot be denied and yet is so hard to get hold of and express. And because we know that the Infinite is inexhaustible, there is always more to comprehend and experience. This challenges and ignites in us a desire to relate to the unity consciousness and therefore to deepen, expand and merge the connection through our Soul Level.

Since the unity consciousness is without form, we need to develop a way to perceive it. When we allow our bodies to relax and our minds to detach from all thoughts, we become receptive to other possibilities and the awareness that comes from the connection to different consciousness levels. Meditation, praying and listening, yoga, walking in nature, automatic writing, enjoying music, drumming, expressive painting, and creative imagination all develop receptivity. Only through trial and error do we determine the circumstances that put us in a space to perceive the unknown.

We all need to find several different ways to become receptive. Depending on our day and life events, we may be more open to one method over another at any given time. *What do you need to be receptive? When have you allowed yourself to have space to clear your mind and emotions? When do you allow yourself to wonder what it would be like to live from your soul perspective? When do you allow yourself to depend on your intuition?* Accepting our Intuitive Level means that we respect, use, and actively seek to develop it. Once we develop an intuitive sense of connection, we need space to deepen it, form symbols to strengthen it, expand it, and make it more real. Light is a universal symbol for higher consciousness. Think of its enormous effect on the world. Without sunlight, we would not be here—in this form, at least. If we use light as a symbol (it comes into our bodies to welcome and receive the highest level of consciousness or infinite energy), through time and practice we develop an awareness of subtle change in our energy fields. *How does light affect your life? How does it affect your body, living or work space, moods?*

Symbols are a powerful way to develop our intuition. These can be every day, concrete objects to which we assign meaning in order to help us with the invocation of our Intuitive and Soul Levels. For instance, when I take a shower, I simply ask for a cleansing on all levels to allow the light of the Infinite to freely flow to and through me. I imagine the water as light, and I see it in my mind's eye and feel it go on and through my skin.

When we choose and assign meaning to symbols, they aid in our spiritual journey and then become expressions of the connection consciousness. They trigger emotional responses which pitch us into the Intuitive Level and prepare us to receive the messages from our soul. Our soul guides us to what we are ready to connect with for our next learning. Magic starts happening in our lives as soon as we connect to our Intuitive Level in our spiritual bodies. *What inspirational symbols do you use in your life? What do they mean to you? How do you experience being part of a bigger picture? For you, what is the difference between religion and spirituality?*

## Mental body

The most evolved aspect of our mental body in the Intuitive Level is knowingness. We might not know how we know something; we just know that we do. Knowingness appears with surety but without will or determination. It might come when we are confused about a personal problem or a professional project. Most often it comes in an unexpected realization, an "aha" moment that spins our world and shifts our perspective. When knowingness appears, we have clarity. In my private practice, I hear such comments as, "So, that is why I was married to Mark." "Now I see. No wonder I couldn't make the project work." "I get it! Now I don't have to carry this guilt. I can . . ."

Since clarity from knowingness arrives unpredictably and out of our control, the more concrete part of our Intuitive Level in the mental body is our imagination. We do have some control over that by choosing to use strategies to develop it. Take the time to mentally play with possibilities. Asking ourselves, "I wonder if ....?", challenging ourselves to see another way in our mind's eye and being triggered by something that catches our attention. All of these techniques develop our imagination and help it become a habit. It's like building muscles--the more we use them the stronger they become.

Imagination is a treasure to hold in our hearts and minds. It is triggered through our knowingness, which is in turn is activated by our soul. Imagination helps us to develop our visions and ideas. Spiritual development is the choice to participate in developing these visions, images and ideas. If we do not develop them, they become lost to us and given to others who choose to bring them into expression. Unfolding the images, symbols, and visions that come from the soul through our imagination requires time and reflection. Sadly, I hear comments such as "I don't have the time to waste" and "What's the point? No one wants to hear my ideas anyway." "I have too much to do." "Right! I can see bringing up something I imagined in my team meeting. I would be laughed out of the room." All of these, opportunities lost.

## Check It Out!

**Imagination is not mysterious. It is a component of our human and spiritual nature. Everyone has the ability to imagine.**

- What attitudes block you from imagining?
- How much time do you allow yourself to imagine?
- What do you do with your imaginative ideas?
- How do you create space to imagine?

**If imagination isn't part of your everyday thinking then the separation consciousness is holding you too tight. Practice imagining using any topic that interests you. Imagine a new concept for cars or houses, decorating your house, dancing, doing extreme sports, writing a screenplay....anything. Just practice imagining.**

## Using affirmations to develop the mental body

Once we derive ideas from our imagination, we then choose the thoughts, values and beliefs that will help us implement them. One way to open up to new beliefs is to make an affirmation of what we believe is possible. Using the pronoun, "I" announces to our mind that we choose the statement. Then putting it in the present tense helps us experience what it feels like to think in certain way. This links the emotional energy with the mental energy, making the belief more real. Even though we might not fully believe an affirmation today, we try it on when we say or write it. This linking of the mental and emotional body helps us get intuitive information from both bodies about the aptness of the affirmation. Experiment with different words and simplify what you write. Keep playing with the words until you feel that click of rightness for you.

Words are so important because they are energy that holds a certain vibration. They are sounds that carry an idea. Writing is the annotation of the spoken word. Both are associated with cause and effect. Through the choice of our words that hold high vibrations, we effect changes in others and ourselves. Examples of high vibration words are love, courage, commitment, loyalty, trust, compassion, gratitude, and joy. Just saying those words aloud and drinking them in shifts us to a higher consciousness. We feel this shift in all of our bodies. Stand, close your eyes and say these words aloud. Notice how your body holds itself differently. *What did you observe when you said those words? How did you feel? How many of the words that you chose are also associated with the beliefs of the connection consciousness?* We must choose our words carefully, not only when we are making affirmations, but also in our everyday interactions.

**Below are some examples of affirmations that represent different levels of connection:**

- I am a light within the greater light
- I am a representation of an aspect of God
- I am a spark of the Divine
- I accept my Divine Power
- I AM

- I am connected to all that is known and unknown
- I chose to be who I am meant to be
- I am a creative person
- I choose to implement my creativity now
- I am an intuitive person
- I am connected to God
- I align my personality, intuition and soul
- I am a part of the grand design
- I have a place in this world that only I can fill
- I am a unique expression of God
- I know that I am guided
- I choose to experience life
- I am alive
- I trust my connection to the Oneness
- I support life, and life supports me
- I have within me everything I need to create a life that has heart and meaning
- I align my wants and desires with my soul
- I open up to live a life of joy, love, compassion and gratitude
- I receive the love of God through me
- The Source is within me
- I accept the flow of my soul's expression
- I receive support from my soul
- I merge the separation, connection, and unity consciousness within

Affirmations are a link between our spiritual and mental bodies. They make more real the possibilities that our soul activates through our intuition. As we spend time with the concepts in affirmations, it shifts our perspective. Our imagination takes the statement and expands upon it through symbols, images, thoughts and feelings. What would our life be right now if we lived from the perspective of the chosen beliefs that life supports us or that we have the opportunity to live a life that has heart and meaning? Take some time to imagine how your life would be if you lived from the perspective of one of the affirmations you created for yourself.

In fact, that is really what we are doing now. We all create our lives from our values and beliefs. Whether or not we are aware of them does not matter. Take any situation that is difficult or painful for you. *Ask yourself, "What is causing the problem?"* As our mind starts answering that question, we come up against values and beliefs that are causing us to act in certain ways. What is so amazing about the subconscious mind is that it remembers everything it was exposed to and everything that entered it, whether real or not. Our subconscious cannot distinguish between what is a real situation, what was imagined, what was read, and what was seen on TV, at the computer or in the movies. Recall when we are looking at old photographs. After a while, the pictures and our reaction to them become indistinguishable from the real event. Alternatively, think of a dream or story we told someone in the past. As time goes on, it becomes more difficult to ascertain what was real, actually experienced and what was the story or dream. We must be the guardians of what goes into our subconscious mind, for that is the program that influences our reality.

Observe what you imagine—your thoughts, feelings and behaviors. *From what values and beliefs do you think you are living? Is there a discrepancy between what you think is important and how you are actually living? Do you need to change those beliefs and values? What behaviors do you need to change? What have you learned from them? What is a new possibility now?*

Think of what imagination has produced in our world. Revolutionary ideas start with dreams and visions. We need to dignify the intuitive process and imagination in our world. Why aren't the skills of imagination and intuition being taught in our schools? What we receive through our knowingness and develop with our imagination today becomes the reality of our lives tomorrow.

## Aligning our mental body

Once we set our intention (see Chapter Four) we bring to bear all perspectives of our mental body to hone in on actualizing our dreams. We enlist our creativity, allowing our imagination free reign to gather and configure ideas and concepts. Then we form thoughts to express what we gleaned from our imagination. Finally, from our thinking process, we figure out step-by-step how to implement our vision. At this point, we have a mission statement and a procedural plan. We utilize all parts of our mental body, which strengthens our laser beam of energy. *What part does your imagination play when making a plan for your intention or vision? What are the ideas that support your vision? What concepts are needed? What are your thoughts? What affirmations do you need to support your emotional body when it becomes reactive? What beliefs do you hold that help you align with your soul during the implementation process? What strategies or plans do you construct to manifest your intentions?*

## Emotional body

In the separation consciousness, the emotional body helped us to learn about ourselves as we reacted to the world around us. We learned about our fears, needs and wants. One of the dictates of the Personality Level was to control our emotions for fear of being criticized or rejected for being out of control. Most often in the Personality Level, emotions are hidden, denied, minimized or expressed inauthentically. Displaying feelings that are unacceptable according to our social institutions is considered a weakness.

*The process for dealing with emotions at the Intuitive Level is to identify our feelings, own them, trace the beliefs that caused them, and then decide how, when and why to express them.*

If we align the beliefs from our soul and intuitive level and then implement them we have gained self-mastery. While emotions are still teachers at this level, our new skill set will support us to deepen the use of the emotional body.

## Developing the emotional body

Developing our emotional body helps us express the full range of emotions. Feelings are the common language of the human experience—our recognition of the way we connect to each other. Since they shape the way we see the world and our place in it, the more we experience and understand them the richer our internal and external lives.

We cannot recognize and connect with emotions that are foreign to us so if our emotional repertoire is small, we are limited. Experiencing all emotions facilitates a better understanding of others and our self.

We all sense the same emotions although we do not necessarily share the same beliefs. Review interactions you've had with different people. *Who did you feel closer to after the interaction? What made that possible? What feelings did you share?* In the Personality Level, it is difficult to trust our feelings, since they are suspect in our society. If we express strong emotions we become vulnerable to the reactions of others. This dampens our desire to come forward since the situation becomes too risky. We may also fear that once we feel an emotion, we will get stuck in it. We are afraid that we will become victims of emotions that we can neither handle nor dissipate which activates a sense of powerlessness.

Our feelings also make us vulnerable, causing us to fear losing face. This stems from the pressure at the Personality Level to appear cool and competent. We want to project that we are unaffected by anything thrown at us. Our social institutions tell us that, no matter what, we are not supposed to succumb to feelings.

In the Intuitive Level, our relationship to feelings shifts. We value learning and rearranging ourselves as we journey toward becoming who we are meant to be. All experiences have value. Identifying our emotions allows them to become our teachers. They help us interpret the state of our internal and external realities. We identify them and own them as ours. No one else makes us feel a certain way. This is what taking responsibility for our self means. Identifying and owing our feelings so that we can learn more about ourselves renders unnecessary denial, suppression, and being out of emotional control. Now we can make statements about how and why we feel the way we do instead of dumping and leaving others to react to our upset. "What you are doing is making me angry, and I need time to figure out what is going on inside me." "I hate that tone of voice you use when you are angry. It is triggering a memory I need to get in touch with." "I'm so hurt. I am blinded right now to what is causing my intense reaction." "Some of the feelings I am having are beyond the scope of this situation so I need some space. I'll talk with you later."

Once we identify and own our feelings we expand our emotional body. This provides the opportunity to make new connections by developing our present relationships and connecting with new people and to our different levels of consciousness. With a developed emotional repertoire, we have a solid base from which to understand and respond to others.

## Check It Out!

I have a list of one hundred feelings that I give to my clients. I ask them to check off how many different feelings they experienced in a week. I am always amazed how few are checked. Not only do people limit themselves to same old emotions; they also do not recognize the nuances, shading, and intensity to the ones that are familiar.

- List how many emotions you felt today.
- Which ones did you chose to express?
- Which ones did you chose to ignore, deny or hide?
- What made you decide to express or keep emotions to yourself?

Consider the emotion of anger. Write the word ANGER on a piece of paper. Remember all of the emotions you felt before actually becoming angry. Some might be frustration, hurt, irritation, disappointment, annoyance and anxiety. Then remember how you expressed anger and how it accelerated.

- What comes after anger for you?
- Do you experience rage, violence and depression?

Each of us has our own continuum of intensity of feelings. The range is triggered by what we perceive and how that perception aligns with our internal reality—the sum of all the conclusions we made either consciously or unconsciously about our life experiences and our self. Becoming aware and reflecting on the thoughts, values, and beliefs that trigger emotional reactions is the way we create openings to change them.

## Creating our emotional field

Our willingness to investigate the reasons behind our feelings is the first step in creating our emotional field. For every thought there is a feeling, and for every feeling there is a thought that causes the feeling. The acceptance of this simple yet profound connection between our thinking and feelings (our mental and emotional bodies) is the key to managing and creating our emotional field.

Remember a time when you were angry, hurt or sad. *What expectations did not get met? What did you think should have happened but didn't? What thoughts and feelings caused you to expect the situation would go your way? What control did you really have? Could you have gotten the other person or the circumstances to change?* Now look at the situation from another perspective. This only happens when we release the emotion and become calm and objective. *If you let go of your expectations, what is your view of the situation and other(s)?* We may get angry because a friend or coworker didn't treat us with respect. Maybe he or she didn't defer to our personal power so that we felt invisible. We all have expectations of how we are supposed to be treated. As we saw in the Personality Level, exercising our personal power and having our needs met by others was key to our motivation.

In the Intuitive Level, the task is to acknowledge, identify and satisfy our needs through the conscious choices that align with our soul. When we start living from our soul emotions, our perspective changes. Compassion and unconditional love leave little room for feeling unworthy, so we don't then need to flatter the boss, flaunt our wealth or carry the latest designer handbag to get approval from others. Once we choose to look behind our reactivity and ask for the thoughts that caused it, we are free to create the emotions that support our living from the Intuitive and Soul levels. Reactivity reminds us that we are viewing our situation from the Personality Level and our soul cannot reach us if we if we accept only the existence of our Personality Level.

Our soul energy vibrates in our emotional body as it does in all of our bodies. The soul creates emotions that reflect themselves in ways that are available to us at the Intuitive Level. We label these soul emotions as our most noble: peace, joy, commitment, courage, humility, unconditional love, compassion, acceptance, generosity, gratitude and trust. The true soul energy within these emotions expands our hearts and minds. To optimize growth, we choose one of these emotions to actively live within us at all times.

We may not know the depth and scope of all of the soul emotions. However, if we choose one that we are more receptive to, we can ask our soul for assistance to understand, and feel the others. This is done in a simple meditation. *Choose an emotion you want to explore. Sit quietly and imagine a beautiful forest scene with a waterfall. Instead of water, see it as a waterfall of light that represents your chosen emotion. Walk to the waterfall and stand in it. Imagine the light saturating you inside and out. Focus on the emotion and sense of its vibration within you. What images, thoughts and feelings come to you?*

Along with invoking these soul emotions in a meditation, we can remember when we felt them in the past. As we activate a specific memory and relax into it, we feel the corresponding emotion—another confirmation of the connection between thinking and feeling. This simple technique makes the emotion we want to explore more available to us.

At first, we might need the memory of a particular situation to activate the emotion. This need for others to help us feel a certain way is the basis for all love relationships. We love how we feel when we are loved and in love. As we evolve spiritually, we maintain that love vibration on our own, freeing ourselves from dependency on others. We have to be the love of our own lives. Only then is it possible to truly love another person. We may still choose to be in a love relationship, but we have internalized the energy vibration of love and can choose it at any time. Dependence on others for our self-esteem and sense of well-being occurs when we do not take responsibility for our emotional field. When we do, we activate our soul emotions and live from our highest level of consciousness.

Before I meet with a client, whether for business consulting, personal counseling, or a reading, I make sure that my soul vibration is activated in my emotional body. I always evoke the feelings of unconditional love, trust, compassion and acceptance. I become an open channel, because I am focused on my soul vibration, not my personality. Indeed, I surrender my personality to my soul. After thirty years of working with people, it still amazes me how my personality, language, and gestures change for each person with whom I interact. I become flexible in personality because my soul connects with the soul of the other.

Just as we choose values, beliefs and thoughts that represent the Soul Level in our mental body, so do we need to choose Soul Level emotions for our emotional body.

## Check It Out!

**Too often we don't think about how we feel or else identify just the one obvious emotion without taking the time to feel the rest. The more you take the time to allow yourself to feel the more opportunity you have to know yourself better.**

- What emotion are you most familiar with? Trace the history of that emotion.

- What event in your life caused you to have such a strong attachment to the emotion?

- Review a day that had a strong emotional component to it. List all of the emotions you experienced from the most intense to the least.

- To facilitate this, after identifying each emotion, ask yourself: "What else did I feel?"

We fall back on the emotions we are most familiar with. That is why it is important to start exploring Soul Level emotions that you do not have much experience with.

### Trusting our gut-level feelings

As we recognize the diversity, nuances, and intensity of all feelings, we develop the ability to sense the ones that emerge from the Intuitive Level. We feel emotions in our bodies, and as we become more aware of the obvious and subtle vibrational differences among them, we discern our gut feeling.

Take the time to feel the following emotions: fear, anger, sadness, joy, and love. Notice that each feels differently in our body and produces a specific physical reaction. *Does your heart race when you feel fear? Is your body relaxed when you feel love? Which emotion constricts your body? Where in your body do you carry stress from the fear of unworthiness?* The more we stay in the emotion and observe how we feel, the more sensitive we become to its energy. When we are able to feel the subtle sensation of emotions, we then discern the vibrational range of our Intuitive Level. Sensitizing ourselves to our emotions helps us interact with our intuition. It is a skill to observe our reactions, reflect on our experiences and take the time to feel our emotions. These sensations affect our thoughts, which in turn impact our outlook and our physical bodies. Conflicting emotions put our bodies into great stress, which can compromise our health by interfering with our immune system. Choosing to express the highest level of consciousness available to us strengthens our bodies.

Understanding our gut level feelings is essential in our search to know what is right for us. As we feel the vibrations of our Intuitive and Soul level emotions we speak our truth. We must hold and feel those vibrations within, then act. This assures us that how we express ourselves demonstrates respect for ourselves and others.

## Check It Out!

**Our willingness to express authentic emotions invites our soul to participate in our lives. It is a spiritual act.**

- What causes you to leave a situation without authentically expressing yourself?

- What communications skills do you need to help you express yourself in a way that is authentic to you and respects others?

- What does it feel like to express your emotions authentically?

- If you are not feeling differences in your physical body from your emotional body then you are shut down. What fears do you have about feeling your emotions?

Always keep a Soul Level emotion handy to use when you are experiencing strong feelings that unbalance you. Use it as lifeline so that you will not drown in the intensely negative feeling. You might feel bad, but at the same time you can reach for the soul emotion.

## Engaging our emotional body

Once we have set our intention and feel that it is right for us, we plan our strategy to fortify our emotional body for the process ahead. We choose feelings that support us as we move forward toward our goal. Yes, there will be delays, unexpected detours, disappointments, frustrations, and doubts that cause us to question our direction. During these times, we activate the soul emotions that support us. We use an affirmation that strengthens our emotional body and gives us the courage to investigate problems. Our soul sends intuitive messages and magnetizes people and situations to provide what we are missing. That is the reason why we must learn to live from our Intuitive Level. *What emotions and feelings can you create that will support you in living the connection consciousness? What emotions can you depend on for support? How do you go about creating the emotions that represent the connection consciousness? How do you check in with your emotions? What is your strategy to manage disappointment, frustration, and unrealistic expectations?*

## Physical body

Listening to the wisdom that our bodies innately hold supports the development of our Intuitive Level. This attunement is actually our intuition. Our bodies support us to function in this world. They let us know how we are balancing our lives and how well we are using our four bodies. Discomfort, stress, pain, and disease alert us to disharmony among our four bodies. These messages tell us we are not listening from the Intuitive Level to our four bodies about our decisions. When we connect to all of our four bodies at the Intuitive Level and respect the wisdom of each, we are balanced. No one of our four bodies is over-stressed nor does its specific point of view dominate.

Relying on one or more bodies to the exclusion of the others distorts our perspective. In fact, we become separate from all of our parts, which then leave us feeling incomplete and self-doubting. This produces the sense of emptiness as expressed in statements such as, "Is that all there is?" To fill this void, we look for something that assuages our anxiety. This is when the Personality Level becomes seductive. Since social institutions tell us what and how to do things, we become dependent on their dictates to fill the vacuum.

Imagine a body cell that has at least two conflicting directives, one from the Personality Level and the other from our Intuitive or Soul Level. Each has its own vibration. One directive is in charge of eight to ten hours of work a day for five days a week. It demands that we act, think, and feel in accordance with society's demands. The body responds accordingly. But when we get home and look to the beliefs of the connection consciousness as we seek to be responsive to our families and our own personal growth, we put different demands on the body. Of course, there is also a third directive: that of our internal world where we hold our dreams and secret wants and desires which come from the unity consciousness.

All of these realities represent different vibrations that the cell must negotiate within the cellular walls. It takes enormous energy to integrate them all. And, if the dissimilar realities spin into view frequently, the cell cannot assimilate the fluctuating energy vibrations. This results in a breakdown of the function of each cell, which in turn leads to stress and illness.

Our personalities, intuition and souls are designed to function as a whole, connecting to and using all of our four bodies in the Intuitive Level. In order to live from realizations made from the integration of our four bodies, we must respect our physical body as it monitors the balance in our lives. This means we need to take care of it, eating and exercising properly. If we overload with improper food and drink, it must devote energy to clearing the effects of abusive eating. Consequently, it won't have the energy to receive and process intuitive messages from our soul.

When we take the time to listen to our body and do what it says, it tells us what foods it needs. Experiment with listening, trying out what the body says and then observing the results. *How often do you listen to your body? What prevents you from valuing what your body tells you? What foods give you energy? Which make you dull and listless? What is the difference in your energy level when you are taking care of your body?*

Eating is a representation of our lifestyle, so choosing the right foods that maximize health becomes a commitment to supporting ourselves. Our bodies don't require some bizarre, extreme diet. They want variety and mostly natural foods. We all must take responsibility for what we eat, for food is the fuel and medicine for our bodies. *What is your relationship to your body? What do you do to support it? What is your body image? How do you abuse your body? What causes this? How can you meet your needs in other ways? What behaviors, attitudes, thoughts, and feelings do you need to get in sync with your body?*

Think of all the clear ways our body tells us its preferences and all the obvious indications that we are overstressed and abusing ourselves: indigestion, allergies, tiredness, gas, lethargy, aches, pains and disease. As we move away from forcing our body to function without regard to what it is saying, toward listening and following the clues it gives us, we get in touch with our own internal rhythm—something we must respect. *During the day, when are you most alert? When do you need a few minutes to revitalize yourself? At what time is your blood-sugar low? What is a healthy way to handle it? When are you most likely to be irritable? How do you function after you eat?* We all know instinctively what we need. But this intuitive connection to the body is only as valuable as our willingness to trust the information we perceive and act on it. And as trust grows, we continue to connect to more subtle vibrations that bring in new perceptions.

Energy is constantly flowing through our bodies from our soul and also from responses and interactions that we encounter daily. All energy is stored and interpreted by our four bodies, but this can only happen when they are in optimal condition. That means that we need to engage the personality, intuition, and soul in the processing. That is why paying attention to our intuition and observations from the Personality Level is so important. When we don't reflect upon our experiences, feelings and thoughts, the energy of our interactions lingers. The body holds the unprocessed energy and layers it. Eventually, the layers slow and become solidified. Extra fat is usually the form unprocessed energy takes.

Think of how our minds keep us awake because we cannot shut off our thoughts, or how our feelings keep us in turmoil if we have not come to terms with our expectations. Unresolved thoughts and feelings affect the body by keeping it in a state of stress. Conversely, processing our emotions and thoughts and resolving our problems by incorporating the perspectives of our four bodies, supports the body's proper functioning.

Now, imagine standing in a different waterfall. This falls symbolizes the flow of energy and our body represents unprocessed energy. Notice what happens to the water. It is diverted in many directions as it hits the solidity of our bodies. It changes course and scatters from the original flow. Unprocessed energy is like the mass of our body. We lose our energy and our connection to our four bodies when we don't process it. *Every day we need time to listen to our four bodies and review our day. Did you recognize and understand your feelings? What did you create today? How does your body feel?* Reflect, observe, and then let the energy go. Any movement such as yoga, biking, walking, or dance relaxes the body and releases energy. Unprocessed energy creates an environment for disease because it stresses the body, causing our energy field to be out of balance. Unprocessed energy is stored in our bodies for years. It can come from our childhood or early school experience but also from a highly charged current situation that was so impactful, we tried to dismiss or deny it before we processed its ramifications. Whatever the situation, we need to process our experience from the input of all four bodies. Many types of bodywork (including Shiatsu, Reflexology, Yogi, Reiki, EMDR, massage, acupressure and acupuncture) support energy release and create balance. Often we become aware of the issue we didn't process as we release the energy during this work. A great deal of information about these different kinds of bodywork can be found in books and online.

When we routinely care for our bodies by processing the configurations of energy that arise from our interactions, they become accurate interpreters of our surroundings. They let us know whether our environment is safe. Our instincts, which are an expression of the Intuitive Level in our physical body, will automatically act to protect us. Our bodies also know what is right for us as we learn to live from our three levels of consciousness.

As the physical body matures into the Intuitive Level, we trust our instincts more and more. This development is necessary as we embrace the Soul Level in the unity consciousness. It is the receptor for all energy including the energy of our soul. Although this energy of the unity consciousness is hidden from us because it resides in the unconscious, we can still assess it from our intuitive relationship to our four bodies. Actually, all of us can feel the dissimilar vibratory rates of different levels of consciousness. Sensing the shifts within our body concretizes and validates our connection.

## Check It Out!

**Becoming aware of sensations is a great way to start tuning into your body. When the wind is blowing through your hair, focus in on the sensation. Become aware of the range of tactile feelings that are available to you. Touch different plants, animals, bark on trees, materials, fruit, shells, rocks—and learn to feel textures. Develop your sense of smell —smell the ocean, fruits, wood, and spices. Stop to sniff often. Do the same with your sense of taste.**

- Can you taste the different ingredients in your food?

- How do the textures feel on your tongue? Can you describe them?

- What is your relationship to sound? Can you hear silence? Can you hear a bird, water running, wind on water, rustling leaves, a baby's sigh, the fall of an apple from a tree?

- When you look at a rose do you see the color or do you also see the veins in the petals? Do your eyes sweep over large areas or do you see detail? Do you notice subtle hues of color?

Every sensation gives us valuable information and connection to ourselves and where we are at any moment. How we respond helps us know ourselves. Using the abilities of the body is a gift.

### Energizing our physical bodies

We need physical energy to manifest our intentions. Our body instinctively knows whether our intentions are aligned with our soul. If we are misaligned, we will end up using our will to force our bodies into a situation they reject. This stresses us and depletes our bodies' energy. It's as if we are constantly swimming upstream. In fact, when we struggle with physical pain, the first culprit is the mismatch of our four bodies within the consciousness level we are operating from. If we do not make sure our thoughts, feelings and actions are congruent each of our four bodies will operate at a different vibrational level. The result is the fragmentation of our laser beam of energy which then weakens our magnetism.

Chaos then takes over. We are no longer focused, causing our energy stream to dissipate. Checking often for alignment among our four bodies and making necessary adjustments, keeps the energy flow strong and magnetic. *What behaviors represent the consciousness level you choose to identify with? How do you support your physical body? What thoughts correlate with emotions you use to support yourself? How do you use your body to help pace yourself and set your priorities?*

### Choices and Clarity Create Authenticity

In the connection consciousness we accept responsibility for the choices we make in order to build an authentic life. Each becomes a reflection of our values. *What beliefs are important to you now? What values are you currently trying to live? What is your intention for your behaviors in your personal and professional life? What attitudes do you espouse? What do you stand for? What is your worldview? What messages do you want to share about it? What are your hopes? What do you trust?* Valuing and learning from our experiences as we attempt to live from our Intuitive and Soul Levels becomes our inspiration to make mindful, authentic choices. The perspectives of our four bodies are necessary in the decision-making process. This enlightens us about the consciousness level they reside in. We then align our thoughts, feelings, beliefs and actions so one is a reflection of the other and also represents the consciousness level we choose to express. This gathering and sorting process is essential to clarity. We periodically review, reflect upon and update our self-created criterion.

We need to clarify how we think, feel, what values our behaviors represent, and our intentions. We need our own clarification process.

## Invoking our Soul Level in the unity consciousness

The transition toward becoming a spiritual human being requires our commitment to live from the highest level of consciousness we can connect to at any given moment. We recognize and implement the optimal conditions in our lives, which make us receptive to messages from our Intuitive and Soul Levels. We want to obtain the most expansive perspective. Only with the alignment of the Soul, Intuitive and Personality Level are we actually using all parts of ourselves and interfacing with all that is. Without invoking our Soul Level to participate in our lives, we limit our reality to just the separation consciousness and occasional glimpses of the connection consciousness. That means our imagination is reduced to probabilities instead of possibilities and potential. The support and activation from the soul set up the consciousness levels that manifest our intentions. It stimulates our four bodies in the Intuitive Level. Think of it as a start button that kindles the clarification and manifestation processes. Preferences, images, concepts, thoughts, gut-level feelings, emotions, and instincts ignite. It is up to us to integrate the messages from all of our four bodies to get the complete transmission from our soul.

Here is how this works in practical terms. We may think we want to be a singer and invoke the soul for support. The soul in its wisdom takes the energy from our desire and aligns it with our connection and expression in the unity consciousness. At this level we are using our unique potential. That means even though we want to be a singer and dedicate ourselves to this pursuit, what we learn along the way is actually the main event. Indeed, we may not become a singer but rather, discover that we have talent as a songwriter. Once finding our way into songwriting, we are joyous. The soul authenticates our intentions. However, our desire to sing might actually come from a wish for fame. Since this is a Personality Level motivation, it blinds us to our real creativity and authenticity. Of course, if our needs and wants operate from the Personality Level, our power will devote a great deal of energy toward our making a living as a singer. Sooner or later that power supply diminishes leading to a limited life. Aligning our three levels of consciousness brings grace into our lives.

Our soul holds more potential for us than we can use in a lifetime. When our personality and intuition work in concert with our soul, we provide it a structure from which to express itself. *What consciousness level do you identify with? What are the premises you hold about the consciousness level you choose to live from? What kind of a ceremony, statement, prayer, or ritual can you develop that signifies asking your soul for guidance?*

### Concretizing values of the connection consciousness

Soul expressions such as unconditional love, compassion, gratitude, commitment, courage, joy, trust, peace, and humility are emotions as well as concepts. They form a state of being that includes: an invocation of the desired value, summoning its emotional intensity, thoughts that express it and behaviors that implement it. The congruency of thinking, feeling and doing equates to living the value. This is when mystery and magic happen. We are using all of our four bodies and focusing our energy toward living our Intuitive and Soul Levels. Review how you live your daily life. *What values do you choose to live by? What are the thoughts, feelings, and actions necessary to bring the vibrations of the value into form? What specific values guide you now? How do circumstances and roles change your values? What are your intentions? From which level of consciousness does your intention emerge? What is your motivation for this intention? How do your intention and motivation align with your Intuitive and Soul Level? What values does your intention reflect? What soul emotions are activated? How successful are you at sustaining your intentions?*

### Checking Congruency

The awareness of the congruency of our thoughts and feelings is extremely important. As we connect to our own interior, we find the essence of who we are—our soul. This deepening is made possible by our willingness to be mindful of how congruent we are with the expression of our four bodies, and especially the mental and emotional bodies. Since thought and emotion are energy, the more aligned our thoughts and feelings, the more power our energy field has to magnetize and connect with like energy. This renders our connections greater in scope and depth. If our thinking and feeling are disparate, we send conflicting messages that cause our energy field to wander onto unintended paths. Our ability to attract necessary connections diminishes dramatically.

Awareness and expression of our thoughts and feelings define who we are becoming. Even though we speak a common language each word we use has many subtle connotations. Ask ten people what "power" or "authority" means and what emotions they activate, and you will have ten different responses. Each of us is unique. We must be aware of our own thoughts and feelings in order to communicate authentically with others. It is so important for us to pick words that accurately describe what we are thinking and feeling. They help us connect our thoughts and feelings, our hearts and minds. They also encourage others to speak from their hearts. Choosing our words and emotions is choosing the consciousness level we live from.

## Check It Out!

**It is powerful to use the Intuitive Level to change our association with words we automatically use and then to imbue them with the vibration of the connection consciousness. Using visualization with symbols that hold the meanings we assign them changes our energy field.**

- Think of the word and see it in your minds' eye.

- Imagine the letters connecting and becoming a line. See the line turning into a triangle.

- Imagine a higher level of consciousness represented as any color you want. This raises the consciousness level of the emotion and thought associated with the word. Slide the color you choose from the apex of the triangle to its perimeter.

- Move it around faster and faster until the triangle collapses and become a circle of light.

> • Put the light in your heart and feel the new emotions and thoughts that are imprinted in the word. Now when you use the word you are expressing a higher level of consciousness. Create your own visualizations to reprogram the emotional and thought content of your words.

Misunderstandings occur when we assume that others share our emotional imprinting and thoughts. We must express ourselves clearly and authentically. Using the clarification process becomes our criteria for evaluating how we are doing. It helps us discern which beliefs of the connection consciousness are evident in our lives and what draws us back to the separation consciousness. It helps us set up guidelines to focus our thoughts, feelings and behaviors until our internal reality becomes our external reality. And when we check to see if our four bodies are engaged at Intuitive Level then it signifies that we are merging into the connection consciousness.

### The Scope of the Connection Consciousness: What looks familiar?

The connection consciousness is expansive and comprehensive. When we are first connecting to it we simply accept the concept of a bigger picture and something greater than ourselves. Soon we more fully trust our intuition in all four of our bodies. We feel more alive, appreciate all that is, and create a life that brings the expression of our soul into form. The scope of the connection consciousness is beyond a single definition. Below are some of the many ways we recognize the presence of the connection consciousness in our lives. How many are operative in your life right now? Then make your own list.

- Recognizing there is a higher power
- Setting intentions
- Desiring to bring love and joy into our and others lives
- Living a graceful life
- Creating a life that is based on our spiritual values

- Congruency between our internal and external perspectives: no fronts, roles, personas. "What you see is what you get." We act and are the same in every situation
- Intuition becomes our guiding force
- Being able to feel calm at will
- Being objective and acknowledging our part in any situation
- Owning and accepting our feelings and behaviors
- Separating our feelings from others–knowing what we feel and what others feel are independent of each other
- Desire for growth
- Trust that our life is unique and of value and cannot be compared to anyone else's life
- Acceptance that we are a light within the greater light
- Feeling compassion to all living things on this earth
- Seek to learn instead of judging
- Wanting to find another way
- Trusting our gut level feeling
- Knowing that what we feel is a wakeup call for us to look at our lives
- Knowing what we think and how we feel
- Recognizing how our intuition operates in our four bodies
- Fulfilling our dreams
- Accepting our sense of knowingess and acting on it
- Feeling supported and guided
- Becoming who we are meant to be
- Seeing life as a support system
- Knowing we do make a difference no matter the size of the deed
- Speaking and living authentically
- Clarifying the values we choose to live by
- Recognizing that our life is rich with choices
- Making changes that expand our lives
- Rejoicing that we are soul
- Being compassionate instead of judging
- Being grateful for what we have right now

- Letting go of ideas, feelings and things that no longer support us to align with our souls
- Treasuring special moments that open our hearts
- Being receptive
- Questioning ourselves to understand and acknowledge our motivation
- Accepting, loving and respecting ourselves
- Responding instead of reacting
- Choosing to actively overcome our fears
- Noticing the change in our perspective
- Being objective
- Taking responsibility for the life we create
- Doing what is right for us
- Self-respect
- Self-love
- Self-acceptance
- Self-confidence
- Recognizing our worth
- Not personalizing interactions and events
- Being our own self-authority
- Developing our imagination
- Interpreting symbols
- Looking behind our five senses
- Seeing the co-existence of shadow and light in all
- Deleting assumptions
- Walking the unproven roads
- Asking questions of ourselves and others
- Learning from all of our experiences
- Accepting that we are human and spiritual beings

## Chapter Six Exploration and Discovery Activities

### Points to Ponder
**What do you think and feel about the following statements?**
- Our soul authenticates our intentions.
- When we are clear about the motivations behind our intentions and align them with our Soul Level, our energy fields become stronger and more magnetic.
- It is the nature of the soul to be a change agent.
- Being understood makes people feel valued.
- Speaking authentically gives others an opportunity to speak their truth.
- Words and their inflection are a window into our internal perspective.
- Clarity within each of our four bodies supports authenticity.
- Making conscious choices supports clarity.
- The words we chose and the style of delivery tells our story to the world.

### *Developing the Connection to the Intuitive Level in Your Four Bodies*

It is our job to ascertain the clarity of our four bodies and provide an opportunity for us to pay attention to the state of each. But at times, they reside in different levels of consciousness or are not as consistently clear within the same level. This means we need to listen and process any thoughts, feelings, and behaviors that prevent us from being in the Intuitive Level in all of our bodies. **Our hope is for all four bodies to reside in the highest level of clarity in the Intuitive Level so that we are an open channel for our souls.** You can use the suggested exercise below to process an issue that needs clarity. Do I stay in my job? Is this the person I want to marry? Is a divorce necessary or do I need to take more responsibility for myself? What are my expectations and how real are they for me now? All of these questions and the multitude of others we ask ourselves are resolved in a satisfactory and joyous way **ONLY** when we involve our four bodies at the Intuitive and Soul Level.

**Activity 2. Imagine that you are sitting at a conference table conducting a meeting of your four bodies. Personify each (spiritual, mental, emotional and physical) to make this exercise easier. Ask each body:**
- What is your perspective on the issue?
- What are your expectations?
- What do you want?
- What do you need?
- What is your hope?
- How can you help each other? How can the others help you?

**Activity 3. Invoke symbols to activate a higher level of consciousness. You might get the answer immediately. Or if you need to integrate and clear other issues, you might get the answer tomorrow, next week, or next month. Remember the answer will be waiting for you in your subconscious when you are ready to use it.**

**Activity 4. Find a comfort place where you can relax without interruption:**
- Ask for a symbol of each of your four bodies
- Imagine a beautiful container. (Allow your imagination full expression.)
- Put the symbols of your four bodies into the container.
- Imagine diamond-like sparkles raining on the container. Watch all the symbols and the container melting into a burst of light.
- Now ask your soul for a symbol of this energy field. It represents congruency between the four bodies in the highest consciousness level available.
- Put the symbol in your heart.
- Take a few deep breathes and as you exhale, allow this symbol to become bigger and bigger until you are standing in it.
- Stay with this image until you feel the new vibration.
- Know that the wisdom of the consciousness will reveal itself to you when you are ready to receive it.

**Activity 4. Becoming receptive-count the ways!**

**There are many ways to become receptive just as there are many roads that lead to God.** Some suggestions that have worked for others include: meditation, listening when praying, yoga, walking or sitting in nature, journaling, listening to music, drumming, dancing, expressive art, creative visualization, imagining, being in the zone during a physical activity, reflecting on dreams, and writing stories or poetry. Experiment to discover the many ways you can pitch yourself into a receptive state. The more methods you develop and practice the easier it is to stay connected and evolve.

**Activity 5. Merging into the connection consciousness**
**Look through a kaleidoscope. While the elements are the same, unlimited patterns emerge as you turn it. This becomes a symbol for merging into the connection consciousness. Let's investigate your reactions and responses.**

- What are your immediate feelings?
- What are your immediate thoughts?
- What are your reactions from each of your four bodies?
- What are your fears?
- Do you have any resistances and where do they come from?
- What responses can you create that support each body?
- *To which* symbols *can* you assign meaning to remind you to check with your Intuitive Level?

## Staying in the connection consciousness

**Integrating and living from the connection consciousness takes an investment of time and energy.** But the rewards are so great and each step so enlightening that this journey becomes wondrous. Actively engaging all of our four bodies in our Intuitive Level assures living in the connection consciousness. **How do you connect with your four bodies every day? Here are some suggestions:**

*Spiritual Body:*

**Activity 5. Create an affirmation that invites your soul to participate in every moment of your day.**

I choose to align with my soul. I am a point of light, love, and power, through which my soul energy flows. I choose to become who I am meant to be. I am a channel for the light.

**Activity 6. Use a symbol.**

See the sun as a symbol for your soul. Place your own sun in your heart. As you breathe, expand the light and stand in it. Walk in the light all day. Or, imagine the air contains glitter. As you breathe, visualize the glitter becoming the soul energy in and around you.

*Mental Body:*

**Activity 7. Set your intention for the day.**

What do you want to create? This can be clarification of what is most important for you to do this day. It must be in the format of "I choose to..." This helps ensure that every thought and action aligns and contributes to your soul focus. If so, there will be guidance when you need it.

**Activity 8. As you think of your day make sure you choose the words you use.**

Remember for every thought there is an emotional charge and for every emotion there is a thought.

*Emotional Body:*

**Activity 9. Invite your soul's emotional expression into your heart and body.**

These are higher ground emotions: courage, awe, trust, joy, compassion, love, humility, commitment, gratitude, acceptance, generosity. Ask to see the vibration of one of these emotions in a certain color. See the color inside and outside your body. Keep saying the word until you actually feel it.

**Activity 10. Choose what emotional state you want to stay in during the day and summon it up.**

Even if you become reactive, you can get back to being in charge of your emotional field. If you aren't able to feel it, use a memory or an object that you imbued with the emotional state you want. Just like thought memories, we have memories of how emotions feel. Start tuning up the memories of your soul emotions. The more you practice, the easier it is to change your emotional state.

## Physical Body:
**Activity 11. Eat healthfully and get enough sleep.**

Food is medicine. It's not as if you can't have an ice cream cone now and then. But after about six weeks of choosing healthy foods, you really won't want one. So many books on health can guide you. Buy a few and study them. Figure out what is right for you.

Sleep is not only for resting and repairing your body. It's also for processing problems in the unconscious. Before going to bed, ask your soul to resolve an issue that has been bothering you. Keep a pen and paper next to your bed. You will be amazed at how much information is available upon first wakening. In that in-between stage of waking up and getting out of bed you are in a very receptive state. Use it! If you fully wake up and start your morning rituals and then write, many thoughts and ideas will be lost.

**Activity 12. If you are uncomfortable in your body–do something about it!**

We need to be spiritually, mentally, emotionally, and physically powerful. Make sure your body is a reflection of who you are becoming. Can you depend on your body? Is it strong? Do you feel its power? Work out. Set and achieve physical goals that demonstrate your strength. If the clothes you wear are no longer comfortable or don't express your new sense of self, donate them to charity and create a new look. This has nothing to do with fashion but is all about your personal creativity and values.

*The scope of the connection consciousness*

**List occasions when you used your intuition and lived from the connection consciousness. Reflect on each of your four bodies for each instance you listed.**

- What were you thoughts, feelings, actions, motivation, and intention?
- What patterns do you see?

# Chapter Seven

## Challenges of Shifting to the Connection Consciousness

Merging into the connection consciousness is a heroic journey. While it is filled with surprises, insights and joy, like most journeys it also has stumbling blocks, emotional upheavals, and downright discouraging times. It takes commitment, courage, and trust to go the distance. Through the symbolic language of our intuition, we develop awareness of ourselves as spiritual beings existing beyond the separation consciousness. Connecting to and acting on the continuous insights we receive from our Intuitive Level demonstrates the power of our soul energy to guide us to our unique potential. But our challenge is to move from familiar beliefs that no longer support us toward the unfamiliar territory of the connection consciousness.

### *Identifying and Accepting the Challenges*

Merging with the connection consciousness is a process. Our soul magnetizes us to specific challenges for our learning. These are based on soul themes such as integration, gratitude, connection, love, courage, authority. They can affect all areas and situations in our lives. The challenges they bring are based on our readiness. While we do not have control over these learning opportunities, we do choose how we respond.

The attitude from the separation consciousness is that we should overcome challenges in order to prove our worth. In the connection consciousness, on the other hand, the main event becomes what we learn and how we apply this learning in our lives. The outcome is just another element in the learning process. To transform a challenge into an asset, we must accept it, trust that it is a learning opportunity, and open to our Intuitive and Soul Levels for interpretations and guidance.

Discouragement with our spiritual development sets in when we assume that once we confront an issue such as relationships, we banish any additional problems in this area. However, we have multiple lessons to learn about relationships, and each one is different. In fact, we keep learning within the same theme that the soul designates until we reach clarity and alignment within the four bodies in all three levels of consciousness—an "aha" that is inclusive and comprehensive. All of our experiences now connect, and we see how each contributed to our newfound wisdom.

Spiritual life unfolds for every one of us in a unique way. Judgment about how we are doing, where we should be, and the difficulty of the journey just stress us and make us susceptible to the doubts and fears of the separation consciousness. All concerns are part of the path. Whether we meet a fear and conquer it immediately, chip at it for months or even years, it is the exact process we need. We decide to be hurt, angry, and take things personally or to welcome the learning and wonder of what can be. This is a shift in attitude from "I don't want..." to "I want..." which demonstrates our belief in self-authority.

## *Check It Out!*

**Learning our lessons is a fertile time for us to take another step in creating who we are meant to be. It is definitely a moment for reflection and clarity.**

- What is happening? When is it happening? Where is it happening? Who is involved? What do your reactions and responses tell you about the event or situation?

- What does your current situation tell you about your attitudes, beliefs, and thoughts? What might be some emerging values?

- How do you choose to respond to the situation? How are you acting? What do you need to change? What are the new perspectives and beliefs you now need to adopt?

- What beliefs of the separation consciousness are defeating you? Which characteristics of the connection consciousness do you need to apply in your life now?

## The Challenges on Our Journey in the Connection Consciousness

### *The challenge of blocks: an opportunity for growth*

As soon as we perceive an intuitive message, the soul provides the initial energy. Participation of each of the four bodies doing their specific function keeps the energy flowing in the right direction for implementation. However, in the process of realizing our intentions, we experience blocks in the form of resistance or obstacles. These are unprocessed energy configurations–separated parts of our self that divert the Soul and Intuitive Level energy from flowing to support the manifestation of our intentions.

We may feel stymied by these blocks, but they are opportunities for learning the lessons our soul knows we need to clarify. The identification of blocks helps us recognize those parts of ourselves that are still actively expressing the separation consciousness. They appear as insecurities, self-doubt, lack of resources, defensive behaviors, the inability to get cooperation from others, abusive use of power, fear of rejection, fear of success, procrastination, frustration, and disappointment.

Getting the permits from the city to open a drug rehab center is time consuming, frustrating, and wrought with red tape. Learning the software for an accounting system is confusing and tedious. Being overwhelmed by the decisions to find the right location and set up a business requires resources and effort and brings uncertainty. We need mental and emotional fortitude to learn new skills, develop and implement plans, and calculate risks.

Fears divert our creative energy to thoughts and behaviors that defend us from these undermining feelings. They distort our perspective and move us away from trusting our intuition and soul. We are unable to distinguish what is causing our fear and what are realistic possibilities. We lose direction and become confused. We diminish ourselves when we think about and are afraid of defeat. Eventually these thoughts and feelings become our reality. At this point, we are cut off from the hope of what can be. This causes us to be fixated on the past and catapulted to the fear of the future. We can't see beyond the energy of fear, since it wraps around our bodies. It restricts and constricts us and thus cuts off our lifeline–our soul. The natural tendency for energy to reach out and connect is sabotaged by our concentration on fear. So instead of creating, we use this essential energy to shore up our battered self-image. These diversions are blocks to clear.

Think of something you wanted to create that didn't happen. *What ideas or dreams once excited you? What happened to them? What did you say to yourself to make it okay to let them go? What did you say you would do but didn't follow through with? What thoughts and feelings were the obstacles? Where did your energy get diverted?*

When I first started writing, I felt insecure. Even though I experienced a flow of creative energy I couldn't just sit and write. Instead, I often used that energy to cook, run errands that suddenly seemed so important, and impute ordinary situations with too much drama. I was emotionally drained and had the cleanest house ever! These and other behaviors were my attempt to ignore the uncomfortable feelings of being emotionally disconnected from my soul because my emotional body is weaker than my other bodies. I therefore became mistrustful of my innate connection. I hung onto my self-doubt. I started thinking I was inadequate. I worried what people would think of this idea. What will happen if I fail? How will I feel about myself if my project doesn't work? Will my self-image withstand criticism? Can I risk losing face with my family, friends, and people who know me professionally? And if I lost face, would I recover?

*What do you do when you feel vulnerable, powerless, doubtful, or defeated?* Fears can seem so real. At times, we act from courage and determination to overcome minor blocks and continue on our course. These cause only temporary delays. We overcome them by simple mental adjustments such as eliminating expectations and remembering to choose the emotions that sustain us. However, there are blocks that cause necessary detours, because the lesson is significant for our growth.

In order for me to write, I had to build a relationship between my soul and my emotional body to loosen the energy that was stuck in fear. I held conversations with my soul and emotional body; meditated; wrote in my journal; deleted beliefs that were no longer right for me; imagined, envisioned, and entertained new possibilities; interpreted my dreams; observed life from a symbolic perspective; walked on the beach for hours at a time; and practiced creating soul level emotions within.

Fear separates us from our intuition and also plays havoc with our four bodies. It creates physical symptoms such as rapid breathing, sweating, and an adrenaline rush in the physical body. The emotional body feels the concrete response of the physical body and fans the fear. The effect of the emotional body's response on the mental body is to undermine our thinking and sense of competence and worth. As a result, the spiritual body begins to distrust the process and losses faith in our ability to create.

Whichever body reacts first to the fear affects the others. For example, if the emotional body is overwhelmed by the fear of changing professions, the mental, physical, and spiritual bodies are left to process the blocks created by these fear signals. But while these three bodies use energy to dissolve blocks, they also must nourish themselves and strengthen the connection to the emotional body so that it can take another step closer to trust. Valuable energy that is otherwise needed to move forward in order to manifest our creation becomes scattered in many directions.

Depending on the intensity of our block we may be diverted for long periods or even permanently from what we intend. However, when a client feels pain because of a block, I acknowledge it. And then I also express my excitement about this wonderful opportunity to choose a response that supports growth. When a block confronts us, it is a signal from the soul that we are ready for a change.

Emotional blocks dissolve when we become more attuned to our feelings and practice the skills to manage them. Also creating the Soul Level emotions inside us strengthens our emotional body and starts the soul connection.

## Check It Out!

**Review your life.**

- What area do you think and talk about the most?
- What areas evoke the strongest emotions and reactions?
- What are your recurring issues (relationships, work, creativity, relationship to authority and institutions, physical illness)?
- What blocks can you identify?

As we participate in bringing our vision into implementation by using the Intuitive Level of our four bodies, we are getting the necessary information as well as channeling the necessary energy. We are the vehicle for changing the consciousness of energy into matter.

## The challenge of limitations: an opportunity for guidance

Although the desire for human and spiritual growth may burn within us, it will not automatically eliminate real or self-imposed limitations. These play important roles in our lives. They direct us to the path that provides the optimal conditions to experience, expand, and express ourselves.

Theoretically, we are unlimited; that is, the part of us that exists in the unity consciousness is without limits. However, if we were only in the unity consciousness–the world of energy–we would be without form. Since we also co-exist in the connection and separation consciousness, these levels make their limitations felt.

Self-created limitations might be fear based. We believe we could be rejected if we don't go into the family furniture business. We may doubt that the software games we design are good enough to compete in the market. We are afraid that if we have to constantly come up with unique recipes to open the café we dream about that maybe we will run out of ideas. These fears frustrate us and cause pain but never take away the longing to manifest what is burning within us. This longing hurts us until we stop to look for the cause of the pain. Once we accept our fear is at the root, we find movement in our lives.

We then process our fear and replace it with hope and trust-based thoughts, feelings and behaviors.

Self-created limitations can also be caused by the behaviors we invent to protect ourselves against feeling powerless to move in the direction that is right for us. Brenda, a client of mine had two half brothers that mirrored their father's large athletic body and competitive attitude, while she inherited her mother's petite body type. The frequent teasing that came from both brothers about her "shrimp, stunted" size put her on the defensive. She tried to show how strong she was by arguing with them on all subjects that she had an opinion. This need to win the verbal arguments became so much a part of her everyday behavior that it affected her interpersonal relationships for many years. Her marriage became a battleground, she controlled her children to the point of their rebellion, and her work life was a series of lost jobs. While she felt powerful whenever she got her way or proved herself right, her true caring and loving nature was suppressed. She was unable to risk living this more positive perspective. These defensive behaviors may or may not be justified, and whether or not they work isn't the issue; the fact is that they limit us. To surpass these limitations the beliefs and function of the Intuitive Level are our hope.

Real limitations are on-going. We might have thought we could revamp the Medicare system because we have experience in the field and some great new ideas. However, the collective consciousness of those in the United States might not be ready for it. Just because we think we have skills and come up with ideas doesn't guarantee success. We live in a greater context, and therefore the readiness and conditions might limit our endeavor. We need to sort out our expectations versus the direction and intention of our soul.

Real limitations can cause repeated failure. Nevertheless, they also get us to wake up and reassess our direction. Ryan wanted to be a professional baseball player. He played from childhood hoping to get a college scholarship. His mother told him he could do anything he wanted if he worked hard for it. He practiced and practiced. No college scholarship. Ryan was crushed, but then he convinced himself that he would get to the major leagues by trying out for a minor league team. His determination continued even though his manager told him that the owners would let him go at the end of the first season. Ryan talked his way into another year's contract, again convinced his time had come. But finally, the ax just fell. Ryan just wasn't good enough and his limitations finally stopped him.

He returned home defeated and holed up in his room, making up songs on his guitar. One week turned into a month and then two. He felt good writing songs; the lyrics poured out of him. On a lark he recorded a couple and gave them to the father of one of his friends who knew someone in the recording business. Ryan became a famous singer, lyricist and musician.

Sometimes, real limitations nudge us to walk on our unique path.

*Check It Out!*

**When we encounter limitations, our first task is to access from the Intuitive Level the reality of our situation. Think of a time when you felt limited:**

- What thoughts are causing your fears?
- Are these feelings a reaction to what you are doing?
- What is your motivation? What is your intention?
- What is causing you to feel limited?
- What control do you have in the situation?
- What has been difficult for you to accept?
- What do you have to fear?
- What is your objective perspective about your fears?
- What are your limitations telling you?
- What is your truth?

We know the difference between real and self-created limitations in our heart and soul. Bless those limitations that are real, for they are part of our guidance system. Each of us has within us a unique potential, a Divine Blueprint that we weave through our three levels of consciousness. These abilities, talents and insights are all within waiting for us to bring them into form. Developing these special talents brings joy and satisfaction.

## The challenge of emotions: an opportunity for self-mastery

While we might not be in control of the challenges our soul designs for us, we are in control of how we respond to them. This gives us an opportunity to incorporate the beliefs of the connection consciousness to support us as we transform challenges into personal strengths.

Here are some of the emotional challenges that may present themselves as we progressively live in and integrate our Intuitive Level:

## Defeat, fear and self-doubt to self-trust

Thoughts of defeat caused by the fear of inadequacy make us question our ability to accomplish what we set out to do. To relieve us of these uncomfortable feelings and distorted thinking that tortures us, we create irrational excuses to protect ourselves from failure. All of a sudden, it is the world, "they"–the system, the recording industry, the corporate games that must be played, publishing houses–that is the problem. They are against us. They won't let us succeed. With those attitudes, we give up after a single rejection, a single bump in the road. It is as if we were looking for something to blame in order to justify "inevitable" defeat. This is a separation consciousness attitude–we are a victim.

Memories of actual failures also keep our thoughts and especially our feelings stuck in the separation consciousness. However, those arising during childhood come with the emotional impact of a child's perspective. Nevertheless, we as adults accept these experiences as predictors of our present and future. *Think back on your childhood. What defeated you? What were your feelings? Did you tell anyone about the situation? What did they do to help you through the situation? If you didn't tell anyone, what did that feel like? What conclusions did you come to from that situation? How did you feel about yourself? Can you identify any attitudes, beliefs, thoughts and feelings that remain today from this incident? Are those thoughts and feelings still valid?*

Also, it is especially painful to experience defeat in a quest that we strongly believe in and feel is important to ourselves as well as others. Defeat undermines us and makes us feel alone. We believe that who we are becoming and what we want to create has no place in the world. This leads to negative thinking that reopens old wounds. We start to fear that history will repeat itself and that we are destined for failure. This puts us in a powerless state, which in turn activates the limitations of the separation consciousness.

When we become paralyzed by fear, we must go back to the basics. We must reestablish the bond with our intuition and soul. We do this by connecting with the Intuitive Level of our four bodies. We find our spiritual body by meditating, praying, reading spiritually inspiring material, reviewing our beliefs about connectedness and being totally honest with our review of our internal world. One way to get support from our mental body is to write and say affirmations; another is to reflect on our thoughts and determine which come from the separation consciousness and which represent the connection consciousness. Confronting our expectations of how things should be and then throwing them out the window helps to clear our thinking. Also, reviewing our self-talk clarifies which thoughts are moving us toward the connection consciousness and which are activating the separation consciousness.

Our emotional bodies can balance defeat by activating the hope that we can effect changes in our lives no matter how small. Also, getting in touch with all the feelings that link us to our Intuitive Level helps to change the energy field. Even connecting to the Intuitive Level of at least one of our four bodies restarts the process. One body influences the others. We can use our imagination and envision the life that is aligned with our soul. By experiencing the feelings that go along with these images we are reminding our emotional body of emotions that support us. Our soul connection is always there. It is up to us to be aware of it again.

## Check It Out!

**Think of your adult experiences with self-doubt and defeat.**

- When have you been defeated?

- How did self-doubt contribute to your defeat? How did you deal with it? What hurt you about the defeat?

- What negative conclusions do you still hold from this experience? What are some of the rationalizations you use as a result of this experience that prevent you from risking something new?

- What process do you use to symbolically release the energy that still holds these thoughts and feelings?

- How did each of your four bodies react and respond to the situation? What thoughts and feelings do you need to activate to make you feel connected? Which body was receptive to support?

Feeling defeated is a separation consciousness belief. In the Intuitive Level, we turn defeat into finding the lesson we need to learn. We want to know what is causing us to feel defeated so that we can correct our limiting beliefs and choose ones that support us. It is an act of self-responsibility to grow and embrace our potential.

### Disappointment to self-acceptance

As we travel on the path to realize our dreams, disappointments are bound to appear. It is part of life. But it also gives us another opportunity to connect with the energy frozen in the emotion and transform it to a higher consciousness level. Disappointments make us feel fragile and vulnerable. They may come from many directions: seeing the support we thought we had from others crumble; underestimating the effort, time or resources it would take to reach our goal or underestimating the opposition; being unrealistic about our abilities; losing focus; and encountering unforeseen obstacles. In short, our anticipation of just how our path should go crashes right into life, and suddenly we're facing a reality we never expected—or wanted.

We start all new intentions with such hope, and when we are disappointed, we feel a personal hurt that makes us ask, "Why me? What did I do wrong? Why is the world against me? My idea came from my desire to help others; shouldn't it be easy?" Such pain, when deep and prolonged, easily turns into despair and depression. This is also a sign that we are moving toward the separation consciousness and away from the connection consciousness. When disappointment is not easily shaken by the activation of hope, we need to check our clarity. We might be mistaking hope for a mixture of expectations and denial.

Hope is easily confused with expectations, for they are so intertwined. Hope comes from our bond to our intuition, which makes us feel our spiritual connection and our power to make a difference. With this sense of spiritual power, we imagine how things can be. However, there is a fine line between where our hope stops and our expectations begin. Hope sets a direction and focus. Expectations demand a certain outcome, achievement, and a specific kind of validation from others. Part of experiencing our spirituality is to let go of expectations so that we can live in the flow of our soul energy. We learn to detach from what we create. Our soul gives us the consciousness. We take this energy and shape it into some form. However, if we are emotionally attached to the outcome, instead of staying strong in the knowledge that we are creating something as an expression of our soul, then we do become disappointed if we don't find success.

The separation consciousness operates whenever we have expectations for outcomes. Indeed, the belief that things should work out because we are coming from a spiritual perspective can lead to discouragement if we falter. The hurt is more personal because we have already opened up to the new connections with our soul. We feel betrayed.

This is to be expected, for in truth, as we explore the connection consciousness through our emotional body, we become more sensitive and therefore more vulnerable. However, if we don't feel this link, only our mental body is engaged within the connection consciousness and all we do is theorize and talk. The feelings of the connection consciousness are those beautiful emotions that express the soul vibration such as love, joy, compassion, courage, trust and humility. Because we are learning to feel deeply, when we are hurt, it *really* hurts!

Fortunately, one of our bodies may be clearer about the connection consciousness. This helps us quickly process our hurt and vulnerability. In fact, that is one of the differences between the separation and connection consciousness. We feel emotions in both, but in the connection consciousness we process them faster and learn the lesson in minutes, whereas in the separation consciousness we easily get stuck in the emotion to the point where we believe the emotion is reality. It takes much insight and time to process through the heavy vibration of emotions at the separation consciousness level. The connection consciousness vibrates at a higher frequency. The energy oscillates faster and therefore is not as dense. The negative emotions only last if we put energy into continuing to feel them and hold onto the thought that generated them in the first place. Therefore, in order to stay in the connection consciousness it's essential to practice the power of changing our thoughts so that they align with our soul. When we have a strategy and a willingness to manage our emotions we can accept our process. We have shifted into a reality that jettisons expectation and embraces process. This supports us to accept ourselves and put events and situations into a wider perspective that that incorporates all three levels of consciousness.

## Check It Out!

**Accepting ourselves means that judgment is no longer a productive means for growth. In the connection consciousness we reflect and learn from our experiences. Having some compassion for ourselves helps us to recognize and dignify that the journey we are on no matter how hard, convoluted or smooth is our journey, our story, our life. We accept what is and choose how to respond. That is core for self-acceptance.**

- When have you felt disappointed and hurt? What were some of the expectations you held when you felt this way?

- What body can you align with to help you process this emotion?

- What body or bodies do you align when you need to accept yourself?

- What expectations do you have for your spirituality?
- Which bodies are prone to set expectations?

Emotional pain is a reminder that we are personalizing the situation. This then becomes the time for our emotional body to reaffirm our intuitive and soul connection by shifting the negative to a more hopeful, positive perspective.

## Anxiety and frustration to self-respect

Frustration is caused by the discrepancy between our desire to do something and our fear of our own incompetence or our actual incompetence. These fears make it difficult for us to honestly assess our abilities, learn the necessary skills, and create a plan to get us moving in the right direction. What should we be doing with our lives? Do we have what it takes to get where we want to go? Are we correctly interpreting the political ramifications of the situation? Or we become frustrated when we start acting on our desire and are overwhelmed by the difficulty or other unforeseen factors. *"Why didn't I see that? I can't do this. How was I supposed to know? Who am I fooling? I don't have the right.... education, contacts and/or experience."* These thoughts cause a downward spiral when we are frustrated.

We feel an inner tension to do something, but since we are unclear about what to do and how we should do it, we become even more exasperated. This leads to anxiety. In this state, we are getting unclear messages from all of our bodies as to what direction to take, how to get unstuck, and how to regenerate ourselves to access the new. We are cut off from our Intuitive Level.

This leads to our questioning our creativity. It is a difficult time because the interplay of frustration and anxiety continues to build. We become restrained externally, while inside the pressure keeps festering—an internal volcano is being created. At this point we can move into self-pity and act as if we are victims. This further amplifies the irritating energy field surround us. Our lives get ugly and self-destructive. The anxiety builds to the point that we feel we will explode in rage.

We rail at the world, circumstances, God, our loved ones, coworkers and life in general.

We alleviate frustration when we surrender to our soul by accepting the situation and where we are now. With this act, we acknowledge that we are not in control of circumstances, timing, resources, other people, or opportunities. Maybe we don't yet have the skills we need; maybe our intentions are not in alignment with our soul; maybe we thought we were doing something noble, but our actions really grow from an ego need; maybe the timing is wrong; maybe we don't have the cooperation of all four of our bodies; maybe we need more emotional fortitude, maybe ... maybe ... maybe. We can try until the end of time to analyze "why or why not" things are not working out for us.

Surrendering is the acceptance of what is and the humility to ask for guidance. Until we surrender through acceptance, we get sucked into the separation consciousness one more time. What were our expectations? What were we thinking? What is the range of our feelings? What is an accurate picture of our abilities, skills and talents? To which false beliefs and expectations are we attached?

Surrendering through acceptance and self-acceptance is a deliberate choice to identify the consciousness level from which we are operating. After we reestablish our connection and see the situation from our intuitive and soul perspective, we can then take the necessary steps. We might doubt that our goal is in alignment with our soul because of the way things are turning out. Finding what is true for us is one of the lessons to learn through our intuition. We intuitively know when we are on the right path, so if we need to go step–by-step to improve our skills, take a class or even get another degree, then that is what we need to do. We might have to narrow our scope and use incremental phases to move in the direction we desire. Whatever we need to do is a valuable learning opportunity.

Frustration dissipates when we stop to gain clarity. Our soul helps us to accept what we need to know. If we handle frustration and anxiety by facing a problem, processing it, asking for guidance from our Intuitive and Soul Level, choosing our direction, and learning from the experience we enhance our self-respect.

*Check It Out!*

**Self-respect starts with being honest with ourselves. Then acting from that honesty in accordance with our soul enhances our worth.**

- What does frustration mean to you? How do you handle it? What has frustration prevented you from doing?

- What does anxiety do to you? How do you handle anxiety?

- How do you go let go of frustration and anxiety? How do you reconnect with your Intuitive and Soul Levels?

- What does self-acceptance mean to you? How comfortable are you with self-acceptance? What associations do you have with self-acceptance?

- What thoughts and feelings do you need to create to bring your attitudes about self-acceptance and self-respect fully into the connection consciousness?

- How do you recognize and acknowledge when you respect yourself?

## *Worry to self-confidence*

We worry about possibilities that we don't want to happen—and most often about possibilities over which we have no control. Like all emotions, worry has its light and shadow sides depending on the level of consciousness in which we reside. It can alert us to potentially negative situations and can help us adequately prepare for them. However it can also drain our energy and close off the connection to our intuition. If we are worrying about the unexpected drop in our monthly income, a constructive use of this energy could be to review our marketing strategy and also find a short term line of credit. Taking those steps would turn the worry into solutions. If we are worrying that our college freshman daughter will be partying, drinking recklessly, and skipping class even after our lectures and threats, then we are wasting time and making ourselves miserable. Her behavior is now out of our control. No matter how much we worry, she will do what she wants.

Worry splits our energy field by causing a preoccupation with either the past or the future. This strains the part of our energy field which is still operating in the present. If we are thinking of the past, we actually re-create the energy configuration of that time, which is of course different than the current situation. This makes it seem as if the past is still our reality. Since the energy field of the present is different from that of the past, we feel disconnected from ourselves and confused about where we are. Getting back to the present and allowing the past to recede in its dominance takes much effort.

When we worry about the future, we project our present fears and embellish them. This activates reactions from our emotional and physical bodies, which adds yet more energy so that we anticipate the future with even greater fear. Again, we are disconnected from the present, which is the only reference point that connects all parts of ourselves.

The energy we need to shift from the past to the present to the future is enormous. Indeed, the degree of energy we leave in the past and project into the future is the degree to which we are absent in the present. The result is that we are not fully connected to our intuition and soul. Dancing from past to future to present wastes energy that might have been available to overcome our worries to begin with.

We are pulled to the past because we have unfinished business. We did not process the lesson the first time around—we just didn't get it yet. But we will not find our answers in our past or by projecting into the future. Answers come from the present. When we stay in the present we are connected to our intuition which will provide the needed perspective to solve problems.

Putting worry in a larger context, one that is aligned with our Intuitive Level is an act of self-confidence. We know that on any path we will meet with challenges that cause worry. However, through our self-confidence, which combines with our self-respect, self-trust, and self-acceptance we are choosing to identify with stronger, clearer parts of ourselves. Also, when we affirm our self-confidence by staying in process (especially where learning is available), we actively participate in life instead of worrying about it.

> ## *Check It Out!*
>
> **If worrying causes paralyses then it is time to determine which body is stuck in the separation consciousness.**
>
> - What do you worry about? What does worry hide from you?
>
> - Where do control and worry come together?
>
> - What is the problem that is causing you to worry? What are some solutions? Which solution will you pick? What would prevent you from taking action on the solution?
>
> - What are you confident in about yourself? What skills, talents, beliefs and values give you self-confidence?
>
> - What actions that you take do you justify is right because you worry about it?

## *The challenge of grandiosity: an opportunity to learn wonderment*

Grandiosity is self-inflation that emerges from pretentious, exaggerated and overblown thoughts, feelings and behaviors. And yet if our thinking and feelings connect with our Intuitive Level for even a little while, we may have seen a vision that inspires us. Within the grandiosity may be a seed of inspiration.

Grandiosity may also come into play as we walk our spiritual path and recognize evidence of our connection to our Intuitive and Soul Level: when we received guidance so that our dependence on others for validation turned into self-acceptance which gave us the confidence to sell our art work; when we took on a mentoring perspective with our troubled teenager instead of being dictatorial; when we acknowledged that we needed classes in business finance and therefore reigned in our excitement about opening our business. All of these are the result of our connection to our intuition. And since these situations worked well we might have easily activated a Personality Level belief that we should be able to do anything we chose if it comes from our intuition and/or spiritual perspective.

Self-imposed expectations about our spiritual journey of merging into the Intuitive and Soul Level can set up grandiose ideas. Unfortunately if we act on expectations, we create inflexible rules for ourselves that bind us instead of supporting us. The separation consciousness is at play again. Here is a conglomeration of false beliefs that I've heard from my clients as they started their journey. *If I am spiritual then I must:*

- *Never show anger or doubt*
- Be a vegetarian
- Visualize what I want
- Be joyous and grateful for everything in my life
- Feel my center at will
- Be able to solve world problems
- Be intuitive in all situations
- Make things "happen."

However, if we do anything, no matter how spiritual it sounds from the perspective of, "If I do this, then I will . . ." we are setting ourselves up for disappointment. Whether we choose to meditate, show compassion, or change our values, spirituality becomes an expression of how we are feeling, not an action to earn or prove our connection. Self-righteousness about meditating, praying, and doing good deeds are not an expression of the connection consciousness.

Grandiosity about what we should be able to perceive, feel and access because we are intuitive results in despair when the task cannot be accomplished. Yes, we may be connected to our Intuitive Level, but that doesn't mean that we can cure all the diseases known to man and bring peace to the world. We may have valuable political insights, but that doesn't mean the United Nations will be giving us a permanent seat on the Peace Council.

True alignment between the personality, intuition and soul is from the inside out. I see too many people who want to cure the world of something as a sign and validation of their spirituality while neglecting their own personal inner work. Maybe the task has merit, but it cannot sustain if there is a disconnection between our three levels of consciousness. We need the "how-to" from the personality, the vision from our intuition and the energy from our soul. If our personality is unclear about our alignment to our intuition and soul, then the grandiosity of our ideas crushes our mission and sends us into despair.

But, after the balloon pops and we have wallowed in the murky waters of depression, hope does emerge. We pick up the pieces that are salvageable–those parts of our ideas and the strengths that come from the authenticity of the connection consciousness–and wash them off. We ask our soul for the antidote to our confusion. The lesson the soul offers is the emotion of wonderment.

Wonderment is the innocent, childlike part of us–the child that is untouched by disappointment, hurt, anger, shame, or any circumstances that cause bitterness, defensiveness, or pain. It is a space filled with possibilities and potential, free from all limitations that we or others put on ourselves. We are in a state of wonderment when we are joyously absorbed in an act of creativity and lose sight of time and surroundings. It is an altered soul state. Wonderment is the desire to express, experience, explore and discover. Here are wonderment statements:

- "I wonder what will happen when I use resin with the pigments I made."
- "I wonder how to teach kindergarten boys and girls to respect each other through play."
- "I wonder how flying wind turbines can bring rain to drought areas."
- "I wonder what the common denominator sound for the earth is?"

Wonderment emerges from the Soul Level while grandiosity comes from the Personality Level. Between these is the bridge of the Intuitive Level where we have the room to clarify our thoughts, feelings and actions.

## Check It Out!

- What grandiose ideas are still operating in your life?

- What happened to past grandiose visions? How did they turn out? What did you learn?

- How did grandiosity act as defense mechanism? What were you defending yourself from? How is that a form of conditionality?

- What is your understanding of wonderment? When have you been in a state of wonderment? How can you make it a larger part of your life?

- What activities in your life bring wonderment?

## Dealing with Challenges: The Reality of External Support Systems

We all want the comfort and support that comes from being part of a group or family and having a significant other or special friend. Depending on how intimate the relationship is, we get the benefits of being accepted and loved. In all relationships there are spoken and unspoken exchanges going on.

Before we ask someone for support, it's important to evaluate our relationship. We form and stay in relationships only when there is a continuous exchange of energy. Sometimes this is helpful and sometimes dysfunctional. For instance, Marcie and Linda are friends because they feel safe venting their frustrations to one another about their husbands. They really don't want to face their marital problems with their spouses. During their joint gripe sessions, they get relief from their pent up feelings and they also gain sympathy, which makes it easier for them to avoid the risk of approaching their husbands with their issues. They continue their dysfunctional relationships with their husbands, and when they need a release, start the venting again.

Marcie and Linda are on the hamster wheel. Their relationship is based in the Personality Level through their emotional bodies.

A limited friendship is all they can expect. Although this kind of support can help them through a difficult period, it may also be a form of denial and/or dependence. They may get temporary relief from a show of empathy, but they are not addressing the real problems in their lives.

Conversely, a healthy relationship with our significant other is connected through our four bodies in the Personality, Intuitive, and Soul Levels. The more energy vibrations that we put into the common energy exchange, the more intimate the connection and the greater potential for learning and growth.

Every person has a concept of what support means to them. *What does support look like to you? Who supports you? How? How do you support others? How does your support change depending on the person?* Based on our perception at that moment, we may think that support from others is essential to our well-being. If we do get support, and it relieves our immediate fears, it is easy to depend on it. However, it is not enough just to get relief from our anxiety. We must face our challenges and make the necessary changes that bring us into alignment with our Personality, Intuitive and Soul Levels. To determine what kind of support we need and who would be the best person to give it to us requires reflection and clarity. *What do you want the support for? What do you want it to do for you? What does it look like? What personal price are you paying to stay in a relationship that you perceive gives you support?*

Another way to ensure that we get support is to conserve the relationships we are in. If we change, we might risk losing the support we need. We then subject ourselves to the expectations embedded in the relationship from the start. This leads to predictable patterns of behaviors. Think of the last business meeting or family interaction you had. Did anyone act unexpectedly? How did the group or the individual react? Can you describe the predictable behaviors of each person in the interaction? Patterns of behavior become predictable to ensure that we stay connected. Many relationship books label behavior patterns with terms such as: "people-pleaser," "dominant power style," "the whiner," "martyrs," "killjoys," "intuitive thinkers," "the visionary." All of these are evidence of how people take on specific, long-practiced behaviors to fit into a group. Unfortunately, the pressure from others to stay within the bounds of predictable behavior interferes with authenticity and growth. It prevents energy fields from shifting vibrations that bring about change.

Giving support authentically from our internal reality affirms our choice to express the connection consciousness. Receiving support from a higher consciousness level than the one we are currently inhabiting reveals alternatives and possibilities. We feel hope.

Once we experience the benefits and limitations of support between another and ourselves, we are ready for our next step: finding our own support system within. This takes a desire to connect with ourselves more comprehensively and to experiment in order to discover what works. The most important step is to give ourselves space to listen to our intuition and soul.

## Checking the Reality of External Support Systems

When consensus and conformity to roles brings us support, the price may be too high as the support may also include dependency. In fact, support and dependence are easily intertwined. We need to clarify the difference for ourselves as well as our relationship to the people from whom we want support. The following are questions that help with this differentiation. As you use these questions to illuminate your thinking and feelings, be aware of the unspoken as well as the spoken interactions.

### The Price

*What do you have to do to continue to get support? What happens to the relationship if you make some changes? Is there one person in the relationship who is the "authority," or is there mutual sharing? Can you share all parts of yourself with the person, or are you limited in your interactions? What percentage of your relationship is focused on your problem? Does the other person reveal his or her issues? Does the person worsen your problems? Does the person see the situation through your eyes or his or her own issues and biases?*

### Type of Support

*What do you want from the person who supports you? Does the person listen and reflect back to you? Are you asking the other person for solutions or for emotional support? Are you getting unsolicited advice? What happens if you don't take the person's advice? How did you communicate to the person what you need and want?*

## Ego Placement

*Where are the egos of each person involved in your support system? Who is getting what out of the situation? What is the motivation of the person who is supporting you? What is your emotional need for support? What are you hoping for? What are you getting from the relationship?*

### Support at the Intuitive Level

Mutual respect and compassion characterize appropriate support. No one makes a decision for us or tells us what to do. We need support so we can be courageous through the process of clarifying our own truth. Asking someone to listen to us as we clarify our thinking and feelings is what's called for. And if that person poses some open-ended questions to assist us with our process, then that is helpful.

Encouragement is also a part of support at this level. Here are some encouraging statements: "I know this is a difficult time for you, but I also know you will be able to sort this out in your own way." "I see that you are hurt. Would you like to talk it over with me? May I listen to whatever you are thinking and feeling?" "I have seen how your intuition guides you at other times. What are some of the messages your intuition is revealing to you now?" "I would like to sit here quietly so you can listen to whatever messages are available from your intuition." And, "I don't know why this is happening to you. I trust that you will come to peace with this in your own way and in your own time." A nonverbal expression of support is a hand on a person's shoulder or forearm as we listen.

The highest level of support we give is to witness a person's journey. We listen nonjudgmentally and with compassion. We know we must trust the other person's relationship to his or her intuition and soul instead of supplying answers. Setting aside our own agenda and needs, we are fully present to receive guidance from our soul and the soul of the other if appropriate. Objectivity is important as we support others, for it is their life journey that we are witnessing.

Challenges are opportunities to learn about our Intuitive and Soul Levels. We are launched out of our habitual behavior and look for new answers. This is when the soul sighs happily and says, "Finally!" There is space and room to flow soul and intuitive energy since we are not focused on maintaining the status quo. Inhaling new scents, viewing new horizons, responding to new opportunities is akin to breathing in the energy of the soul. What wonderment—a new day, a new cycle in our lives, a step closer to understanding what it means to be a spiritual being. What a joy to stretch our consciousness of who we are. What excitement is in store when we master a challenge.

## Chapter Seven Exploration and Discovery Activities

### Points to Ponder
**What do you think and feel about the following statements?**
- We are the channel and the vehicle for changing the consciousness of energy into matter.
- As we participate in bringing our vision into implementation by using the Intuitive Level of our four bodies, we are gaining the necessary information as well as channeling the necessary energy.
- Anxiety is the state of energy waiting to be focused.
- Surrendering to our soul through acceptance of where we are now alleviates frustration.
- Any expectation about how our spiritual journey should look or feel puts us in the separation mentality and prevents the unfolding of our journey that naturally develops as we choose to connect to our intuition.

### Activity 13. Developing self-mastery and self-authority
A solid foundation of self-mastery and self-authority is necessary to become who we are meant to be as spiritual beings. We must develop

our skills, abilities, and an appreciation of our life experiences. Mastery of the following components ensures self-authority:

- Self-respect: (What actions demonstrate that you respect yourself?)
- Self-worth: (Can you recognize the divine in you? What values do you live by? What do you stand for? What do you do that you feel has worth?)
- Self-love/appreciation: (Do you love who you are becoming? How do you show yourself appreciation that you are courageously walking on your path? How do you nurture and care for yourself?)
- Self-confidence: (What talents and experiences can you acknowledge and rely upon?)
- Self-trust: (How well do you recognize and use your intuitive and soul guidance?)
- Self-acceptance: (What is your ability to accept what is in front of you with wonderment and with the knowledge that this is an opportunity for learning?)

**Activity 14. Make a chart of the above components of self-mastery. Answer the questions below for each. Remember to use your four bodies from your Personality and Intuitive Level perspectives.**

- What is your definition of the above components?
- What criteria do you use to evaluate your development in these areas?
- Which have you mastered?
- Which need development or fine-tuning?
- Identify who around you has mastered these components. What do you notice?
- Which of your thoughts, beliefs, feelings and actions represent each of these components?

**Activity 15. At the end of each day, record in a journal what you did or said that enhanced one of the components for self-mastery and self-authority. Do this exercise for one month. Skip a month and do it again. What did you notice when you started your journal for the second time? What have you learned?**

**Activity 16. Reflect on a relationship in your life.**
- What is your intention for the relationship?
- What is you motivation?
- What do you need from this relationship?
- How much self-responsibility are you taking in the relationship?
- What are you expecting from the other?
- What consciousness level(s) are you using to connect with the other?
- Which of your four bodies is engaged in the relationship?
- Which ones are not engaged? Why?
- If one of your four bodies needs help, can you look to the others for support and clarity? What is missing?

**Activity 17. Remember a time when you needed support.**
- What emotional state were you in when you decided to seek support?
- What did you seek support for?
- Who did you ask? Who gave you the kind of support you needed?
- What was the outcome?
- Was there a price to pay? If so, what was it?

# Part III.
# The Unity Consciousness And The Soul Level

## Chapter Eight

### The Unity Consciousness: What is it?

The separation consciousness is what is realized, the connection consciousness is what is possible, and the unity consciousness is potential waiting for interpretation and form — a world of transcendent and universal energy that exists everywhere in everything. All form comes from this energetic impulse that radiates within and around us.

Imagine a world that recognizes the inherent guidance and self-authority we all have within us to create a civilization based on acknowledging intrinsic talents and abilities and valuing beliefs that support them. Think of a world that doesn't require as a sign of success our fitting into a rigid structure based on the control of a few. Instead, imagine a world that supports flexible social structures that meet the needs of people to evolve. Contemplate a higher perspective that creates from a position of trust not fear, that believes in and works for abundance and rejects reacting to scarcity as a justification for control, that cherishes the exploration of ideas and expressions of innovation and creativity as responding to human needs and relinquishes the glorification of materialism and media hype. Imagine creativity being honored and valued in society for its ability to support human evolution without the exploitation of it to generate money. This is the world as it could be – the potential is in the Unity Consciousness.

### The Unity Consciousness is a World of Energy

The unity consciousness, the world of energy, is the fertile essence that holds potential for all that is and all that can be. It is everlasting, mysterious, powerful - omnipresent, omnipotent, and omniscient. It is the consciousness that is in all. Creating from the unity consciousness is akin to participating in a runaway atomic chain reaction — it is uncontrollable and knows no boundaries. Every action affects the whole energy field of all that is and is not.

The vastness of this level of consciousness is incomprehensible to our individual minds, so we only access it through our soul. This is our energy adaptor. It customizes and steps down this incredible living pulse into a miniature that we can grasp. We are our soul's expression in this universe, galaxy, planet, species, evolutionary epoch, location on earth. Our soul also expresses itself through our connection to the collective unconscious and our history, gender, the structure of our brains, our physical bodies, cultural identity, genealogy, genetic heredity, associations, and more. In essence, our soul connects us with the time and place and the matter called "us." Our soul configures energy specifically and expansively so that it coalesces from a pulsating point to matter that operates within an interdependent energy web.

When we are aligned with our soul and expressing the unity consciousness, we never know the full impact of our actions or creations. During a simple conversation, our soul might guide us to express a thought that vibrates an alternative energy offering our friends another possibility. Whether or not they consciously accept it, the energy transmits to each of them, creating a chain reaction. Think of dropping pebbles in a pond. Throw in one pebble, and we notice expanding concentric circles. Toss in several, and we see the concentric circles intersecting one another. Each has its own path and yet interacts with the others. Imagine each pebble as a person's energy field. What is the effect of these expanding, intersecting circles as they interact with others? Energy interactions between our Soul Level and other levels within our self and among other people produce unlimited configurations that we perceive, imagine, think, desire, and ultimately fashion into multitudes of enormous and miniscule forms of matter. This is the interdependence and ever protean nature of our energy field. The power of the exchange and reconfiguring of energy is awesome. The flutter of the wings of a hummingbird in the aviary in Hong Kong affects the energy field on the Serengeti in Tanzania.

Expressing the unity consciousness through our soul, becoming who we are meant to be, living our unique potential, affects the gross, subtle, and not yet defined elements of our natures. We are intertwined by an energy field that is common to all forms in existence—even those that are still only energy.

Scientists are trying to understand this level of energy interaction. They call it "the science of everything." String theory suggests that this energy is like a woven field of flexible impulses: imagine a huge volleyball net that is not confined to one shape. Another theory posits that the most fundamental energy impulses create membranes that contain a certain consciousness.

Understanding energy interactions at this elemental level reaffirms the existence of multiple consciousness levels beside those of which we are aware. The unity consciousness is a breathing, expanding, expressively creative impulse of aliveness. Throughout history, religions, cultures, and scientists have named this comprehensive energy as the Supreme Being, God, Jehovah, The More, Great Father, the Source, the Presence, the Theory of Everything, the Tao, and many other names. We accept the existence of the unity consciousness since we are aware of a natural order in our existence–there is some design, a self-organized system, a grand scheme that is greater than ourselves and beyond our understanding. Naming this level is the way we accept and come to terms with the unknown and the unknowable. *What is your relationship to any concept that denotes the unity consciousness? Who is your God? How do you explain or handle the anxiety of the unknowable? What influence does the unity consciousness have upon you?*

The unity consciousness may or may not manifest into form. To turn this energy into something concrete requires that our Intuitive and Personality Levels be attuned to our Soul Level. It is the soul's function to interpret the unity consciousness. The Intuitive Level creates symbols from the energy patterns of the soul consciousness. These symbols develop into insights. Then our intuition guides our personality to develop the specifics which create form. The unity consciousness magnetizes the specific energy connections to bring the consciousness of the soul-driven energy into forms. The unity consciousness is so vast that we cannot comprehend the totality of its essence. We are left to describe the experience of connecting with it. Of course, this description is only a representation of the experience, for the entrance into the unity consciousness goes far beyond the limits of the spoken and written word. It is intimate, personal and sacred.

Let the beliefs of the unity consciousness stir wonderment and kindle our desire to experience it. Let them ignite possibilities as they flow through you.

### Beliefs of the Unity Consciousness
### Elemental energy

The unity consciousness is pure, universal energy. There is nothing concrete for our five senses to identify. It is the fertile field, the raw material of creation.....the fountainhead of existence. It is the alpha and omega. It is the OM. It is the All. It is the ultimate mystery, the beyond, the more.

Our acceptance that we are all made up of energy that we will never fully comprehend paves our way to connect with the unity consciousness. Everything that has form—brothers, tulips, puppies, rocks, Mars—are unique configurations of particles of this elemental energy. Its consciousness is the creative principle, the urge to experience, express and expand in infinite ways. Anything that we create into form has a place on this earth because of the expansive and inclusive character of the unity consciousness. Just this concept alone eradicates any self-doubt and personalization of events.

All of our creations are valued, and used for learning on every level of existence and beyond.

## Channeled by soul

The soul channels the unity consciousness through itself and then adapts it to vibrations that the Intuitive and Personality Levels can connect with. We can think of it as making sure the electrical current from two or more energy frequencies modulate so that one frequency doesn't blow out the wiring of the others. This soul flexibility changes and rearranges our energy field in order to accommodate new levels of consciousness.

Our lives in the Personality and Intuitive Levels have given us skills that serve us well in this new exploration of the unity consciousness. We need a strong sense of who we are. We are competent masters of our thoughts, emotions and behaviors. This creates a foundation for a sustainable connection to the unity consciousness. Yet we also know that surrendering our perspectives, thoughts, feelings, attachments, and identity when appropriate keeps us flexible to receive guidance from our intuition and soul. In short, our experiences provide a sense of peace with the choices we make for ourselves and an acceptance of who we have become and are becoming. Only then are we ready for our soul to connect us to the unity consciousness in the world of energy.

The power of the unity consciousness is profound. When our soul channels it, the foundation with which we are familiar is blown away. Our personal preferences, daily routines and relationships seem to fade into the background as we are focused on this shift into a higher level. While nothing destroys our past experiences and memories, they make way for the new. Therefore our "blown-away" foundation serves as a flexible structure for our soul to use, rearrange and expand as the unity consciousness remakes us through its expression. It is said in the Indian culture that Shamans, medicine men, can actually shift shape when connecting to spirit world. Their bodies change form from man to animal and other entities. This is a symbol of expressing the unity consciousness.

When the soul channels the unity consciousness and we are aligned with it on the Intuitive and Personality Levels, we experience a vast energetic shift. This brings a new perspective and consciousness that demands to express itself. Suddenly, our thoughts, feelings, and preferences are aligned with this soul-driven desire to create. I have experienced personally and have seen in my clients the effects of the shift of energy when connecting to the unity consciousness. Not only do beliefs, attitudes, responses and feelings change, but the physical form also changes. A nose isn't quite as prominent as it was; the skin glows and becomes more elastic, posture straightens, there is a spring to our step. We are more "energetic" and healthier.

People frequently are befuddled when interacting with others who are allowing the unity consciousness to be part of their lives. They see something is different, but they don't know what. They ask questions as they attempt to figure it out. "Did you lose weight? I like your new hairstyle. Is that a new outfit? You look so relaxed; where did you go? That color looks good on you. You look ten years younger." Truly we are different. The unity consciousness activates a vibration within us that physically alters our cells, organs and bodies. The changes are even more powerful in our unseen spiritual, mental, and emotional bodies.

## Check It Out!

**The unity consciousness expresses through the Soul Level of our four bodies. It is comprehensive in its effect. If we open our hearts and souls to this level, it penetrates any areas and configurations of energy we are holding onto in the conscious, subconscious, and unconscious levels that are not beneficial to our spiritual growth. We are penetrated and reconfigured by the power of our soul expressing the unity consciousness.**

- Do you respect yourself? Are you comfortable being you? Are your life and lifestyle authentic? How do you think and feel about who you have become?

- What are your concerns for yourself and others when you accept your ability to channel and interpret many different levels of consciousness?

- What is your concept of soul? How do you think it functions?

When we accept our co-existence in many levels of consciousness we are ready to align and merge with our soul. *Are you ready?*

## Universal perspective is created

Our desire to connect with the unity consciousness starts with the wish to live from a spiritual perspective. Imagine the possibilities that exist if all people in positions of authority–politicians, judges, corporate leaders/managers, religious leaders, fathers and mothers–made decisions from the unity consciousness perspective. They would create an environment that supports human development and encourages our expression as spiritual beings in which we can all attain the world of Unity Consciousness I described earlier.

This kind of perspective supports us to evolve into spiritual beings.

*Check It Out!*

**With the unity consciousness motivating us, we find new solutions. We stop repeating humanity's sad history in which certain individuals and nations abuse, rationalize and justify power to control others. We all know the sadness and tragedy of war.**

- Do we really need to hang onto the fears and beliefs that result in war?

- Can we justify excluding groups and nations of people from sharing the decisions that affect them?

- What is so precious about keeping the world order just the way it is?

**Unfortunately, those who don't want change try to convince those who do that chaos will reign if they tamper with the status quo. However, in the unity consciousness, change means transformation and evolution. There is always space for gathering new perspectives and guidance.**

- What fears do you have about personal and societal change?

- How are change and chaos perceived in your world?

- How does anxiety affect your attitude toward change?

Wondering how you can change your life so that you move toward being more authentic is a sign of opening to different consciousness levels.

## Detachment from the external world

We establish integration with the unity consciousness by detaching from the reactions and outcomes of events in the external world. But detachment is not about going to live on a mountaintop and having our food helicoptered in every month. Rather, it means that after fully participating in an experience, we then loosen the energy connections and reside within our own energy field once again–a fertile ground of inspiration and enlightenment.

We are able to detach from the external world when our internal world is strong and developed. This comes from our learning as we explore our personality, intuition, and soul. Detachment is the ability to choose to interact with people for stated intentions whether that means we're kicking back and relaxing or solving the world's problems.

While we process all experiences, our internal world is a self-created state that reflects the highest level of consciousness we understand. Being attached to the external world–friends, objects, and situations–puts us once again in the separation consciousness. Attachment is all about the beliefs that we have tried at the Personality Level such as judging, conditionality, using others to validate ourselves and.... Unfortunately, many people are caught in attachments that fuel their fears of loss, separation and unworthiness. But recognizing that we have everything we need inside ourselves allows for detachment.

## Integration of polarities

Polarization sets up an energy structure for exploring and experiencing possibilities and potential within a range of opposing ideas. If we know one perspective, we then can imagine its antithesis. One point helps create its polar opposite. The space between the two stances becomes an expression of their relationship. These points set up a design from which we identify variations within the energy structure and help contain the energy.

In the separation consciousness, polarities are limited to an either/ or mentality. One person has a definite position and anyone with a differing opinion is dead wrong. This creates opposition. At this level, needing to have the one right answer motivates behaviors. This strengthens a position which paradoxically reinforces the other side as well, creating a power struggle—a tug-of-war. Compromise is difficult and is used as a temporary strategy to maneuver toward the ultimate goal of having our perspective adopted as the "right way." Any shades of gray are dismissed—the center becomes a veritable no man's land. Safety in the separation consciousness comes with a definable position. Fear of losing ground prevents us from seeing the many opportunities for shared beliefs available in the connection consciousness.

However, at this next level, we welcome the guidance we receive from our intuition since it helps us to escape from our fixed perspectives. We may start from a polarized position and then dance between the polarities to learn self-mastery. Trying on new beliefs, thoughts, feelings and behaviors expands our repertoire of insights and provides avenues for growth. We are more willing to look for common ground and perceive that no man's land as fertile territory for shared possibilities. Indeed, when we tackle polarities from the unity consciousness, we may start at one point, but as we move to the other side, we find ourselves at a clearer consciousness level. We now have a new attitude, as we're perched at a higher plane from which to view the issue. As we continue surveying the situation from this higher level of consciousness, what initially seemed to be a linear, black-and-white question of right or wrong now becomes a ball of energy that includes every potential experience that might occur between the original polarities. This universal perspective includes the potential in every level of consciousness for every person who has ever and will ever live. It is the complete understanding of what is possible for us humans. Wow! The enormous task of identifying, processing, and exploring these infinite possibilities and variations is just too overwhelming to contemplate.

This kind of insight into the depth and scope of human behavior can only come from the Soul Level. But our lives are too short and our learning too slow to master the totality of even one polarity in a single lifetime. There are too many nuances and variations to consider.

Nevertheless, bringing in an alternative perspective from a higher consciousness level changes the dance. It is not a hop to one side or the other that we learned in the separation consciousness. Nor is it the expansive stretch to include all possibilities in the connection consciousness. Indeed, most of us will dance between the polarities we need in order to learn self-mastery at this level. At the unity level, the dance is actually creating possibilities from a different consciousness. While connecting with the unity consciousness how we dance, be it a waltz, quick step, or rumba will be determined by our soul.

This blended energy is contained in order to create configurations that allow us to understand and experience all the possibilities that can arise. This brings depth and scope to each energy field within every level of consciousness. To better grasp this concept, let's look at the polarity of fear and trust.

If we simply understand fear and trust without appreciating the nuances of these emotions or by using the tension of polar opposites, then we don't fully experience the possibilities of that continuum. We need to recognize the constructive and destructive aspects of each emotion.

Fear in its most constructive form slows us down and makes us become more objective and observant of our behavior and circumstances. We become more mindful of our intentions and what we choose to create. We look at the situation more profoundly and seek to recognize every element that may help us grow. We discern real obstacles versus fear-based feelings. This moves us to creatively decide how to handle the situation. If used in this way, fear supports us. On the other hand, if fear causes us to feel separated, prevents constructive action, causes self-sabotaging and hurtful behaviors, then it can hold us hostage and imprison our soul.

Using trust to keep our hearts open, no matter how difficult the circumstances, is constructive. This kind of trust allows us to stay connected to our soul and the higher levels of consciousness that provide support and guidance. It nurtures the thoughts, feelings, and behaviors that keep us moving and creating. However, if trust is blind, it leads us to hide behind hope and deny the reality of situation we are facing. Trust then intertwines with fear, leading to separation from our self which thwarts growth. We become stuck.

Our soul determines which piece of the ball of energy representing the polarity we must process for our development. We are bestowed with the wisdom of the totality of the ball to manifest our soul's expression. What a gift.

For us to live our potential and transform into a spiritual beings, the most important polarity to contemplate is that of separation and unity consciousness. The connection consciousness integrates these polar opposite perspectives. The soul is a representation of the unity consciousness, whereas the personality is the representation of the separation consciousness. Our intuition represents the connection consciousness, which integrates and supports our movement between the two. It's like baking a cake. Put some premises and affirming statements of trust in the bowl; flow feelings of hope and excitement; stir in a few grains of fear for discernment; and put it in your heart to blend and bake. See what comes out.

## Check It Out!

**Identify the polarities that you feel you have experience with and start integrating them.**

- What parts of your understanding that gave you insights beyond your actual experience come from the unity consciousness?

- What part of your life was created from the Soul Level in the unity consciousness? What does it feel like?

- What issues in your life are emotionally charged and causing you pain? What is the opposite polarity?

- What is your relationship to each side of the polarities?

- What is your present range of movement between the two points? Which polar point pulls you the most?

- What options can you create that integrate and lessen the range of movement between the polarities?

There is no judgment about polar opposites on a continuum. We just need to determine what range we want to dance within. Our soul provides alternatives we may never have thought about.

When our external and internal reality is congruent, we are truly connecting to the unity consciousness.

## Co-existence in Unlimited Consciousness Levels

To fully accept the premise that we co-exist in unlimited levels of consciousness, we must accept that the origin of form is energy. This must be part of our everyday thinking because it keeps our lives and intentions in context. We exist as energy, consciousness or essence as well as physical form. In fact, we exist as pure consciousness at the same moment that we exist in a physical form. This allows us unlimited possibilities. We function and express ourselves from different levels of consciousness as our soul creates various energy configurations to manifest a specific intent. Our physical form becomes a suit that our soul creates in order for us to participate in the separation consciousness as well as the other levels that don't have form. When we are creating from a certain level of consciousness and find ourselves without another alternative, or if we've exhausted the possibilities available from the level of consciousness we are aligned with, we move to the next higher level. This might be a shift within one of the three consciousness levels or from separation, to connection, to unity consciousness.

When we shift from one consciousness level to another to receive insights that we then turn into form we avail ourselves of unlimited resources. To make this shift takes both thoughts ("I am soul," "I AM," "I merge with my soul," "I choose to align with my soul," "I ask for soul vision," "I accept and receive my soul's wisdom") and feelings like courage, commitment, compassion and love. In combination, these move us to the Soul Level. The intention to actively align ourselves with the Soul Level dissolves the thoughts and feelings that hold us to a reality that is not true to our self. We are never stuck in only one reality. The more we are willing to try on the beliefs of our three levels of consciousness, the wider the scope within ourselves, the world, and the vast beyond.

Our heritage is co-existence in unlimited levels of consciousness.

## *Check It Out!*

**The acceptance of the unity consciousness allows us to trust in ourselves and in life since everything–bosses, oak trees, glaciers, and tigers–is created from the same elemental energy—only in different configurations.**

- How do you experience shifts into different levels of consciousness?

- What conditions in your life support you to be open and see your life and situations from different perspectives?

- From what level of consciousness have you created from? What did you learn?

- Where in your life do you create from the Soul Level?

- When are you pitched into a higher level of consciousness?

Check your attitudes and the conclusions that you have held for a long time. If you can identify the changes you made in your conclusions about yourself and others when you feel a connection to your soul, then the unity consciousness is a part of you.

## State of being

Being is a state of existence. It affirms that we are alive in the here-and-now. Expressing our individual reality is evidence of our existence. The journey to explore, align and merge our three levels of consciousness with their levels of expression–Personality, Intuitive and Soul–is unique to each person at the unity consciousness. At this level, we fashion our own reality by creating the internal state of being in which we chose to live.

The energy field of our internal reality emanates from us and magnetizes people, circumstances, opportunities, resources and timing that support our visions to come into form. These forms, along with our internal energy field represent our being's level of consciousness. Our energy then radiates out and affects energy fields around us. The degree to which it impacts those around is the degree by which we effect change. Change does not come immediately; it depends on the readiness of others. However, others register and connect to our energy at their Soul Level. It stays in their subconscious minds waiting for them to choose to interpret it. Of course, they may need to do personal work to remove any blocks that prevent them from connecting with their soul. Their own energy shift depends on their willingness to connect with their Soul and Intuitive Levels to utilize the consciousness that we transmitted through our energy field.

Beingness is an active state. We create joy, trust, compassion, courage, love, gratitude and grace from the unity consciousness. These are expressions of aliveness, heightened awareness and maximum sensuality. It is as if we are in the eye of the storm. No matter the circumstances around us, we recognize them as a configuration of many energy fields projected by everyone and everything that exists. As we look around our world, we observe the configurations that are being expressed.

People who believe in religious absolutism, rigid ideology, judgment, alienation, and hierarchy of authority figures are still testing and learning the consequences of these beliefs. As we know, these are some of the characteristics of the separation consciousness.

At the same time, we can observe configurations of energy expressed by the connection consciousness. We notice people who accept that no force in the external world can make them be anything other than whom they choose to be. As we accept this reality and utilize the beliefs of the connection consciousness, we can live our unique potential which is ignited by the soul. We can be an artist, inventor, entrepreneur, dancer, salesman, quantum physicist–anything that is true to our heart and soul. We can challenge failed ways of being in work or personal relationships and create new ones. It is our choice to learn from the separation consciousness and try out life from the connection and unity consciousness.

Our world is composed of people living from the three levels who are figuring out how our infrastructure of personality, intuition and soul operate. By interpreting higher levels of consciousness and bringing them into form, we actively contribute alternatives to how people choose to resolve problems. Killing other people isn't the best that spiritual beings can come up with. Raising our own consciousness level raises the levels of all, since our energy field radiates out and connects with like vibrations. We hope that through our own evolution we can offer another example to others to commit to utilizing their three levels of consciousness.

## Check It Out!

**From the perspective of the unity consciousness, we accept that lessons are being learned from all levels of consciousness. What is true for us is our Soul Level in the unity consciousness.**

- What is true for you?

- How do you create a space for yourself in chaotic situations?

- What do you do to create an energy field around you that supports communication with your Intuitive and Soul Levels

> while allowing participation in the circumstances that surround you?
>
> - What optimal conditions do you need to support your creation of a state of being that is right for you?

The state of being created in the unity consciousness is our core, our essence and our soul.

## Spiritual being

The most fundamental statement we make about ourselves is that we are souls. As such, we exist in the unity, connection and separation consciousness. Each of these levels has the potential of expressing our soul reality and connection to the unity consciousness. We need all the levels and the infrastructures that represent them to bring the energy of the soul into the form. Any action, thought, feeling and experience we have is an affirmation of our existence in one of the unlimited levels of consciousness in which we co-exist. Choosing to live from the unity consciousness aligns our Personality, Intuition and Soul Levels. Living from this merged perspective confirms our evolution from a human to a spiritual being who reflects and holds a universal perspective.

If we consider ourselves spiritual beings, then our perspective is a universal sense of self. We no longer perceive personal, community, state, national, international and intergalactic situations from an individual perspective. In the unity consciousness we are concerned about the commonalities and universal truths that apply to all of us. These are global patterns that the mass consciousness of man is working to resolve. The unity consciousness asks the question: What would serve mankind's highest good? That includes how we organize and distribute resources as well as the values we support for our survival, social needs and creative impulses.

I have travelled many places in the world while conducting spiritual psychology workshops. This put me in contact with many peoples. Listening to them, confirmed for me that when we connect as spiritual beings, we create the optimal conditions for growth and evolution.

However, even though the impulses that come from the unity consciousness dwell in a universal perspective, our efforts don't have to be worldwide. One client opened a hula school where she conveyed the spiritual teachings of the Hawaiian culture through the sacred movements of the dance. Her intention was clear and her heart was open to her soul. This made the energy field her students entered a sacred space. Another became a photographer. While shooting pictures, he was in a state of wonderment and love. His work inspires awe in all who see it. The clarity of our creative process to make form from soul energy raises the level of consciousness within the mass consciousness. Each one of us is extremely important.

We must choose to recognize the difference between the unity, connection and separation consciousness. Let's explore the concept of compassion to observe how it expresses itself differently at each level.

Compassion is a Soul Level emotion that expresses the unity consciousness. No matter how available or buried this emotion is, it resides in all humans. In fact, it is one emotion that describes our growth toward becoming spiritual beings. Compassion resides in the same emotional state as unconditional love. From a compassionate state we accept and love ourselves and others no matter the circumstances. We see the soul within others even though they express the darkest facets of their personalities. We see their light and hold it as a reflection for them in the hope that it will lessen the darkness.

Compassion means that we experience difficult situations in order to transform into spiritual beings who see life through a universal prism. We can bear witness to others, but we cannot shorten or lessen their suffering or even change their experiences. From the soul perspective, we emanate compassion. We do not want to diminish their experience and hence their learning. We remember that we are only experts in our own lives. Our compassion transmits from our soul to theirs. They may grow if they choose to connect with this higher level of consciousness. Empathy is the Intuitive Level of compassion. We understand what others are feeling—we share their emotions without creating them. While empathy can relieve the emotional pain for the moment it also keeps the person who receives our empathy susceptible to dependency on others to feel good. Empathy can interfere with growth if it is not used wisely. It's okay to support others as they explore their feelings, but it is not okay to wallow in them or believe that merely expressing them resolves an issue. This is only the first step.

On the Personality Level, compassion is expressed as sympathy. Ironically, this actually creates more problems than it solves. When we sympathize with someone, we feel their emotions since we are in agreement with them. But all this does is add our energy (of the painful feeling) to their energy field. So now we just have more hurt, rejection, and sadness energy around the hurting person. This intensification of sympathy makes a person stuck since it focuses on the pain.

## Check It Out!

**We are all capable of becoming spiritual by choosing the beliefs of the unity consciousness that support all.**

- Think of a time when you were in your spiritual being consciousness. What were you doing?

- How did it feel?

**Since living from the Soul Level in the unity consciousness is so abstract and can only be interpreted by ourselves, we can start our understanding by identifying our own definitions.**

- What do you perceive are the universal truths of man?

- From observing world events, what do you recognize are the issues we are working on?

- What is one universal perspective that you hold and live from?

- Who in the present or in history do you think worked from this universal perspective?

## Creative principle: creation and destruction

As quantum physics and nanotechnology advance, we are learning more about the profound effects of the manipulation of energy on forms. Energy itself is a form, but the one element that is at its base has yet to be identified. Energy and form represent yet another polarity that helps us understand the depth and scope of our existence. The continuum of consciousness between these points represents what is not and what is. And any point within can be in the separation, connection or unity consciousness. As we explore the unity consciousness through our soul, our understanding of energy increases. All energy is an impulse, constant movement, aliveness. This impulse is what keeps our heart beating, our lungs inhaling and our brains thinking. We are energy and contain the creative impulse in every fiber of our beings. We create our own reality. And with higher levels of consciousness we co-create what is and what will be. This is our potential for aliveness.

Creation and destruction are polar opposites. But at the unity level, "destruction" may not hold the same connotation that it would in the separation consciousness. Here, destruction allows for the constant movement of the cosmos. Energy is freed to reform at another level of consciousness. This polarity is the life of transformation. The forms that are created eventually are destroyed—the cycle of birth, death, and rebirth of all living things. While we cannot experience a cosmic or even a geological cycle within our lifetimes, we know that they still exist. As spiritual beings we grow as we create from our soul perspective. Creation brings us the fulfillment of using our potential. It is the gift we offer others. Once our learning is realized, it's time to let go, melt down the form and create again with a new configuration of energy, this time at a higher level of consciousness. Creation and destruction are at every level of consciousness since they are so fundamental to producing form from energy.

But whether our gift has a life of its own has nothing to do with us. Investment in sustaining what we create is part of the separation consciousness. The value of creating is what we learn in the process. Therefore we no longer need to sustain our creation. The pure joy of creating is the gift to our self. It aligns us with the unity consciousness. It keeps us moving: it is life: it is evolution.

> ## Check It Out!
>
> **Removing all the beliefs of the separation consciousness from your thinking will greatly enhance your creativity. Incorporating the connection consciousness beliefs will support your creativity. We are all capable of the joy of creating from the unity consciousness. Try it!**
>
> - How do you define creativity for yourself? What is your relationship to creativity?
>
> - What spoken or unspoken messages did you get from people in your past about your creativity?
>
> - Have you ever longed to create something? What was it? Why did you or why did you not do it?
>
> - What is your hope for your creativity?
>
> - What do you trust about your creativity?

When we understand that the unity consciousness is unlimited, this allows us to trust in life and in ourselves. We are the integrators among the consciousness levels. Our shifting reality and our ability to do this is the basis of our unlimited potential. We are both unrealized and manifested energy. The art of integrating and creating from energy is our purpose in life. The degree to which we do this is the degree to which we merge our three levels of consciousness.

## Moving From Separation to Connection to Unity

The separation consciousness is what is realized, the connection consciousness is what is possible, and the unity consciousness is potential waiting for interpretation and form.

The external world is a laboratory that provides opportunities for us to decide how we want to be in relationship to everything around us. We choose our intentions, beliefs and actions. We observe what exists and then decide how to respond. This enables us to understand how our beliefs create our reality. We live a multitude of experiences that help us clarify and modify our perspectives. Creating our lives through conscious choices allows us to try on and live from different levels of consciousness.

As we progress in learning from the separation and connection consciousness toward unity, we grasp the available possibilities and experience the gift of life. We even come to appreciate the necessity of learning from the separation consciousness. A mirror that reflects what we recognize about ourselves on conscious and unconscious levels, it supports us to understand how our reactions to the world of form have created our beliefs, feelings, and behaviors. Continuing on our journey, we enter the connection consciousness and develop intuition—and the beginnings of an internal reality. As we acquire self-mastery and self-authority, we rejoice in our innate ability to freely create our lives.

Then, through experience, we accept that our lives are based on our internal reality. We react and respond to the world outside from this perspective–no person or external force is doing anything to us. Indeed, our reactions provide a playing field upon which to understand our psyches. But our ability to shape this internal perspective which then affects our external lives becomes more real to us as we move through the separation and connection consciousness. We are then ready to understand and develop our creative abilities by merging with our souls.

Aligning with the unity consciousness means that we have accepted that our internal and soul realities are one. One becomes an expression of the other. The purest interpretation of the unity consciousness demands that it be through the Soul Level, which has no attachment to the external world created by the collective unconsciousness. Although creativity is a part of all levels of consciousness, at the unity level, what is created (whether it's a technological advancement, an artistic expression or a physical feat) comes from our soul intention. Therefore, it is profound and acts toward the betterment of mankind. Humanity can recognize such creations as genius. However, our innovations may also be so unique and enlightened, that society may not fully understand or accept them.

When the soul energy flows completely through the Personality and Intuitive Levels, it shapes them. Our individual perspective ceases to exist and is only activated in those particular areas that we need to bring through its representation and creative flow.

The reality we experience when we are living from the unity consciousness is different than that of our everyday lives. Indeed, connection to the unity consciousness as our creativity flows is often described as being inspired by the muses. Writers, artists, and inventors–all those who create from an internal perspective and allow a uniqueness to come from within–know how this altered state feels. They lament when they cannot reconnect to the flow and despair when the connection fades. And, of course, they rejoice and feel that fortune smiles on them when they are in the zone once again.

Whatever is created from the unity consciousness raises the vibration of the mass consciousness. Think of Pascal, Socrates, Michelangelo, Tesla, Archimedes, and Boyle. All of these geniuses opened up to the unity consciousness in their own ways. No matter how they identified it, they trusted this connection to flow through them and the activate parts of themselves that expressed their connection to the unity consciousness through their soul. They tapped into raw potential and shaped it.

It brings such joy to know that each of us, through our willingness to accept our internal reality, surrender to our soul, and clear limitations, can also connect to the unity consciousness and become creators of unlimited potential. When we acknowledge the geniuses of the world for their achievements, we are also acknowledging that each has brought the unity consciousness into the mass consciousness. This kindles the realization that this level of creation is within us as well.

Life is the context in which we experience the worlds of form, symbol, and energy. It is the framework for an energy field that was created from a particular level of consciousness. Some parts of this are seen in the world of form, whereas others are unseen. We are integrators among the unmanifested consciousness levels and those that are manifested. This shifting reality and our ability to alter consciousness levels is the basis of our potential. We are both unmanifested and manifested energy. The art of integrating and creating from energy is our purpose in life.

> ## Check It Out!
>
> **When we connect with the connection consciousness we get glimpses of our potential. What can be isn't a walk through fantasyland but a vision for us to manifest.**
>
> - What is within you that yearns to be expressed? What do you perceive is possible in your life? What do you perceive is your potential? What do you recognize as your potential?
>
> - Is something is in the way of that expression? If so, what is preventing you from aligning with the unity consciousness?

Deciding to live what you know you are capable of means that you need to deal with any obstacle to manifesting your potential. Review the beliefs of the separation consciousness and check if any of those are the boulders in your way. Then substitute a belief from the connection consciousness to change your perspective. This process to clear limitations that prevent you from using your potential is worth the effort. Feeling the transcendence of living from your soul is beyond description. Experience it for yourself!

## Chapter Eight Exploration and Discovery Activities

### Points to Ponder
**What do you think and feel about the following statements?**

- Acknowledgement of God, the unity consciousness, and all forms that refer to a Higher Being is based on the acceptance that some grand design which has a natural order is greater than our self and our understanding of the world and cosmos beyond.
- Anything that we create has a place on the earth because of the expansive and inclusive character of the unity consciousness.
- We are penetrated and reconfigured by the power of our soul expressing the unity consciousness.

- The separation consciousness is what is realized. The connection consciousness is what is possible, and the unity consciousness is potential waiting to be interpreted and formed.
- We create the emotional state we choose to reside in. No matter what is happening around us, we create our own space.

**Use the continuum between separation and unity consciousness below to chart the range you are living now. Reflect on changing decisions in your life. Where would you put them on the continuum?**

Separation              Connection              Unity

# Chapter Nine

**The Soul Level as a Reflection of the Unity Consciousness**

The ways of the soul are mysterious, magical, and elusive, yet at the same time specific. The soul sees the bigger picture and is an active co-creator in expressing the unity consciousness. It is versatile, magnificent, ever changing, existing in levels of consciousness that never may be known to us and yet are so available to us. Our soul and we are one in the unity consciousness. The Soul Level is our hope for mankind—the next step in our evolution.

Our souls hold the most expansive consciousness available to us. They are energy apparatuses that connect to specific levels of consciousness. They format and configure energy for us so that we can interpret and implement their wisdom in our everyday world.

Here is a good way to visualize this concept: Pretend you are a small circle on a piece of lined paper. Randomly make dots on several horizontal lines that represent different levels of consciousness. Connect the dots to the circle. Now connect the dots to each other. The energy created by this configuration of dots linked to each other and to the circle represents a specific consciousness. The energy within this shape is the full potential. The mixture of different levels of consciousness and how we integrate, internalize and express their wisdom makes us unique spiritual beings.

At this level of growth, we accept that we are our soul, and our soul is us. We dance among the three levels of consciousness and trust that our Soul choreographs the dance to suit the task we focus on. This is the miracle, wonder and potential of human existence. While we are human beings we are also spiritual beings. We can choose to live from the soul perspective with every thought, feeling and behavior. Everything we do can represent the Soul Level in the unity consciousness.

Our soul is a container for all of our experiences as human and spiritual beings and whatever other forms we experienced in this cosmos. It activates and structures our Intuition and Personality Levels to prepare the lessons we need to learn. Our job in life is to merge with our Soul Level, so that our Intuitive and Personality Levels become the structure through which it expresses itself in our physical existence. In common terms, we can call this: "becoming who we are meant to be," "loving what we do," "being guided by destiny," "expressing our unique potential," "living our bliss," and "finding our calling."

Since the soul is timeless, it allows us to grow at our own pace, knowing that all experiences are valuable and worthwhile as we learn about our potential. Free will at this point in our journey means limiting our life experiences in the patriarchal world of form (the separation consciousness) and choosing to listen to the songs of our soul that inspire us to live in accord with all aspects of our potential. It means living in harmony with all living things, earth, our fellow man, and spirit forces.

The energy that the soul configures is constantly rearranging itself, depending on the present moment—the eternal now. Past and future do not affect it. Time belongs only to the separation consciousness. That is why it is so important for us to live by our intuition and allow our soul to form our personality; we need all of our abilities to express our souls in our physical existence. *What skills are you willing to offer to your soul for use in creating a Soul Level vision? What talents are you willing to develop for your soul to use? When have you felt an inner shift to a higher consciousness? What calls to you now?*

We do not know the soul's limits or its vastness. Many religions teach about certain levels of the soul and their specific functions. I prefer not to label something our rational minds cannot fully understand. Instead, descriptions of the unity consciousness allow all of us our own experiences. Who among us can be the experts on the totality of soul consciousness? We are only authorities for our own realities. However, as we all share our experiences, we glimpse more of the soul. That is as good as it gets. We know viscerally and cerebrally when we are operating from the soul. No one needs to sanctify or verify our experience. It is personal and life-altering.

The effects of our soul consciousness express themselves in every aspect of our lives. When we are attuned to the soul, everything–from the color of the clothes we wear to how we design our home—matters, for our internal and external worlds at this level represent each other.

The soul expresses itself through our four bodies as we create form from consciousness. Our spiritual body receives the revelations from an energetic perspective. We feel currents, subtle energy shifts of consciousness that are sublime. Connections to our unconscious minds and other consciousness levels make us view the physical and non-physical world differently. Our mental body has an inner eye that sees visions and symbols, as well as a sense of knowingness. We then use our imagination and creativity to make meaning from these symbols and visions. Our emotional body experiences our soul through feelings that uplift and fortify us. And our physical bodies hold the consciousness of our soul in the cellular memory that we interpret through instinct. We feel energy shifts in our internal reality when the soul is adapting a level of consciousness for us to interpret.

## Check it out!

**Looking back and reviewing the changes in our attitudes demonstrate our commitment to growth as we mature spiritually.**

- What obstacles and limitations did you overcome? What events were painful yet offered you learning opportunities? What did you learn from them?

- As you have grown spiritually, what behaviors can you now recognize were good intentions that didn't help the situation?

- What image did you have of a spiritual person? What does it mean to you now to be a spiritual being?

- What thoughts and feelings activate when you ponder the fact that the soul and you are one?

- Who in your life would object to that? Why?

### *Living in the State of Trust*

Living at the Soul Level means permanent residency in the state of trust. This translates to certain premises that we live by with certainty.

- We are soul and soul is us.
- We are life and life is us.
- We are creators and co-creators at all three levels of consciousness.
- We make a difference by our existence.
- We are spiritual beings in an ever-expanding spiral of evolution.
- We are integrators of spirit and matter.
- We discover ways to manifest endless possibilities.
- We are channels for the transcendent.

As we live from these premises, they shape our perspective and worldview.

Trust at the Soul Level is the foundation for living as a spiritual being. Without it, we can easily pitch back into the Personality Level and the psychology of fear. When we live from the Soul Level in a state of trust, everything we do is sacred. We are open channels for the transcendent.

This state of trust expresses itself as specific thoughts and feelings that shape our Intuitive and Personality Levels.

The state of trust has several functions at the Intuitive Level:

- It activates the courage so that we can live from the unseen world of symbols.
- It supports self-trust as we gain self-mastery and self-authority.
- It eliminates our need to know and to see results from every action.
- It supports us in living in the present.
- It emphasizes valuing the process of creativity.

At the Personality Level, the psychology of trust supports the development of competency and self-confidence. We accumulate experiences and skills that when accepted, developed, and integrated, set a firm foundation from which we can express our Intuitive and Soul Levels.

> ## Check It Out!
>
> **Trust ignites all expressions of the Soul Level. With trust we love, are compassionate, have courage, show humility, are committed, exude joy, focus our power and light, and demonstrate gratitude. Trust is the great connector and initiator.**
>
> - What is your relationship to trust? How does it support you?
> - What spiritual beliefs do you trust in?
> - Looking back at your spiritual development, what beliefs about trust changed?

Trust in a belief is similar to a support system as it keeps the clarity of our intentions in the fore. Check to see if you feel viscerally and cerebrally what you trust in. If you don't, then talk with your four bodies to find any incongruencies among them.

## The Purpose of the Soul

The creative principle is the underlying common bond among all living things. From the various worldwide creation myths to our projections of God and Supreme Being as a creator, we reference our accomplishments and the worth of our lives from what we have created. Indeed, we are living in a cosmos that is the creative principle in action. Being creators of our own lives, creating life and being creative are inherent to us.

*The purpose of the soul is to present us with opportunities from which we can learn in order to become the creators we are meant to be.*

Creativity not only assures our survival, it validates that we exist. And as we express our creativity, we become familiar with its reciprocal nature. What we create supports life, and life supports us. An exchange of awareness takes place in the process. It's like a brainstorming session. One possibility ignites another, which then ignites another–and on and on. Creating from the soul expands consciousness, which supports evolution. It is a celebration of life, the human spirit, and man's potential.

The need to create exists in all consciousness levels, and what we create represents the consciousness level in which we choose to live. It acts as a mirror of our progression toward becoming spiritual beings. When our Personality, Intuitive and Soul Levels are out of alignment, we create only from the consciousness level in which we reside at in any moment. And usually nothing is accomplished if we don't sustain an energy field long enough to bring it into form.

In the Personality Level we create by imitation. Our inventions reinforce what is already in existence. They are dominated by the demands of institutions in which we live and our own striving for personal power and are subject to all of the beliefs of the separation consciousness–appraised for monetary worth. If the elite (whoever is valued, such as critics, media, or other authority figures) judge our creations favorably, many others will seek out our creations.

When we choose to create from the Intuitive Level, our creations are inspired from our desire to express our authentic selves and to join with others for a common cause–we manifest from a bigger picture that has value to us personally as well as to others. Although these impulses come from within, they expand our perspective. We experience this when we solve a problem in a team meeting, find the reason for the inconsistent performance of a software game we originated, conceive a new way to teach word problems to eighth-graders, design an appliance that is both beautiful and efficient, or write a screenplay whose theme is courage. The Intuitive Level provides us with personal growth through our creativity.

At the Soul Level, we are co-creators. Our energy and creativity come from the unity consciousness–a universal perspective. At this level, the personality is malleable and uses abilities and talents as necessary. We all know of astonishing feats that occur at the Soul Level. For instance, compelled to put hands on his wife's pregnant belly as she was starting to miscarry, a geologist was startled and humbled when he stopped the bleeding and healed her. Receiving abstract and specific messages from the soul and acting on them moves us out of all personal thoughts and feelings. Accepting that we are soul and soul is us provide the freedom to act on soul messages and directives without self-doubt or judgment. At the Soul Level, we are messengers to individuals, groups and humanity at large. Our message is part of the next step in humanity's evolution. Here, our creations are channeled from a transcendent, universal perspective.

*Check It Out!*

**The ramifications and potential to expressing our soul are endless. We need to look inside ourselves and give space, silence, and time to listen to the exquisite song that originates in our soul.**

- How do you honor yourself by recognizing that you are a creator?

- How do you facilitate your understanding that you are soul?

## Defining Questions

### How can I serve my fellow man and earth?

In the Personality Level, we believed that the source of personal power was our will. We created a life based on external values. In the Intuitive Level, we unite our personal power and will with self-trust and trust in the beliefs of the connection consciousness. We create lives based on internal values. Both levels taught us about power. Merging with our Soul Level means accepting ourselves as spiritual beings. We trust ourselves with power and never fear abusing it. Role, gender, age, religious and cultural identifications are meaningless. We are no longer seduced by the external world. We are in accord with our species in our place on this earth in this universe. Our motivation becomes, "What can I do to serve my fellow humans and serve this earth?" Once we take the arduous journey to connect, align and merge with our souls, creating becomes a joyous experience.

As we expand our consciousness, there will always be space to bring this wisdom into form. All levels of existence expand through the creative principle. We are in this evolution together, whether we are human, animal, the earth, planets, stars, the universe and beings without form.

From the soul perspective (which is to serve our fellow man and the earth), we must produce the conditions for individuals to grow. This means living the principles of the unity consciousness in our everyday lives. If we are in a conference with our business associates and our soul guides us to speak, we must. The soul knows the synchronicities of the situation. What we say could be a spark for change.

As we live from a soul perspective and express the beliefs of the unity consciousness, our creations are gifts to be offered. We are ready to present alternatives to problems that society faces. The reality that corporations and other businesses must make a profit to survive is not the issue. The differences between living from the unity and separation consciousness is the beliefs upon which the premises of the business is based. *What are the intentions of businesses? What responsibilities do they have for using natural resources? Can businesses care for the environment that supports us as people? How can we as individuals and collectively support the business world to earn a profit, provide jobs, and also have a social conscience? What attitudes need to be embraced? How can businesses make products that respect the earth? What work environments are needed to invest in human resources?*

Incorporating more connection consciousness beliefs while loosening the hold of the separation consciousness is the basis for creating a new reality which allows for the evolution of man. This can only happen from the inside out. When we experience the vitality and authenticity that come from our connection to our intuition and soul, we are compelled to apply these in all areas of life. Whether we are a secretary, janitor, or the president of a company, when we live from the intuitive and soul perspective, we can create lives based on unity consciousness beliefs. We become the living testimony that there is always another way.

It's time for those who connect to the Intuitive and Soul Levels to trust the values from these corresponding levels of consciousness. Every word we speak in our professional and personal lives must represent our relationship to our Soul Level. That affords the best possibility to take the next steps in the evolution of man and our world.

## Check It Out!

**Our institutions sustain values that diminish the human experience instead of supporting it. It is time to trust living from values such as courage, commitment, trust, compassion, humility and joy that are all part of the soul perspective.**

- What truths do you hold in your heart? What have you done about them?

- How can you identify with the concept of being a universal, spiritual being?

- Accepting that you are soul, what changes will you make in your life?

- How do you support life? How does life support you?

**Each day we are responsible for our behaviors and what they contribute to the mass consciousness. Use the questions below to determine what you contributed.**

- Did we live the values that we say are important to us?

- What consciousness level did we create from?

- Did our Personality, Intuitive and Soul Levels align?

- Were our four bodies congruent? Why or why not?

Making changes in this world starts with everyday decisions. We must check whether these decisions represent the Soul Level and are authentic to our alignment with our personality, intuition and soul. We need to put into organizational structures the vision, premises and procedures that support us to live from a soul perspective in all of our institutions as well as in our individual lives.

## How can I live from my Soul Level perspective?

Living from our Soul Level perspective means living in this world without defenses. We possess a connection to our intuition for guidance. Also, through experiences, we have a foundation of self-trust and trust in our co-existence at different levels of consciousness. No matter what life presents, we have the ability to respond. This allows full participation in life. Staying in the now, trusting the process of creation, choosing which state of being in which we wish to live, committing to discover who we are meant to be, and desiring to serve humanity are all necessary components. At this level, we know the answer to, "What is enough?" We manage our spiritual, emotional, physical, and mental bodies in an authentic lifestyle. This allows us flexibility to fully express our Soul Level.

Surrendering to my soul perspective led me to walk many different paths. I have been a stockbroker, eighth-grade teacher, school counselor, business consultant, Marriage and Family Therapist, spiritual advisor, soul reader, spiritual psychology workshop leader, and author. Each of these forms of creativity had a specific focus and message. However, underlying all the messages (which were spoken in vocabularies appropriate for each audience), were the beliefs of the connection and unity consciousness. No matter what the situations and circumstances we are in, no matter how many personas we need to adapt to in order to deliver our message, our essence *is* soul–the consciousness of unity.

The degree to which we integrate and apply the characteristics of the separation, connection, and unity consciousness is the same degree to which we fully develop the potential of our personality, intuition and soul. However, it is at this Soul Level that we are most aware that we coexist in three level of consciousness. While we are washing the dishes, our soul still sends us messages. As we talk with others, we still listen to our soul voice. All three consciousness levels, and the realities we create from them, are operative at all times, even as one level may be more dominant (depending on the agenda at hand). The eternal now is constantly in accord with our soul, and it discerns when and what to respond to.

We must remember that even though we may be connected to someone from the Soul Level, it does not mean that everyone chooses to be connected to their soul. Nevertheless, I trust that what comes through me emerges from my soul. It is an exchange from the connection between my soul and that of the other. For instance, Frank's soul might tell mine that only by raising my voice would he pay attention to what I am saying. It's almost like being an actor; the soul essence is within me as I act out an emotion. Our soul helps us express all emotions in ways that others can receive them. In this situation, my soul is supporting Frank's efforts to ignite an awakening. If it were left to me, I would not raise my voice. Yet I know that as it gets sterner, louder, and I use direct communication and intense eye contact, my behavior is still coming from a soul vibration of love and compassion. Both my soul and Frank's understand what will work best far better than I do at the Personality Level. There are always opportunities for opening, and souls always use what is available to help us to grow.

When we merge our personality and intuition with our soul agenda, the soul uses our personality in the most effective way. Our messages may be inspirational, emphatic, didactic, emotional or even neutral. We must trust that what is channeled through our souls to our intuition and personality is what needs to be said and acted upon. Our soul is connected to the souls of all the people with whom we communicate at any moment. They work together for a common purpose. This interaction is part of a bigger picture.

## *Check It Out!*

**To discern when we are living from our Soul Level purposes, we must reflect on our intentions and identify which beliefs of the unity consciousness are operational in our lives. Use the questions below to help you to determine if are living from your Soul Level perspective. As you ponder your responses, look for the beliefs of all three levels of consciousness.**

- What are your intentions?

- What are your motivations?

- Do you have a personal agenda, a desired outcome?

- What are your personal needs? How will they be satisfied? How will you chose to satisfy them?

- What is the gain for you and others?

- What purposeful behavior did you create and put into action?

- What is in front of you?

- What do the intuitive messages from your four bodies tell you?

- How are you interpreting the signs you are given?

- Are your internal and external realities in alignment?

- Are you seeing movement? (circumstances, opportunities, changing and rearranging)

- How are you using fears and doubts? (At this level these act as reminders to make us check out our intuition in all four bodies.)

- Are you listening with your internal ear at all times? (We can be fully participating and keeping our internal ear open at the same time. That is one of the many benefits of coexisting in different levels of consciousness.)

- How does this serve humanity and/or the world?

- Does this align with the truth, as you perceive it from your soul?

- Do your actions promote self-respect and a feeling of authenticity?

- What level of consciousness are you living in? Are the conditions and premises from that level operational in your life? Are they operational in your four bodies?

- What is your connection to those who have power in this situation?

- Does your compassion for others facilitate connections?

- How do you express respect for your opponents as fellow human beings with a right to their perspective?

- How do you demonstrate flexibility and inclusiveness of others' ideas?

- How do you create connections among people of different consciousness levels?

- Does it open your heart?

- Does it bring joy?

## How can I channel the transcendent radiance?

Channeling the transcendent radiance of the unity consciousness comes from the commitment to live a spiritual life and attain the wonderment of becoming who we are meant to be. It is the tapping into the potential of humankind and creating possibilities to bring into some kind of form. For this to happen, our lifestyles support us to live the beliefs of the unity consciousness.

Below are three attitudes that support unity consciousness-living.

### Trust.

Living in the unity consciousness means that no attachments, obligations, or personal agendas supersede the messages our soul gives us. Trust fortifies us to intuitively know that the circumstances and opportunities in front of us constitute our direction. For instance, I was scheduled to give a spiritual psychology workshop in Delphi, Greece. Fifty-two Swiss and German people signed up and were eager to attend. But then the first Gulf War broke out. I am an American. My husband vehemently opposed my traveling to Europe because of the possible danger. I felt his displeasure. I spent time in my Intuitive and Soul Level perspectives, checked the congruency within my four bodies, felt the readiness in the souls of those signed up for the workshop, and reviewed my intentions and motivations. I knew that I needed to go. I approached my husband in a state of love and looked him in the eye. I told him, "This is something that came from my soul. I must go." I also heard a voice in my mind that clearly said I would be protected. Trust sustained me as I spoke my truth to my husband. He embraced me and told me that he loved me. The day before I left, the war ended. The workshop fulfilled the intentions of all the souls who gathered there. This is a trust in the soul and the unity consciousness.

## Check It Out!

At this Soul Level, there is no need for validation of who we are. Those issues were taken care of in the Intuitive Level when we claimed our self-mastery and self-authority. We trust that the circumstances and people we meet are meant to be. We do not need be validated in order to feel the rightness, joy and satisfaction of the part we play in the cosmic drama. We simply trust.

- What is appearing in your life right now that is flowing without using your personal will and power?

> - What are you working hard at to make it happen?
>
> - How do you feel when things just flow?
>
> - What are your thoughts when you are in the "making-it-happen" mode? What does it feel like? What is right in front of you?

### Staying balanced.

Staying balanced means taking care of the needs of our four bodies at all times so that one doesn't hijack the other. Consistent practice turns monitoring our thoughts, feelings, behaviors and beliefs into an automatic process. It is our responsibility to make any adjusts that ensure all are in alignment with the Soul Level. From this comes the authenticity that allows our internal and external worlds to remain balanced. Balance supports us to live in our own energy field, be receptive to our soul, and consequently live in the flow. If we become too emotionally charged, too attached to some ideology, too needy or dependent on others, we don't feel our Soul and Intuitive Levels. The best way to stay balanced is to do what I call "trench work." This entails becoming familiar with how we were trained to react to and be in relationship with our parents and caretakers. We then make conclusions about what those experiences were like for us. This reference point, conditioning model, then influences all of our other relationships. Any conclusions we draw that make us feel unworthy and unlovable are distortions from those that reside in the fear of the separation consciousness.

In the Intuitive Level, we are responsible to clear those erroneous conclusions. Because we are committed to self-authority at this level, we examine the belief systems and experiences that influence us. As we make interpretations of the symbols and images that are available at the Intuitive Level we must be vigilant that the effects of our conditioning model are not a part of the interpretation process. Our personal filters can easily get entwined when we use our Personality Level for the implementation of our visions. Asking the hard questions is essential.

Feeling the sense of rightness of what we are doing affords a sensitivity that stops any pollution from leaking into our thoughts, feelings and behaviors. It's also vital to ask ourselves what belief an action or behavior represents. To have authentic feedback from our four bodies in our three infrastructures, we must know what each contributes. What are the attitudes and opinions of all parts of us? When we align all parts then we are balanced, and life is filled with grace. The work at the Personality Level provides the stability for the Intuitive Level and Soul Level to express themselves through us.

Unfortunately, I have worked with people who have announced themselves as spiritual, but were confused that their lives were not what they wanted. All of these people tapped into their Intuitive or Soul Level and felt the joy of these connections. However, they could not sustain living from those perspectives because they had no foundation from which to deliver the wonderful insights they'd received. Their fear of failure, self-doubt, fear of intimidation, or other personality issues sabotaged their attempts to bring into their lives the higher levels of consciousness to which they temporarily connected.

Our three levels of consciousness need to become real to us. That is why we must consciously know and implement the beliefs of the consciousness levels we chose to live and create from. We need experience in deliberately and consistently accessing our Intuition and Soul Levels. Trying to bypass one of our levels only brings disappointment, despair, depression, hurt, and anger. Think of Icarus attempting to fly to the sun with wings he had fashioned of wax and feathers. When we connect to our soul, we feel transcendent. However, the heat of the soul burns off what is not real. If we don't have solid support systems that we have created in advance with the guidance of our soul, we are going to crash and burn.

## Check It Out!

**The work of our Personality Level is to use our skills, talents and abilities to create forms that represent the consciousness level our souls are connected to. Clarity of our personal issues and the degree to which we do our trench work directly affects the clarity of interpreting the consciousness level we are creating from. If we do not master and manage our Personality Level, then our interpretation from the Intuitive and Soul Level will be distorted.**

- How did you get attention from your parents and/or caregivers when you were a child?

- What are some of the patterns of behavior in your family of origin that are similar to your present family? Have you ever heard your mother and/or father in your own voice or the words you use?

- Have you been in a situation that started with a lofty ideal but ended with people acting from their Personality Level? What happened?

- How do you keep yourself connected to your Intuitive and Soul Level throughout the process of vision to implementation? How and when do you check in with yourself?

## *Developing a consistent soul alignment.*

Our ever-developing spiritual identity is the main event and core in our lives. Our soul is the most constant and everlasting part of us. To become spiritual beings, everything we do, say and feel must be authentic and mindful. Being who we are meant to be is a lifelong journey and not a passing fancy. I have worked with clients who were excited by the concept of coexisting at different levels of consciousness and merging with their soul—until they had to make the first change in their lives. "Maybe I don't need to worry about my marriage." "Who has time to do trench work?" "I don't want to dredge up that stuff! It happened so long ago." "It will never work anyway!" Suddenly, personal growth and spirituality were relegated to "when I have time" or "as soon as things settle down ... at work, home, with my partner, with my sick mother . . ."

Consistently living from our Soul Level is the main event in our lives. Turning on and off the connection to the soul is extremely difficult on the physical body. Our bodies respond to our beliefs and internal reality. Switching levels of consciousness means that you are switching different realities. It takes time for the body to process, adapt and respond.

## Check It Out!

**Distraction occurs when our four bodies begin to work on their own agendas and are not focused on the task at hand. Tension in the body is an easy tip-off that we are in this state of confusion. Recognizing the first signs of stress helps us to check in with ourselves and manage what is causing the distraction. We must assess what it is about. It may be from unresolved issues that are presenting opportunities for growth or it may be a thought or feeling that needs to be explored. The real message is: stop and clarify. Don't keep moving like a bulldozer. You might be destroying or hiding what you need.**

- How does your body react when you go through the varied stages of change? What do you need to support it?

- How do you approach an unforeseen problem? How does it make you feel?

- What can your four bodies do to balance and support each other to say in alignment with the Soul Level?

## Motivating Impulse
## Soul Merge

Soul merge means living from the awareness that we are soul and soul is us. When we align our Personality and Intuitive Level with our Soul Level, and consistently focus and utilize our three levels of consciousness, we are merging with our soul. This is the main event! Our realization that the soul is the highest level of consciousness within us becomes a tipping point. We are soul and soul is us because soul consciousness is our potential, our ability to create from the most expansive perspective possible for us in this physical existence.

The rewards are wonderful: being who we are meant to be, living at the highest level of consciousness available to us, channeling the transcendent, and creating a form to represent the level of consciousness we are connected to at any given moment. To be able to create our beliefs, thoughts, feelings and actions from this rarified state of illuminated consciousness is pure joy. It brings wonderment into form.

### Soul Theme

Each of us is given a soul theme. This is the path from which we frame our soul journey. Our soul selected our place of birth, parents, gender, nationality, circumstances, race and time in the evolution of mankind. We were born into this specific energy field that provides us opportunities to learn about our soul theme—the context and focus of this life's learning. If we study our own histories and ask what we have learned from our lives, a theme readily emerges. Our experiences give us ample opportunities to learn more about this theme. It is energized through the circumstances in our family of origin.

For instance, maybe we are prone to being courageous. This is a gift we can use to help with our learning in other areas. Or maybe our soul theme in this life is integration. We may then be plagued by the perspective of either/or thinking so that we can recognize its consequences. We may choose other possibilities like "and" rather than "or." Sometimes things go one way, *and* at other times they go a different way. This softens the either/or trap and creates a third or even many perspectives. We learn how to integrate our four bodies; our personality, intuition, and soul; the differences among religions, and the rigid perspectives people hold about nationalities, gender, and race.

If "connection" is our soul theme, we explore relationships to understand the effects of connecting from different levels of consciousness and clarifying what connection means in relationships. If it is "radiating energy," we learn about the effects of using power in abusive, intrusive, controlling, supportive, loving and creative ways.

To truly understand the theme, we need a multitude of perspectives. Fortunately, humanity is working on many different soul themes at once, so we are connected at the Soul Level to all the other souls on this planet who are developing the same theme. Each is investigating a specific part. Through our soul, we intuitively communicate our learning and transfer information and wisdom among energetic links. The degree to which we connect to our Intuitive and Soul Levels is the same degree to which we benefit from this group soul focus. We really don't have to learn all lessons by ourselves. We are connected! And at some point, there is resolution and clarity. This comes from the collective experiences of all the souls who wrestle with a common soul theme.

If we do not grow in our soul theme, our lives become difficult. But if we take responsibility to learn from our challenges, our lives become joyous. The soul theme is the most challenging and rewarding aspect of life. It is the main focus of the soul and therefore the most energized aspect of our lives.

*Check It Out!*

**Let the follow questions support you to determine what your soul theme is. You are exploring and investigating your soul theme in all aspects of your life. So if you have problems in relationships (a "connection" theme) then you would need to look at relationship issues at work, home, with friends, partners, children and yourself to name a few.**

- In what areas in your life have you felt the most pain? What areas are difficult for you?

- What areas in your life provide the most lessons for you? What are your reoccurring issues?

- Where in your life do you put in the most energy? When you reflect on the most important lessons you've learned what theme emerges?

## Creating

Creating is the process of transforming energy into form or matter. It occurs at every level of existence. It is inherent and consistent. We are creators and also co-creators. As creators, we manifest from our sphere of interest, focus and influence. If we are quantum physicists, our Intuitive Level supports us as insights come more easily, especially if we are already interested in a certain topic on the Personality Level. Functioning in our everyday lives while simultaneously interpreting soul messages becomes second nature to us as we become more flexible in our ability to rearrange our focus from Personality to Intuitive and Soul Levels. We can switch from one level of consciousness to the other without losing who we are. We create the state of being that best reflects our Soul Level at any moment. That is why we are capable of sustaining our Soul Level mission and still mow the lawn, wash the clothes and enjoy a glass of wine.

Our inherent desire to create is the facilitator to our soul mission and the glue that keeps all parts of us together as they reveal themselves. We don't need the drama of having to lock ourselves in our room for seven days to write or paint or ... and ignore or avoid our families.

Creating is a natural state. Therefore, we are capable of being balanced while we create. Staying balanced by taking care of our four bodies during the creative process supports our mission. It takes a great deal of soul energy to keep all parts of us connected and focused, especially if one body dominates the others. When we become unbalanced we may think we are responsible for how others accept our work, develop a messiah complex, or take ourselves too seriously. Whatever activates inside of us increases our vulnerability to distort the message and in the end bungle the implementation of our dreams. If we continue to trust that our soul is who we are, it allows the soul room to maneuver.

## Check It Out!

**The foundation of a flexible and soul-aligned Personality Level is essential for creating from the unity consciousness.**

- What message did you receive from your soul that directed you? What soul messages have you implemented in your life? Have you been compelled to do something? How did it turn out?

- What happens to your creative process from vision to completion? At what point, if any, does your creative process become distorted or derailed? At what point in the implementation process is there a tendency to allow the personality to dominate?

- What is the first red flag you recognize that the personality is splitting with your soul and going in another direction? How do you realign your Personality Level?

- Which of your four bodies has the most difficult time in the creative process? Which of your four bodies is most aligned with your Soul Level?

The creative process is a reflection of your relationship and merging with your soul. Every act of creation is an opportunity to bring your soul expression into form.

Creating and living from the Soul Level is unpredictable and uncontrollable. It is also a joyous, loving, compassionate and trustful place. Enjoy!

## Chapter Nine Exploration and Discovery Activities

### Points to Ponder

**Activity 18. What do you think and feel about the following statements?**

- The soul activates and structures our Intuition and Personality Levels to prepare the lessons we need to learn and resolve. Our job in life is to align and merge with our Soul Level, so that our Intuitive and Personality Levels become the ultimate structure through which the soul expresses in physical existence.
- Free will at this passage in our journey is about choosing what level of consciousness to live from.
- We are life and life is us.
- We are spiritual beings in an ever-expanding spiral of evolution.
- We are integrators of spirit and matter.
- Living from our Soul Level perspective is living in this world without defenses, since we trust our alignment, connection and merging with our soul in the unity consciousness. We are receptive to the messages of the soul through our Intuitive Level. The necessary components include staying in the now, trusting the process of creation, choosing the state of being in which we wish to live, and desiring to serve humanity.

### Activity 19. Soul Merge

- Ask your soul for a symbol or color of the separation, connection and unity consciousness. Integrate these colors or symbols. Put them in all four of your bodies. Now imagine what your life would be like if you allowed your soul merge perspective to take on life. Write a scenario or expressively paint what your life would be.

# Part IV.
# The Next Step

## Chapter Ten

### As Good as It Gets: Merging the Consciousness of Personality, Intuition, and Soul

The sum total of our Soul, Intuitive, and Personality Levels is a mixture of all of our experiences as individuals, members of a certain epoch, and collectively as human beings. Through visions, visions-dreams, clairvoyance, gut-level feelings, knowingness and ways that are indefinable we recognize information that pitches us into alternative levels of consciousness. That is the wonder of the Intuitive and Soul Level.

How does this work? At times, I see pictures in my mind's eye. They are similar to watching movies and give information from the collective conscious, subconscious, and unconscious of man, earth and beyond. In addition, the movies tell a story about events that happened, are happening, and will happen. Also, I see energy configurations-pulses and energy fields within and around people. At other times, I feel energy shifts in the earth and the collective consciousness. Even days before a calamity, I sense oncoming natural disasters and major manmade catastrophes as unease and anxiety.

When I travel, I see the history of the place in movielike images. After presenting a two week seminar in Crete, I was looking forward to going home. Upon arriving at the Athens International Airport, I heard that my flight to Los Angeles would be delayed for five hours. After the initial, "Darn, damn...," I took a deep breath asked my soul, "What's up?" I saw three different wars that had been fought on the very ground upon which I was standing. My heart pounded as I watched the violence and felt the pain and horror of it. Then a soothing energy flowed through and out from me. I spent the five hours with my eyes closed, watching a magical lightshow of healing energy. I was unaware of the passage of time as I surrendered to my soul's intent.

The comprehensive perceptiveness of the soul determines what humanity is ready to accept. Collectively, we individuals decide the direction and rate of spiritual evolution by the choices we make every single day. It is easy to observe what level of consciousness we live from by noticing what we talk about and how we express ourselves.

## Dancing Between Consciousness Levels

*What do I want to create today? What is my soul asking to express?* These questions focus our lives when we live from the Soul Level. As we implement the answers, we weave and integrate an energy field that uses all three levels of consciousness. Our unique interpretation of these levels turns energy into form.

Creation begins with an initial spark of soul energy. Moving forward, each of our consciousness levels radiates and vibrates to align with that spark. This fosters a magnetic configuration of energy which is the blueprint for our creative process. Images, symbols, insights, wisdom, desire, determination, courage, trust, and hope suddenly materialize. Connections to other people, synchronicities, resources, and appropriate timing appear. All of these provide a fertile field of blessings that supports us in our journey to express the unity consciousness.

This is the creative principle in action. When we are acting from the highest levels of consciousness available to us, we generate new alternatives, perspectives and visions for ourselves and for the evolution of man. The soul activates susceptible areas within us. For example, we may feel a visceral reaction when we read about young children who are having challenges fitting into kindergarten. Our compassion for their circumstances stays with us as we go about our lives. But as we consider our desire to open our own business, we remember our concern for these preschoolers. This is the Soul and Intuitive Level igniting ideas. We get an "aha' moment.

However, even before we conceived of the idea of opening a preschool for children with special needs, our soul was seeding us. It activated the circumstances and preferences that led us to have a strong interest in this field. This reaction often stems from our own life experiences or those of people close to us. It also may come from observing our society and wanting to correct an injustice–hoping for something better for man. No matter the source, we know the soul is involved when our concern compels us to act with a sense of urgency. We say to ourselves, "No matter how hard this is, no matter how long it takes, I've got to do this!" This conviction is consonant with the Kabbalistic concept of Tikkun Olam: We are each given the task of healing the world in one way or another.

Our desire is always lurking in the back of our minds. When it becomes strong enough, we reach a tipping point. We focus and give it more attention. Our intentions become clear: we want to help these children! We image what our preschool would provide, start creating a curriculum, envision the services provided, develop organizational systems, decide on personnel, draw the physical set up, and plan the decor. We research testing instruments for assessment, prescription, and accountability.

The Personality Level then steps into the role of project manager. We shift into action. We start visiting other preschools; talk with school administrators, teachers, and parents; and contact our city, county, and state governments to learn the regulations we must abide by. We crunch the numbers and figure out sources of income. We make a budget. And we ask some hard questions: Do we rent or buy a facility? Are federal, state, or local grants available? If we affiliate with a religious or non-profit organization will we be able to secure funds for our school? How do we market this concept? Do we align with other preschools? How do we advertise to therapists, doctors, teachers, and parents? We start making a business plan to organize the information that we've obtained and use this as a flexible structure. We respond with confidence to challenges that appear along the way.

All levels of consciousness contribute. In fact, we jump back and forth among levels. This is the dance on the continuum of separation to unity, of energy to form. Whenever there is movement on this continuum, there is also integration and merging. This expands our energy field and furthers our spiritual development.

You can think of the process in terms of colors. Each represents a specific level of consciousness. We may begin with red but then move to blue. We are now the integration of red and blue—purple. Because this is a continuum, we are also every shade of that color combination—mauve, magenta, violet, lavender. Think of the range. Add to that the fact that our energy field is constantly rearranging itself. We possess the capability to evolve as an every-expanding spiral of consciousness.

When we are creating, we mix many levels of consciousness both unconsciously and subconsciously. We have an awareness of an indefinable shift within ourselves. This pressure builds until we perceive this intangible creative force. Our perception may start as the energy configuration is forming in the unity consciousness. It may appear as a revelation, unsolicited shift of perception that suddenly upends our lives or stimulates an already ferocious desire. The communication from the Soul Level is compelling and becomes the core of our lives. Nothing is as powerful as the pull of the soul.

## Check It Out!

If you deny, minimize or criticize your longings then you may want to investigate which fears are blocking your way. Remember if you respond to your ideas viscerally and cerebrally, chances are they come from your higher levels of consciousness. We acknowledge that moving back and forth on any continuum constitutes the development of who we are meant to be. That is why we must expand at all times. This gives us the opportunities to dance among different levels of consciousness.

- What is your process of creating?
- How does an idea come to you?
- How do you know to take it seriously?
- What do you do with the idea when you first get it?
- How do you develop your ideas?

## Merging the Levels

Another way to understand the concept of merging our levels of consciousness in all of our creations is to answer the question posed by each level.

## Soul Level: What are we co-creating?

This is the affirmation that we are soul. Inherent in our soul is a unique blueprint, a destiny to embrace and live. It is so important that it ignites into action that consumes our energy, efforts, feelings, and time.

The magnitude of this spark forces us to use the power of our Soul and Intuitive Levels while exploring uncharted territory–areas that can be intangible and uncontrollable. We sustain ourselves with courage, wonder, and hope as we experience the unlimited power of the Soul Level. Trust and self-trust support us. The degree to which an alignment and merging exist among our three levels of consciousness is the degree to which we feel ease in co-creating. As co-creators we accept what part we play in the unfolding of a vision. Our Personality Level is stable and we have a reservoir of life experiences and competencies to support us when difficulties appear. However, depending on how our soul expresses itself, we may not know the ramifications of our creation. Once we offer the gift of form that represents the unity consciousness then our part is finished.

The joy of creating brings the gift of aliveness–the main event.

## Intuitive Level: How do we choose to respond?

The challenges we face when we turn energy into form exist for our learning as well as for creating alternatives for others. When we confront a challenge, we choose how to respond. Clarifying what aligns with our soul intention and what does not is crucial. This is an optimal time to sit down with our four bodies and get a point of view from each of them.

Asking for guidance from our soul and intuition and then being receptive to what comes magnetically broadcasts that we would be excited by new perspectives. This understanding of the connection consciousness sets up the optimal conditions for chance meetings, connections, and all kinds of wonderful synchronicities. Magic happens when we actively implement our soul intentions.

After we reflect and decide how we are going to act, we respond. We clarify, become authentic, use our self-authority and self-mastery, and process our experiences to learn whatever lessons are available to us. We are then confident in what we intend to do. *What do you need to feel confident? How do you check for authenticity? How do you know a decision is the right for you?*

### Personality Level: How do we want to react?

At the Soul level, we receive the spark, the inspiration. At the Intuitive level, we prepare ourselves to be ready to act. We are clear on the why's and what's. Now, at the Personality Level, we gear up for the delivery. We create a game plan that helps structure what we want to do. Since we have a flexible personality, we are ready to use those parts of ourselves that are best suited for the task. It is essential to consider our audience and the most effective way for them to receive our message. When we share our ideas with a targeted group, they enter into the mass consciousness. How each of us uses and integrates this representation of consciousness provides an opportunity for the evolution of man.

That is why form and matter are still so important. Whether only a few connect and benefit from what we have created or our vision goes viral depends on the readiness of individuals and the mass consciousness. If our creation resonates with the pulse of the collective mass consciousness it would help with the depth and scope of its integration. On the other hand, our creation may only reach those who are ready for this new consciousness. But even then, it may plant the seeds for others to develop in their own time. If our creation causes an uproar and controversy, it would help people clarify their thoughts and feelings. But no matter how it is utilized, our creation serves a purpose for us personally and others. It supports us to become co-creators and creators and offers to others another way to be in the world.

## *Interacting from a Merge of Consciousness*

Living from the Soul Level involves a constant flux governed by our intentions among consciousness levels. The more we focus on any one area, the more energy we direct that way. Even fleeting thoughts draw energy. Unbeknownst to ourselves, we may still be reacting to the events of yesterday–what we heard on the radio as we drove to work; what we saw on TV, our IPhones or the internet–and to others' emotional fields. These unprocessed and seemingly extraneous thoughts and feelings respond to whatever consciousness level we are residing in at the moment. This is the outer core of our energy field which is most susceptible to the influences of everyday reality.

To focus our entire energy field, we need to align our intentions with what we choose to create throughout the day. If we do not format our energy, we can be sure that something or someone else will. This in turn separates us from our own resources and agenda. Processing the events of the day, every day, and reflecting on what we learned clears our energy field and opens the lines of communication to the Intuitive and Soul Levels. It also ensures that our mental, emotional, and physical bodies remain in the present, which is the best way to access our personalities, intuition and souls. We are then able to live from a soul perspective and create effective and flexible interactions with other individuals, groups, nature, and objects all in accord with the unity consciousness.

Our inner core of energy, the purest form of our Soul Level, is a radiance that is constant, even if we chose to ignore it. Imagine an amoeba. It changes shapes to displace the water around it which causes movement on its perimeter. Its interior seems still to us. However, that is just the limitation of our eye. There is continuous motion at its core. Jellyfish are also shape shifters with a slower core at their center. Both of these creatures illustrate how our energy field looks. The outer edges are the most malleable parts since they interpret the stimulus around us. Our soul is more constant.

The soul radiates, integrates, and expresses the blueprint that is unique to its interpretation of the unity consciousness. This state of being is always active and available to us, no matter what the circumstances. We create any state of being we choose to. That means we decide on our emotional state, even while we are engaged in a task.

But creating our soul emotion does not blind us to their energy configurations. For instance, if we observe that Jim resides in the Personality Level, we ascertain his motivation. Once we detect expressions of absolutism, we can then recognize his need for reassurance. From this information, we fashion our delivery with expressions that he will understand. This establishes a bridge between our energy field and his. Receiving our soul-inspired message cloaked in the more familiar wording of the separation consciousness allows for Jim's growth. But this does not mean we are only giving the message in the separation consciousness. As we go through this exercise, we still remain true to the soul emotion at our core.

Although we present the consciousness level that Jim can receive, we deliver the whole spectrum of energy from the point of contact. Jim accepts what he is ready for consciously and subconsciously. He uses some of the information contained in the energy field immediately. The rest of the energy that may ignite parts of him in the future stands ready for activation. It is like a tiny drop of potentiality, a drop of magnificent light that upon contact spreads, unfolds, and stretches into a membrane in which a completely new reality is created.

Although we use words with which Jim is familiar, we are in a higher consciousness so our words are imprinted at a different level. Connecting with Jim in this way allows him to feel safe. Now he can become acquainted with a deeper perspective. As Jim goes through experiencing, expressing, and expanding, this drop of new potential might be an instant "aha" or a gradual awakening.

We transmit our whole energy field even if we say, "You need to do this my way!" No matter the actual message and the effect on another, interactions provide a fertile ground for transformation. When we are aligned and merged with our soul level, we are in wholeness. We have complete clarity and see all possibilities. If others are not merged with their souls, they can only see part of the whole. Still it is there. On some intuitive level (that they might not even understand) they do see it or a part of it.

It's like standing next to the Dalai Lama. We feel his energy field—we sense something is different. We interpret this difference individually according to our own point of inner growth. It's an offering from one to another.

Indeed, many years ago, I saw the Dalai Lama speak at UCLA. The auditorium was huge, yet as I looked at him from afar, I felt and saw a ray of light coming from his eyes directly to me. I felt my heart expand to the degree that I felt bruised, as if I'd just worked a muscle in the gym. From the moment of this visceral experience on, I lived at a higher consciousness and compassion. The Dalai Lama offered me and everyone else in that vast room the opportunity to connect with his energy field and claim a new perspective.

This carried over to my practice. As I opened the door to my first client following this awakening, I felt my heart opening to the fullest. My whole energy field rearranged itself in order to hold the highest and clearest consciousness which I could then offer my clients. Thereafter, my clients would leave sessions saying, I feel so much better," "I'm so relaxed now," "I feel peaceful." It wasn't only the personality word-driven clarity they received but also an energetic healing. I was connecting with them at every level of consciousness. My energy field was directing itself to certain spots in their energy fields in need of healing. Words were only the entry point in our interactions. Many times, I saw colors and movie-like images. I always felt movement.

The Soul Level is so magical and mysterious. Our energy field emanates from us and dances with those of others.

## Crossroads for Humanity

The human race is at a unique turning point. Our ever swelling population brings unprecedented shifts in the balance between, young/old, majority/minorities, rich/poor, and urban/rural. Globalization created many market economies, new technologies, more efficient energy uses, and farming techniques that increase food production, yet still we are faced with a limited ecosystem to provide resources. Public health is no longer a local, state, or national issue, as infectious diseases and chronic ailments can sweep both the industrial and developing nations. We are coming up against the limitations of institutions that were created from the separation consciousness as they allow too few people to have too much power. No longer can a singular perspective meet the needs of our diverse world. The time for simplistic answers is over. The complexities of a technological and global world demand a new vision to bring more people together to support the changes that are necessary for the survival and evolution of man.

A shift to shared power among individuals and society is the next step for humanity. This comes with our determination to express our three consciousness levels and use our infrastructures of personality, intuition and soul to cultivate alternatives.

When our internal and external realities become congruent and representative of each other then we have merged our three levels of consciousness. This expanded perspective is our hope for the future. Collectively our internal realties give form to public institutions. A reciprocal flow exists among the internal and external realities of individuals and the collective. Groups and nations are constantly changing, rearranging and influencing each other. What we do as individuals is part of the collective consciousness, and the collective consciousness influences us as individuals. The power of this exchange is a fluid state that is capable of evolving us into spiritual beings. We are all together in this experience of life no matter our race, age, religion, socio-economic status, and gender for we all inhabit this earth individually and collectively.

That means every person on this earth needs the following for us to evolve collectively:

### At the Personality Level

In order for us to learn the lessons of the Personality Level, fulfilling basic survival needs is essential. These needs include:

- Enough food for daily meals
- Clean water
- Medicine
- Basic education/skills
- Good governance—a transparent government that welcomes accountability

- Housing appropriate for geographic location
- Trading of goods to flow money

All of the above survival needs are within the capabilities of local communities to provide.

## At the Intuitive Level

In order for us to learn the lessons of the Intuitive Level, we need a more complex infrastructure to support its most essential factor–jobs. Not just menial labor but jobs that match our personal expertise, intention, creativity, and desire. Essential elements for the development of the Intuitive Level include:

- Diversity of job opportunities from individual enterprises to supported creative endeavors such as nonpolitical think tanks, works of art, scientific research.
- Technology for sustaining and distributing resources
- Technology for environmental accountability
- Technology for health
- Flow of money throughout all socioeconomic levels
- Creating new sources of wealth
- Good governance—authority figures working on clearly defined goals for the betterment of humanity

Again, all of these become available as individuals and groups use the beliefs of the consciousness of connection. As a society, we are working on this same list of needs. However, the solutions too often come from the separation consciousness, which will not provide sustainable new solutions. More people creating from their intuition provide more possibilities and solutions.

## At the Soul Level

In order for us to learn the lessons of the Soul Level and truly become spiritual beings, we must raise the consciousness of the world. Soul Level living includes:

- Managing the earth's resources from the perspective of universal good
- Managing outer space resources from a universal view
- Transparent and accountable distribution systems for resources
- Transparent governance based on a global perspective

So many possibilities are available when we incorporate the characteristics of the unity consciousness in our lives. As spiritual beings, we are pitched into a higher perspective. When we observe the world around us, we understand that the themes being played out in local, national, and world events are reflections of those that we as individuals must clarify within ourselves. This is not a battle between individuals and institutions since the world is inclusive. We are co-creators and creators. Through the merging of our Personality, Intuitive, and Soul Levels, we implement our visions and create lives that are rich and that truly make a difference. As we change and take our next step so does the world. What wonderful possibilities!

## What are you going to create? What is your next step? Chapter Ten Exploration and Discovery Activities

**Activity 20. Create a chart for Soul, Intuitive, and Personality Levels. Under each level, make a column for your four bodies: spiritual, mental, emotional, and physical. Below is a starting list of the functions for each body in all three levels of consciousness. Add your own words and interpretation of the function of each. Use your chart to fill in the specifics of an inspiration, idea, vision, and/or image that you want to develop. This will ensure that you are using all parts of yourself in every level that you co-exist.**

- **SOUL LEVEL:**
    - **Spiritual body:** gathers and adapts energy from different levels of consciousness and makes an energy configuration, activates an impulse to create

- **Mental Body:** inspiration, "aha's", realization, epiphany, visions, dreams
- **Emotional Body:** creating the soul level internal emotions such as: compassion, abundance, trust, love, gratitude, humility, joy, commitment
- **Physical Body:** perceiving, experiencing, and interpreting multi-level energy fields within the body and environment

- **INTUITIVE LEVEL:**
  - **Spiritual Body:** interpreting intuitive messages from soul consciousness
  - **Mental Body:** imagination, ideas, images, concepts, symbols, sense of knowingness, looking for different options, seeing new patterns, flexible thinking, setting intentions
  - **Emotional Body:** self-mastery of emotions, creating emotions to fortify self for soul intention, choosing emotional responses, self-authority for motivations
  - **Physical Body:** instincts

- **PERSONALITY LEVEL:**
  - **Spiritual Body:** beliefs we hold about spirituality
  - **Mental Body:** thinking, setting goals, checking for and acquiring necessary skills, timing, systematic plan, assessing and acquiring resources, reflecting, determining what is enough
  - **Emotional Body:** identifying and understanding emotional reactions and interactions
  - **Physical Body:** care and feeding of the body and balancing life within the limitations of physical energy and time

# Acknowledgements

**Gratitude for...**

- Clara, Jordan, Branson, Cooper, John, Delaney and Cate, the faces of the future which inspire me.
- The spirit of John and Vinerella Bodenburg, the light that continues to shine within me.
- John P. Myers, my husband, for his unconditional love and support that continually feeds and teaches me.
- Susan K. Golant, editor extraordinaire and wise soul.

**Connections with Special People...**

- Sydney Mulligan, John W. Bodenburg, Nancy Helmer, John M. Bodenburg, Virginia Craig, Jill Munro, Patti Nunn, Julie Lorenzini, Jan Gray, Larry Horton, John Parrish, Mary Taylor, and Paul Zack.
- To all my clients and students as we learned together.